GETTING THINGS DONE

David Allen has been called one of the world's most influential thinkers on productivity and has been a keynote speaker and facilitator for such organizations as New York Life, the World Bank, the Ford Foundation, L.L. Bean, and the U.S. Navy, and he conducts workshops for individuals and organizations across the country. He is the chairman of the David Allen Company and has more than thirty-five years of experience as a management consultant and executive coach. His work has been featured in *Fast Company*, *Fortune*, the *Los Angeles Times*, the *New York Times*, the *Wall Street Journal*, and many other publications. *Getting Things Done* has been published in more than thirty foreign countries. Allen lives in Amsterdam, Netherlands.

Praise for the First Edition of *Getting Things Done*

"The Season's Best Reads for Work-Life Advice . . . my favorite on organizing your life: *Getting Things Done* . . . offers help building the new mental skills needed in an age of multitasking and overload."
—Sue Shellenbarger, *The Wall Street Journal*

"I recently attended David's seminar on getting organized, and after seeing him in action I have hope. . . . David Allen's seminar was an eye-opener."
—Stewart Alsop, *Fortune*

"Allen drops down from high-level philosophizing to the fine details of time management. Take a minute to check this one out."
—Mark Henricks, *Entrepreneur*

"David Allen's productivity principles are rooted in big ideas . . . but they're also eminently practical."
—Keith H. Hammonds, *Fast Company*

"David Allen brings new clarity to the power of purpose, the essential nature of relaxation, and deceptively simple guidelines for getting things done. He employs extensive experience, personal stories, and his own recipe for simplicity, speed, and fun."
—Frances Hesselbein, chairman, board of governors, Leader to Leader Institute

"Anyone who reads this book can apply this knowledge and these skills in their lives for immediate results."
—Stephen P. Magee, chaired professor of business and economics, University of Texas at Austin

"A true skeptic of most management fixes, I have to say David's program is a winner!"
—Joline Godfrey, CEO, Independent Means, Inc., and author of *Our Wildest Dreams*

"*Getting Things Done* describes an incredibly practical process that can help busy people regain control of their lives. It can help you be more successful. Even more important, it can help you have a happier life!"
—Marshall Goldsmith, coeditor, *The Leader of the Future* and *Coaching for Leadership*

"WARNING: Reading *Getting Things Done* can be hazardous to your old habits of procrastination. David Allen's approach is refreshingly simple and intuitive. He provides the systems, tools, and tips to achieve profound results."
—Carola Endicott, director, Quality Resources, New England Medical Center

Getting Things Done

The Art of Stress-Free Productivity

Revised Edition

David Allen

PENGUIN BOOKS

PENGUIN BOOKS
Published by the Penguin Group
Penguin Group (USA) LLC
375 Hudson Street
New York, New York 10014

USA | Canada | UK | Ireland | Australia | New Zealand | India | South Africa | China
penguin.com
A Penguin Random House Company

First published in the United States of America by Viking Penguin,
a member of Penguin Putnam Inc., 2001
Published in Penguin Books 2003
This revised edition with a foreword by James Fallows published 2015

ISBN 978-0-14-312656-0

Printed in the United States of America
7   9   10   8

Set in Adobe Caslon Pro

For Kathryn, my extraordinary partner in life and work

Acknowledgments

So many mentors, partners, colleagues, staff, clients, friends, and adopters of the *Getting Things Done* methodology around the world over the past decades have contributed to my understanding and development of these principles that singling out particular individuals to thank here is both necessary and unfair. So, my gratitude and apologies go to the many unnamed but still highly deserving in that group (and you know who you are!).

In the early 1980s Dean Acheson and Russell Bishop provided me initial frameworks that seeded my awareness of the powerful methodology that was to become known around the world as *GTD*. Of the innumerable partners and colleagues who have added to this body of work and its distribution over the years, I must give special thanks to Marian Bateman, Meg Edwards, Ana Maria Gonzalez, Anne Gennett, Leslie Boyer, Kelly Forrister, John Forrister, Wayne Pepper, Frank Sopper, Maggie Weiss, and Mike Williams.

> *It's not what we have in our life, but who we have in our life, that counts.*
>
> —*J. M. Laurence*

In addition, many thousands of clients and workshop participants have helped validate and fine-tune these models. Particular thanks go to the senior human resource strategists who in the early years of this work recognized the significance of this material in bringing needed change to their corporate cultures, and who gave me the opportunity to do that—in particular:

Michael Winston, Ben Cannon, Kevin Wilde, Susan Valaskovic, Patricia Carlyle, Manny Berger, Carola Endicott, Klara Sztucinski, and Elliott Kellman. This book could not have happened the way it has without the unique energies and perspectives of Tom Hagan, John and Laura McBride, Steve Lewers, Greg Stikeleather, Sam Spurlin, and my indefatigable agent, Doe Coover. And much credit is due both the editor of the first edition, Janet Goldstein, and my subsequent editor of this new version, Rick Kot, both of whom have provided marvelous (and patient) instruction in the art and craft of book writing.

Finally, deepest thanks go to my spiritual coach, J-R, for being such an awesome guide and consistent reminder of my real priorities; and to my wife, Kathryn, for her trust, love, supportive hard work, companionship, and the multiple forms of beauty she has brought into my life.

Contents

Foreword

BOOK CATALOGS ARE full of listings for volumes that offer advice on how to improve your work habits, your health, your productivity, and your overall success in life.

Some of what they say is typically dressed-up common sense. A fraction of it is baloney. Much of it is worth reading one time, if that, and is forgettable hours or days after you have put the book down.

This book is different. It has sold steadily, in large numbers, since its first appearance, and the audience for David Allen's programs and philosophies has grown in size and international reach. Speaking for myself, I can say that this is a book I read carefully when the original version came out, that I have revisited every year or two since then, and that I was very glad to learn was coming out in the updated and revised version you are reading now.

What makes *Getting Things Done* different? In ascending order of importance, I would list these three qualities, each evident in nearly every chapter.

One is its practicality, by which I really mean is modular and forgiving approach. Many self-improvement schemes work from an all-or-nothing, "everything must be different, starting tomorrow" premise. If you want to lose forty pounds, take control of your financial destiny, straighten out your family, or have the career of your dreams, you have to embrace a radical top-to-bottom change in every aspect of your life.

Occasionally people do make these radical leaps: in programs for sobriety, in commitments to new diet-and-exercise plans after serious health scares, or even going into the monastery after a life in the business world. But for most people, most of the time, approaches that are incremental and forgiving of error are more likely to pay off in the long run. That way, if there is one part of the approach you forget or fall behind in, you don't have to abandon all the rest.

David Allen's ambitions for his readers are in a sense even grander than those of most other books. His goal is nothing less than helping people remove stress and anxiety from their work and personal lives, so they can match every moment of their existence to the purposes they would most like to pursue. Yet with a very few exceptions—for instance, his sensible insistence on developing a "capture" habit, so that you are sure to write down or otherwise record every commitment you make or obligation you accept rather than torture yourself trying to remember them all, and the related insistence on having one central, trusted repository where you keep such data—a great advantage of his system is its modular nature. This book is full of advice that works better if embraced in its totality but is still useful when applied piece by piece.

For instance: If you haven't gone all the way with David Allen's GTD system, you can still find value in his "two-minute rule" for disposing of obligations *now* rather than putting them off. (From chapter 6, the two-minute rule: "If an action will take less than two minutes, it should be done at the moment it's defined.") Or his emphasis, explained throughout the book, on relying on an "external brain"—that is, tools that can do routine categorizing and remembering for us, from simple folders in which to store receipts to established places in which you will *always* put keys, glasses, or other things you don't want to hunt for each time.

This is advice from a man who clearly understands that people are busy and fallible. He is writing to offer them additional helpful tips, rather than to give them extra reasons to feel guilty or inadequate. The book is also written with an understanding that life consists of cycles. Things go better, and then get worse. At some points we fall behind; at others, we catch up, or try to. When episodes occur, as they will for anyone, in which we are overwhelmed or unable to cope, the book suggests achievable day-by-day steps toward regaining a calm sense of control.

A second virtue of the book is its open-ended adaptability. Through the decades since David Allen first began conceiving his approach to work and life, some practical aspects of personal organization have remained constant. There are only so many hours per day, even as we push back the frontiers of sleeplessness. There are only so many people with whom we can maintain serious connections, only so many things we can do at a time. Yet other aspects of the working life have changed radically. When the first edition of this book came out, e-mail was still an exciting new technology rather than a limitlessly guilt-inducing source of work still to be done. One of David Allen's first technological projects was a program called "Actioneer," a task-management system for the early PalmPilot. Now the Palm company and its once-revolutionary Pilot are gone; iPhone and Android smartphones have taken its place; and others now unimagined are sure to follow.

In this new edition of the book as with its predecessor, David Allen is fully conversant with the technology of the moment. But unlike other management books that are closely tied to hardware or software of an era—Filofaxes in the 1980s, spreadsheets or PowerPoint decks more recently—*Getting Things Done* refers to but does not depend on any specific external systems. David Allen has updated the advice in this book to reflect what is different in modern technology and also (in fascinating detail) what modern brain science has revealed. But his outlook is always tied to timeless principles of how people manage their attention, emotions, and creativity. If this book is still being read a dozen years or more from now, as I think it will be, people in that era will be able to skip past the inevitably outdated references to technology to recognize the still-relevant insights into human nature.

Third is a quality I have come to appreciate firsthand, as I have gotten to know David Allen and his wife Kathryn as friends, and that I think other people must have intuited from David's work without ever meeting him. That is the wholeness and authenticity in David Allen's recommendations, the connection between the person and the message he is delivering.

As I learned when writing a profile of David Allen for the *Atlantic* in 2004, he has had a wide variety of careers and levels-of-luck in life. He has been a schoolboy actor, a debating champion, a karate practitioner and teacher, a waiter and a taxi driver and a manager of a lawn-service agency—and all of this before his decades of success as a consultant and productivity adviser. Echoes from that range of experience come through in David Allen's advice, and his manner, not only in the real-world examples he can cite but also in his quite notable lack of self-importance.

There are times when we overlook the personal traits of a creator when assessing the importance of his or her work. For instance: by all accounts Steve Jobs was more admirable as a design pioneer than as a model of personal conduct. In other cases, the integral connection of a person's life and thought add to the power of that person's message. I can attest from personal experience with David and Kathryn Allen something that many readers might guess and most would hope: that he is doing his best to be honest about what he has learned from life.

Some people will think they don't "need" this book, and in a literal sense that is obviously true. Around the world and through the eons many people have led successful and satisfying lives in total ignorance of the "Getting Things Done" approach. But most people I know who have read this book have benefitted from the time they've taken to absorb its messages and their implications. Two of my tests for a book are whether I remember it a month or two after I have read it, and whether it affects my view of the world. By both tests *Getting Things Done* is, for me, a success. I am glad it is being introduced to a new generation of readers.

—James Fallows

James Fallows is a national correspondent for the *Atlantic* magazine and author of ten books, most recently *China Airborne*. He first wrote about David Allen in a 2004 article for the *Atlantic* called "Organize Your Life!"

Introduction to the Revised Edition

WHAT FOLLOWS IS a total rewrite of the first edition of *Getting Things Done*, originally published in 2001—well, a *sort* of rewrite. I actually retyped the original manuscript, start to finish, with the goal of identifying and revising content and language that was either incomplete, outdated, or otherwise not optimal for keeping the book functional as a continuing and "evergreen" manual, one that would be useful globally and remain relevant and applicable for the twenty-first century and even beyond. I also wanted to incorporate the most significant and interesting things I've seen and learned about the methodology that *Getting Things Done* introduced as I've continued to be involved with it, in myriad ways, since the book's first publication. That includes my own deeper understanding of its power, subtlety, and range of application, as well as how it has been received as awareness of it has spread around the world.

What *didn't* need to change as I reassessed the book were its fundamental principles and core techniques. As I crafted this new edition, reacquainting myself with what I wrote then was a gratifying acknowledgment that the principles of stress-free productivity I described and even most of the best practices of how to apply them haven't wavered, nor will they, in the foreseeable future. In order for a space exploration team to land on Jupiter in 2109, they will have to employ the same principles for maintaining control and focus as anyone does today. They'll still need some version of an in-tray (explained later) to capture potentially meaningful inputs they didn't expect, in order to trust their choices about what to focus on during their first excursion. And next-action decision making will always be critical for successful execution of any task, whatever its scope.

Because many elements of the way we live and work *have* changed since the first edition, though, I've made appropriate recalibrations in the fundamental material and will share my thoughts here about things that I consider new and interesting in this arena, offering relevant advice to both those new to this methodology and the GTD* aficionados who may be reading this edition and want to keep abreast of the latest developments concerning it.

What's New

Here are some of the key areas in the "what's new" category that have influenced my revision:

The Rise of Digital Technology

The continuing manifestation of Moore's Law (digital processing power increasing exponentially over time), along with the social and cultural ramifications of the expansion of the digital world into our daily lives, never fails to surprise, delight, and overwhelm us. Because *Getting Things Done* deals primarily with the *content* and *meaning* of what we need to manage, irrespective of how it shows up or gets organized—whether in digital form or on paper—advances in technology are to some degree irrelevant to the essence of its methodology. An e-mail request means essentially the same thing and has to be processed the same way as a favor asked of you at the coffee machine.

But the wired/wireless world has both enhanced and exacerbated how we can apply the core practices of capturing, organizing,

---

*"GTD" (*Getting Things Done* abbreviated) has become the popular acronym around the world for the methodology I describe in this book. This edition uses it frequently as shorthand.

and accessing what's meaningful. While we now have access to lots of supertools and apps that show up on an almost daily basis and do really great stuff, that plethora of options can easily blow our productivity fuses. Staying on top of and leveraging ever-evolving technologies adds significant pressure to getting one's appropriate workflow methodology right.

I've accordingly changed some of my earlier emphases on types of tools that are best suited to particular tasks and acknowledged the ubiquity of our new digital and mobile world. I've also eliminated most of my references to specific software applications that appeared in the first edition. The rate of innovation in this area means that any specific software program can easily be outdated, upgraded, or undermined by the next new thing by the time you read about it. I've essentially hopped out of that fray, opting instead to provide a general model for how to evaluate the usefulness of *any* tool.

For this edition I grappled with how much attention to continue to devote to paper-based tools and materials (especially for capturing, reference filing, and incubating), as many in the younger generations have come to believe they don't have to deal with paper at all. At the risk of dating myself, I decided to leave most of those instructions from the first edition intact here, as many of the potential readers of this new edition around the world will still be at least partially paper based. Ironically, there is a growing resurgence of interest in the use of paper among the most sophisticatedly digital.* Time will tell whether we can ever truly get rid of that in-your-hand, in-your-face medium.

The 24-7 World

I'm often asked what new advice GTD can offer to the mobile, connected, and always-on world.

> Nothing is new, except how frequently it is.

---

*As I write this, I am in the middle of a move to Europe from the U.S., attempting to reduce my physical possessions to a bare minimum. So I scanned and digitized everything in my physical tickler file (which I have used for thirty years, described on page 182). Already I've been frustrated several times with things that would have been much more easily handled had I kept the physical version!

The necessity of dealing with frequent and complex barrages of potentially significant data was probably true in the past for remarkable individuals such as Napoleon as he marched through Europe, or Bach as he composed, or even Andy Warhol as he decided what to paint or show in a gallery. Now, though, the entire world's digitally connected literate population is the recipient of an explosion of nonstop, potentially "important"—or at least relevant—information. The ease with which it can be accessed through technology has made it simultaneously rewarding in its opportunities and treacherous in its volume, speed, and changeability. If you are by nature fascinated by what may be going on when you hear sirens in your neighborhood or wonder what a group of people across the room at a party is excitedly talking about, then you are ripe for becoming a victim of the endless and powerful distractions your personal technology dishes out to you. Whether your experience with it is ultimately positive or negative depends primarily on the application of the practices in this book.

The Globalization of GTD Methodology

I'm often asked if the GTD process can translate into other cultures, and my answer has always been a resounding, "Of course." The core message of the book is so inherently relevant to the human condition that I've yet to experience any cultural bias—nor frankly any gender, age, or personality-type differentials—in the applicability of the methodology. The awareness of the need for it and what purposes it will serve will, of course, be different for each individual. But that is more a function of one's station in life, the nature of one's work, and one's interest in self-improvement than it is any of the other factors. In actual practice you will potentially have more in common with many hundreds of thousands of people around the world in your resonance with GTD than you will with your next-door neighbor or even your cousin Rafael!

Anyone with the need to be accountable to deal with more than what he or she can complete in the moment has the opportunity to do so more easily and elegantly than in the mind.

Since its initial publication, awareness of the *Getting Things Done* message has spread worldwide. The first edition has been translated into more than thirty languages, and our company has established franchises in many countries to provide training programs based on its content. While I was relatively confident about the cross-cultural coherence of this methodology when I wrote the book, the ensuing years have simply validated that confidence, in spades.

An Approach That Is More Inclusive of a Larger Population of Readers and Users

The primary impetus for my writing *Getting Things Done* was to craft a manual for the methodology that I had formulated, tested, and implemented, mostly in the corporate training and development world. In its examples, style, look, and feel (I wore a tie on the cover!), the book was initially and principally addressed to managers, executives, and higher-level, fast-track professionals. While I already knew that the material could be equally valuable for homemakers, students, clergy, artists, and even retirees, it was professionals who at that time were the most aware of the need for the kind of help I was seeking to provide, as a means both to advance their own development and productivity as well as to stay sane in the process. They were at the front lines, the advance guard, in engaging with the impending flood of information and rapid and significant change the business world was experiencing, and also had access to resources to tackle these issues.

> *Getting Things Done* is not simply about getting things done. It's about being appropriately engaged with your work and life.

Today there is a much more universal interest in the results that can be achieved with relaxed, focused control, and the realization that it is not just a one-shot recipe of "time management" tips simply for business professionals, but in fact a lifestyle practice, necessary to deal with the new world most all of us are experiencing. I regularly receive testimonials from a diversity of people around the world in an infinite variety of situations about the life-changing value they have experienced applying GTD principles. This validation of the growing need across the planet for such a model has inspired me to reframe many of my examples and the focus of that text to support it.

From that perspective I have to acknowledge that even the title of this book can be somewhat misleading, giving many the impression that I am somehow advocating working harder and longer to get *more* done. *Productivity*, unfortunately, does have connotations of both business and busy-ness. In truth, this book is not so much concerned with getting things done as it is championing *appropriate engagement with your world*—guiding you to make the best choice of what to do in each moment, and to eliminate distraction and stress about what you're *not* doing. The resulting clarity and psychological space can benefit a much broader range of people than simply professionals on a corporate career track.

Some of the most interesting endorsements of the value of applying the *Getting Things Done* principles and techniques have come from unexpected quarters. The head of the world's largest finance organization, a popular American comedian, the most listened-to U.S. radio personality, the CEO of a major European conglomerate, one of the most successful Hollywood directors—all have attributed huge benefits in their life and work to GTD. Feedback from the clergy of many different religions has also been fascinating. While they're responsible for handling otherworldly matters, they've been starved for ways to focus *more* in that realm with their flocks by freeing themselves of the distractions of the day-to-day business aspects of leading a congregation. Students, designers, doctors—the list of self-identified GTD advocates is endless.

Over the years I've discovered that we're all in this game together; it's now great to have the opportunity to frame an outreach to encompass the full breadth of GTD users.

A Greater Awareness of the Time and Energy Required for the Full Implementation of the GTD Process, and the Behavioral Changes Required to Maintain It

Alas! As easy as it is to actually *do* what I suggest as best practices in this book, I have been rudely awakened to these two phenomena: (1) the amount of information and suggested activities here can easily be perceived as too overwhelming for someone to even begin to implement them; and (2) making some of the fundamental practices habitual can take quite a while for most people.

Because I have continued to resist "dumbing down" this model and its details, I'm not sure I can ever overcome the objection of "too much to absorb." The first edition of *Getting Things Done* included detailed instructions and recommendations about how to fully implement its methodology in your life and work—and I have retained them here. I now know that for many who are new to this game, this will seem more than comfortable or possible to incorporate all at once. But I cannot with integrity hold back the instructions about how to really integrate this method into your everyday life, if you want to "go for it."

Everything in life worth achieving requires practice. In fact, life itself is nothing more than one long practice session, an endless effort of refining our motions. When the proper mechanics of practicing are understood, the task of learning something new becomes a stress-free experience of joy and calmness, a process which settles all areas in your life and promotes proper perspective on all of life's difficulties.

—*Thomas Sterner*

If you were interested in learning to play tennis, I wouldn't want to hold back at least a blueprint of the game, including a vision of excellence and the levels of learning and practice involved to get there. In the newly added chapter 15, I've sought to illuminate the depth and breadth of the game I'm introducing, and to make it more comfortable for you to take what you can and will from what you read and make it OK for you to simply glean and implement whatever you might from it, for now. I have attempted in this version of the book to add more graciousness to respect the potentially daunting task of rearranging your personal practices and systems. It's really all about one step at a time.

In every case, however, a key challenge is applying and sustaining these practices as an ongoing set of habits, to the point that they will require the minimal application of conscious focus, or "juice," and merely become an everyday part of keeping one's mental and physical environment in good order. I cannot pretend to be an expert in how to change one's habits—I've been much more invested in figuring out and refining the practices of stress-free productivity.* The behavioral ingredients of GTD are actually relatively simple and familiar to everyone. How hard is it to write something down, decide what the next step is to move it forward, record the

---

*An excellent resource in this area is Charles Duhigg's book, *The Power of Habit*.

reminder of that on a list, and review the list? Most everyone admits he or she needs to establish a practice like this, and few do it consistently enough to feel good about it. How challenging it is for someone to internalize the need to consistently keep *every* unnecessary distraction out of his or her head has been one of my biggest surprises over the years.

Information from Cognitive Science Research That Has Validated the Efficacy of the GTD Methodology

I no longer feel as much like "a voice, crying in the wilderness" as I did at the turn of the century, for since then scientific data has emerged validating the principles and practices prescribed in this book. The new chapter 14 here ("GTD and Cognitive Science") features an examination of some of this research.

For whatever deserves to exist deserves also to be known, for knowledge is the image of existence; and things mean and splendid exist alike.

—Francis Bacon

If You Are New to This . . .

. . . and if you've gotten this far in this Introduction, you're probably interested in jumping in at some level of engagement. I've structured *Getting Things Done* as a practical manual—much like a cookbook that frames the basic principles, presents many layers of what cooking and serving a meal is all about, and gives enough specific recipes to enable you to make an infinite number of future dinners. If I've done a decent job in crafting this new edition, you can just start at the next chapter and take it from there, as you feel so moved. GTD principles, as they are laid out in the book, have been verified by many as a powerful experience to work through and apply. Or you can simply jump around—skim the text, randomly dive into a paragraph or two. The book has been written to serve you in that way as well.

If You Already Have Some *Getting Things Done* Experience . . .

. . . this will still be a new book. Over the many years that this information has been available in multiple forms, whenever anyone loops back through the material, they invariably have a response like, "Oh my God, this is totally different information and perspective than I could recognize and absorb when I read it earlier." Even people who have reread the original edition of GTD as many as five times have professed to me, "It was a totally different book each time!" The experience is very much like reading a software manual a year later, after you've gotten the basics on "cruise control." You'll be amazed and enthused about all the cool stuff you realize you could be (and could have been) doing, right at your fingertips, but that you couldn't recognize and implement, given the other major issues that needed to be addressed to set things up.

No matter when or how many times you might have read an earlier version of *Getting Things Done*, or participated in any of the seminars, coaching, webinars, podcasts, or other presentations of this material, you will experience a novel and absorbing level of engagement in this revised edition. I promise you that. What will open up in the following pages is a new universe of ideas to incorporate, within the structure and tools you likely already have in place.

Engaging with this book and the information within it will consistently provide a positive and productive mind-set about the aspects of your life and work that genuinely matter.

Welcome to *Getting Things Done*

WELCOME TO A gold mine of insights into strategies for how to have more energy, be more relaxed, with more clarity and presence in the moment with whatever you're doing, and get a lot more accomplished with much less effort. If you're like me, you like getting things done and doing them well, and yet you also want to savor life in ways that seem increasingly elusive, if not downright impossible, if you're working too hard. This doesn't have to be an either-or proposition. It *is* possible to be effectively *doing* while you are delightfully *being*, in your ordinary workaday world.

I think efficiency is a good thing. Maybe what you're doing is important, interesting, or useful; or maybe it isn't but it has to be done anyway. In the first case you want to get as much return as you can on your investment of time and energy. In the second, you want to get on to other things as fast as you can, without any nagging loose ends.

> *The art of resting the mind and the power of dismissing from it all care and worry is probably one of the secrets of our great men.*
>
> —*Capt. J. A. Hatfield*

And whatever you're doing, you'd probably like to be more relaxed, confident that whatever you're doing at the moment is just what you need to be doing—that having a beer with your staff after hours, gazing at your sleeping child in his or her crib at midnight, answering the e-mail in front of you, or spending a few informal minutes with the potential new client after the meeting is exactly what you *ought* to be doing, as you're doing it.

Teaching you how to be maximally efficient and relaxed, whenever you need or want to be, was my main purpose in writing this book. And after many years of sharing this information and set of best practices around the world, in the most varied environments and with the widest range of people of all types and ages, I can unequivocally attest: it works.

How do you know that what you're doing is what you ought to be doing at any point in time? No software, seminar, cool notebook, smartphone, or even personal mission statement will give you more than twenty-four hours in a day, simplify its content, or make this often tough choice for you.

Used appropriately, those kinds of tools can provide support for your decisions, but they don't in and of themselves get you in control and focused. What's more, just when you learn how to enhance your productivity at one level, you'll graduate or be forced to the next accepted batch of responsibilities and creative goals, whose new challenges will defy the ability of any simple formula, buzzword du jour, or new digital mobile device to get you back "on your game" for your next stage in work and life. You may have established personal habits and tools that work for a while, but a major change, such as a big shift in your job, a first baby, or buying a home, will test their sustainability and likely create serious discomfort (if not havoc!).

> *As to methods there may be a million and then some, but principles are few. The man who grasps principles can successfully select his own methods. The man who tries methods, ignoring principles, is sure to have trouble.*
>
> —*Ralph Waldo Emerson*

But if there's no single technique or tool for perfecting organization and productivity, there *are* very specific things we do to facilitate them. Over the years I've uncovered simple processes that we can all learn to use that will vastly improve our ability to deal proactively and constructively with the mundane realities of the world, while still feeling connected to our more meaningful priorities. And those practices have proven to be viable universally across time. They apply if you're trying to manage your homework at age twelve and if you need to regroup about your corporation's strategies after your last board meeting . . . and to everything in between.

What follows is a compilation of more than three decades' worth of discoveries about personal and organizational productivity—a guide to maximizing output and minimizing input, and to doing so in a world in which work is increasingly voluminous, ever shifting, and ambiguous. I (and many colleagues) have spent hundreds of thousands of hours coaching some of the brightest and busiest people you can imagine, "in the trenches" at their desks, in their homes with their doors closed, helping them capture, clarify, and organize all of their work and commitments at hand. The methods I have uncovered have proved to be highly effective in all types of organizations, at every job level, across cultures, and even at home and school. After years of coaching and training some of the most sophisticated and productive professionals (along with their kids!), I know the world is hungry for these methods.

> *Anxiety is caused by a lack of control, organization, preparation, and action.*
>
> —*David Kekich*

Executives at the top are looking to instill a standard of ruthless execution in themselves, their staffs, and their cultures, as well as how to keep their personal lives appropriately in balance and in play. They know, and I know, that behind closed doors, after hours, there remain unanswered calls, tasks to be delegated, unprocessed issues from meetings and conversations, senior-level accountabilities not yet clarified and under control, personal responsibilities unmanaged, and dozens of potentially important e-mails amid their hundreds (or even thousands) still not dealt with. Many of these businesspeople are successful because the crises they resolve and the opportunities they take advantage of are bigger than the problems they allow and create in their own offices, homes, and briefcases. But given the pace of business and life today, the equation is often in question.

And, more critically for many, people are not paying appropriate attention to their kids' school plays, sports games, or going-to-bed questions about life, or they're simply not able to "be here now," anywhere, anytime. An ambient angst pervades our society—there's a sense that somehow there's probably something we should be doing that we're not, which creates a tension for which there is no resolution and from which there is no rest.

On the one hand, we need proven tools that can help people focus their energies strategically and tactically without letting anything fall through the cracks. On the other, we need to create thinking habits and working environments that will keep the most caring and engaged people from burning out due to stress. We need positive work and lifestyle standards that will attract and retain the best and brightest in our organizations, and we need personal and home practices that foster clarity, control, and creativity for those we love and, most important, for ourselves.

We know this information is sorely needed in organizations. It's also needed in schools, where the vast majority of our kids are still not being taught how to process information, how to focus on outcomes, or what actions to take to make them happen. And for all of us individually, it's needed so we can take advantage of all the opportunities we're given to add value to our world in a sustainable, self-nurturing way.

The power, simplicity, and effectiveness of what I'll be presenting here is best experienced as an experience, in real time, with situations in your real world. As you read or skim the book, you will no doubt be motivated to think about how you would and could implement what I'll be talking about. You'll be greatly served by actually doing what you read about, as it occurs. That will take your understanding to a much deeper and more significant level. You'll find it useful to understand the models; you'll likely find it transformational to apply them.

Necessarily, the book must put the essence of this dynamic art of workflow management and personal productivity into a linear format. I've tried to organize it in such a way as to give you both the inspiring big-picture view and a taste of immediate results as you go along.

> Healthy skepticism is often the best way to glean the value of what's being presented—challenge it; prove it wrong, if you can. That creates engagement, which is the key to understanding.

The book is divided into three parts. Part 1 describes the whole game, providing a brief overview of the system and an explanation of why it's unique and timely, and then presenting the basic methodologies themselves in their most condensed and basic form. Part 2 shows you how to implement the system. It's your personal coaching, step by step, on the nitty-gritty application of the models. Part 3 goes even deeper, describing the subtler and more profound results you can expect when you incorporate the methodologies and models into your work and your life.

There will be inevitable repetition in the content, in the three parts. The core methodology is relatively simple, but it can be expressed and understood at many different levels of depth and detail through the various lenses and lessons here.

I want you to hop in, test this stuff out, even challenge it. I want you to find out for yourself that what I promise is not only possible but instantly accessible to you personally. And I want you to know that everything I propose is *easy to do*. It involves no new skills at all. You already know how to focus, how to write things down, how to decide outcomes and actions, and how to review options and make choices. You'll validate that many of the things you've been doing instinctively and intuitively all along are right. I'll give you ways to leverage those basic skills into new plateaus of effectiveness. I want to inspire you to put all this into a new behavior set that will blow your mind.

From time to time in the book I refer to my work with people applying this material. I've been a management consultant, executive coach, and trainer for the past three decades—alone, in small partnerships, and as founder of a global training company. My work has consisted primarily of doing private coaching, conducting workshops, and giving presentations based on the methods presented here. I (and my colleagues) have now worked with thousands of people individually and trained hundreds of thousands in our in-house and public seminars around the world. We continue to engage with some of the best and brightest people all over the world. This is the background from which I have drawn my experience and examples.

I am a fellow student. I throw myself out of control and lose my focus, along with the rest and best of us. I equally must engage regularly with the practices I describe here, to keep myself clear with an optimal presence of mind. As I have described in chapter 15, this is a set of lifelong lifestyle habits that must be applied to engage in the world at more elevated and mature levels. I don't share anything in this book I have not personally experienced and tested for its validity and that I don't continue to use in some form.

The promise here was well described by a client of mine, who wrote, "When I habitually applied the tenets of this program it *saved* my life . . . when I faithfully applied them, it *changed* my life. This is the vaccination against day-to-day firefighting (the so-called urgent and crisis demands of any given workday) and an antidote for the imbalance many people bring upon themselves."

Getting Things Done

part

1

The Art of Getting Things Done

A New Practice for a New Reality

IT'S POSSIBLE FOR a person to have an overwhelming number of things to do and still function productively with a clear head and a positive sense of relaxed control. That's a great way to live and work, at elevated levels of effectiveness and efficiency. It's also the best way to be fully present with whatever you're doing, appropriately engaged in the moment. It's when time disappears, and your attention is completely at your command. What you're doing is exactly what you ought to be doing, given the whole spectrum of your commitments and interests. You're fully available. You're "on."

This is an operational style now critical for successful, high-performing professionals; a necessary mode for the sanity of anyone experiencing overextended life situations; and a fundamental platform to allow all of us the freedom to involve ourselves optimally in our most meaningful endeavors.

> There is one thing we can do, and the happiest people are those who can do it to the limit of their ability. We can be completely present. We can be all here. We can give . . . our attention to the opportunity before us.
>
> —*Mark Van Doren*

You already know how to do everything necessary to achieve this healthy, high-performance state. If you're like most people, however, you need to apply these skills in a more timely, complete, and systematic way so you can get on top of it all instead of feeling buried. And though the method and the techniques I describe in this book are immensely practical and based on common sense, most people will have some major habits that must be modified before they can fully enjoy the benefits of this system. The small changes required—changes in the way you clarify and organize all the things that command your attention—could represent a significant alteration in how you approach some key aspects of your day-to-day activities. But the results are often reported as transformational.

The methods I present here are all based on three key objectives: (1) capturing *all* the things that might need to get done or have usefulness for you—now, later, someday, big, little, or in between—in a logical and trusted system outside your head and off your mind; (2) directing yourself to make front-end decisions about all of the "inputs" you let into your life so that you will always have a workable inventory of "next actions" that you can implement or renegotiate in the moment; and (3) curating and coordinating all of that content, utilizing the recognition of the multiple levels of commitments with yourself and others you will have at play, at any point in time.

This book offers a proven method for this kind of high-performance workflow management. It provides good tools, tips, techniques, and tricks for implementation. As you'll discover, the principles and methods are instantly usable and applicable to everything you have to do in your personal as well as your professional life.* You can incorporate, as many others have before you, what I describe as an ongoing dynamic style of operating in your work and in your world. Or, like still others, you can simply use this as a guide to getting back into better control when you feel you need to.

The Problem: New Demands, Insufficient Resources

Almost everyone I encounter these days feels he or she has too much to handle and not enough time to get it all done. In the course of a single week, I consulted with a partner in a major global investment firm who was concerned that the new corporate-management responsibilities he was being offered would stress his family commitments beyond the limits; and with a midlevel human resources manager trying to stay on top of her 150-plus e-mail requests per day fueled by the goal of doubling the company's regional office staff from eleven hundred to two thousand people in

---

*I consider "work," in its most universal sense, to mean anything that you want or need to be different than it currently is. Many people make a distinction between "work" and "personal life," but I don't: To me, weeding the garden or updating my will is just as much "work" as writing this book or coaching a client. All the methods and techniques in this book are applicable across that life-work spectrum—to be effective, they need to be.

one year, all as she tried to protect a social life for herself on the weekends.

A paradox has emerged in this new millennium: people have enhanced quality of life, but at the same time they are adding to their stress levels by taking on more than they have resources to handle. It's as though their eyes were bigger than their stomachs. The plethora of options and opportunities brings with it the pressures of decision making and choices. And most people are to some degree frustrated and perplexed about how to improve the situation.

Work No Longer Has Clear Boundaries

A major factor in the mounting stress level is that the actual nature of our jobs has changed much more dramatically and rapidly than have our training for and our ability to deal with work. In just the last half of the twentieth century, what constituted "work" in the industrialized world was transformed from assembly line, make-it-and-move-it kinds of activity to what the late Peter Drucker so aptly termed "knowledge" work.

In the old days, work was self-evident. Fields were to be plowed, machines tooled, boxes packed, cows milked, crates moved. You knew what work had to be done—you could see it. It was clear when the work was finished, or not finished. Increasing your productivity was all about making the work process more efficient, or simply working harder or longer.

Now, for many of us, there are no edges to most of our projects. Most people I know have at least half a dozen things they're trying to achieve or situations they'd like to improve right now, | Almost every project could be done better, and an infinite quantity of information is now available that could make that happen.

and even if they had the rest of their lives to try, they wouldn't be able to finish these to perfection. You're probably faced with the same dilemma. How good could that conference be? How effective could the training program be, or the structure of your executives' compensation package? How well could you manage your kids' education? How close to perfect is the blog you're writing? How motivating is the staff meeting you're setting up? How healthy could you be? How functional is your department's reorganization?

And a last question: How much available data could be relevant to doing those projects "better"? The answer is: an infinite amount, easily accessible, or at least potentially so, through the Internet.

On another front, the lack of edges can create *more* work for everyone. Many of today's organizational outcomes require cross-divisional communication, cooperation, and engagement. Our individual office silos are crumbling (or at least need to be), and with them is going the luxury of not having to read cc'd e-mails from the marketing department, or from human resources, or from some ad hoc, deal-with-a-certain-issue committee. Add to that the increasing pull on your engagement with friends and family as distance from them disappears, with even aging parents taking to the Internet and their smartphones to "stay connected."

The ever-new communication technologies have exponentially magnified the lack of clear limits to our commitments and our lives. The second decade of this century witnessed an explosion of concern about the always-on conundrum, fueled by globalization ("half my team is in Hong Kong, and another key person in Estonia"), virtual work and connection capabilities, and not the least by the addiction to engaging with gadgets in our pockets and on our wrists that have more capacity than a room full of computers did in 1975.

So, not only are work and its cognitive boundaries more ambiguous and ill defined, so are the time and space within which we can (and often should) be engaged with it, along with the continuing explosion of potentially meaningful and accessible data that could add value to our lives.

Our Jobs (and Lives) Keep Changing

The disintegrating edges of our projects and our work in general would be challenging enough for anyone. But now we must add to that equation the constantly shifting definition of our jobs, as well as the frequent changes in responsibilities and interests in the broader scope of our lives.

I often ask in my seminar, "Which of you are doing only what you were hired to do? And how many of you have not had any significant change in your personal life in the past year?" Seldom do I get a raised hand. As amorphous as edgeless work may be, if you had the chance to stick with some specifically described job long enough, you'd probably figure out what you needed to do—how much, at what level—to stay sane. And if you could keep life in general more in check—no residence moves, no relationship changes, no emerging health or lifestyle issues for you and for loved ones, no financial surprises, no motivational programs generating inspiring new directions, no career shifts thrust on you—you might be able to create a rhythm and system of managing it that would allow for some relaxed stability.

But few have that luxury, for three reasons:

> Most of us have, in the past seventy-two hours, received more change-producing, project-creating, and priority-shifting inputs than our parents did in a month, maybe even in a year.

> *We can never really be prepared for that which is wholly new. We have to adjust ourselves, and every radical adjustment is a crisis in self-esteem; we undergo a test, we have to prove ourselves. It needs subordinate self-confidence to face drastic change without inner trembling.*
>
> —*Eric Hoffer*

1 | Organizations are now almost universally in morph mode, with ever-changing goals, products, partners, customers, markets, technologies, and owners. These all, by necessity, shake up structures, forms, roles, and accountabilities.

2 | The average professional is more of a free agent these days than ever before, changing careers as often as his or her parents once changed jobs. Even forty- and fiftysomethings hold to standards of continual growth. Their aims are just more integrated into the mainstream now, covered by the catch-all arena of "professional, management, and executive development"—which simply means they won't keep doing what they're doing for any extended period of time.*

3 | The relative speed of changes in our cultures, lifestyles, and technologies are creating greater necessity for individuals to take more control of their unique personal situations, more

---

*The Great Recession, early in this century, added to the uncertainties by creating the need for many to keep working after traditional retirement ages, often requiring the discovery of some other way to make money.

often. Suddenly needing to handle eldercare for a parent, dealing with a kid now back at home without a job, grappling with an unexpected health issue, or integrating a major change one's life partner has decided to initiate . . . all such seem to be happening with greater frequency, with larger consequences, than ever before.

Little seems clear for very long anymore, as far as what to do at the office, at home, on the plane, in the car, and at the local café— on the weekend, on Monday morning, on waking at three a.m., and on "vacation"; and what or how much input may be relevant to doing it well. We're allowing in huge amounts of information and communication from the outer world and generating an equally large volume of ideas and agreements with others and ourselves from the inner world. And we haven't been well equipped to deal with this huge number of internal and external commitments.

Nothing is really new in this high-tech, globally wired world, except how *frequently* it is. When the pace of change in life and work was much slower, once people got past the inevitable discomfort of the new, they could hang out on cruise control for greatly extended periods of time. Most of us are now living in a world that does not afford that time-out kind of luxury. It's changing while you're reading this. And if, while you *have* been reading this, you've been distracted by your mind wandering to other things going on in your life, or you've felt impelled to check e-mail for potentially meaningful new input, you're experiencing a manifestation of this don't-miss-the-train syndrome.

The Old Models and Habits Are Insufficient

Neither our standard education, nor traditional time-management models, nor the plethora of digital and paper-based organizing tools available has given us a viable means of meeting the new demands placed on us. If you've tried to use any of these processes or tools, you've probably found them unable to accommodate the speed, complexity, and changing priority factors inherent in what you are doing. The ability to be focused, relaxed, and in control during these fertile but turbulent and often unstructured times demands new ways of thinking and working. There is a great need for new methods, technologies, and work habits to help us get on top of our world.

The traditional approaches to time management and personal organization were useful in their time. They provided helpful reference points for a workforce that was just emerging from an industrial assembly-line modality into a new kind of work that included choices about what to do and discretion about when to do it. When time itself turned into a work factor, personal calendars became a key work tool. (Even in the 1980s many professionals considered having a pocket calendar the essence of being organized, and many people today still think of their calendar and possibly their e-mail and text in-boxes as the central tools for being in control.) Along with discretionary time came the need to make good choices about what to do. Creating "ABC" priority codes and daily "to-do" lists were key techniques developed to help people sort through their choices in some meaningful way. If you had the freedom to decide what to do, you also had the responsibility to make good choices, given your priorities.

What you've probably discovered, at least at some level, is that a calendar, though important, can really effectively manage only a small portion of what you need to be aware of to feel on top of your world. And daily to-do lists and simplified priority coding have proven inadequate in dealing with the volume and variable nature of the average person's workload. More and more people's jobs and lives are made up of hundreds of e-mails and texts a day, with no latitude left to ignore a single request, complaint, order, or communication from company or family. There are few people who can (or even should) expect to code everything based upon its priority, or who can maintain some predetermined list of to-dos that the first telephone call or instant message or interruption from their boss or spouse won't totally *undo*.

The Big Picture vs. the Nitty-Gritty

At the other end of the spectrum, a huge number of business books, models, seminars, and gurus have championed the "bigger view" as the solution to dealing with our complex world. Clarifying major

The winds and waves are always on the side of the ablest navigators.

—*Edward Gibbon*

goals and values, so the thinking goes, gives order, meaning, and direction to our work. In practice, however, the well-intentioned exercise of values thinking too often does not achieve its desired results. I have seen too many of these efforts fail, for one or more of the following three reasons:

1 | There is too much distraction at the day-to-day, hour-to-hour level of commitments to allow for appropriate focus on the higher levels.

2 | Ineffective personal organizational systems create huge subconscious resistance to undertaking even bigger projects and goals that will likely not be managed well, and that will in turn cause even more distraction and stress.

3 | When loftier levels and values actually are clarified, it raises the bar of our standards, making us notice that much more that needs changing. We are already having a serious negative reaction to the overwhelming number of things we have to do. And what created much of the work that's on those lists in the first place? Our values!

Focusing on primary outcomes and values *is* a critical exercise, certainly. It provides needed criteria for making sometimes-difficult choices about what to *stop* doing, as well as what most ought to have our attention amid our excess of options. But it does not mean that there is less to do, or fewer challenges in getting the work done. Quite the contrary: it just ups the ante in the game, which still must be played day to day. For a human resources executive, for example, deciding to deal with quality-of-work-life issues in order to attract and keep key talent does *not* make things simpler. Nor would there be less to do for a mother recognizing the importance of providing valuable experiences for her teenage daughter in the few vacations left they may take together before she leaves home for work or college. Upping the quality of our thinking and commitments does not diminish the quantity of potentially relevant and important stuff to manage.

Chaos isn't the problem; how long it takes to find coherence is the real game.

—*Doc Childre and Bruce Cryer*

There has been a missing piece in

our culture of knowledge work: a system with a coherent set of behaviors and tools that functions effectively at the level at which work really happens. It must incorporate the results of big-picture thinking as well as the smallest of open details. It must manage multiple tiers of priorities. It must maintain control over hundreds of new inputs daily. It must save a lot more time and effort than are needed to maintain it. It must make it easier to get things done.

The Promise: The "Ready State" of the Martial Artist

Reflect for a moment on what it actually might be like if your personal management situation were totally under control, at all levels and at all times. What if you had completely clear mental space, with nothing pulling or pushing on you unproductively? What if you could dedicate fully 100 percent of your attention to whatever was at hand, at your own choosing, with no distraction?

It *is* possible. There *is* a way to get a grip on it all, stay relaxed, and get meaningful things done with minimal effort, across the whole spectrum of your life and work. You *can* experience what the martial artists call a "mind like water" and top athletes refer to as the "zone," within the complex world in which you're engaged. In fact, you have probably already been in this state from time to time.

> *Life is denied by lack of attention, whether it be to cleaning windows or trying to write a masterpiece.*
> —Nadia Boulanger

It's a condition of working, doing, and being in which the mind is clear and constructive things are happening. It's a state that is accessible to everyone, and one that is increasingly needed to deal effectively with the complexity of life in this century. More and more it will be a required condition for any of us who wish to maintain balance and a consistent positive output in our work and outlook in our life. World-class rower Craig Lambert has described how it feels in *Mind Over Water* (Houghton Mifflin, 1998):

> *Rowers have a word for this frictionless state: swing. . . . Recall the pure joy of riding on a backyard swing: an easy cycle of motion, the*

momentum coming from the swing itself. The swing carries us; we do not force it. We pump our legs to drive our arc higher, but gravity does most of the work. We are not so much swinging as being swung. The boat swings you. The shell wants to move fast: Speed sings in its lines and nature. Our job is simply to work with the shell, to stop holding it back with our thrashing struggles to go faster. Trying too hard sabotages boat speed. Trying becomes striving and striving undoes itself. Social climbers strive to be aristocrats but their efforts prove them no such thing. Aristocrats do not strive; they have already arrived. Swing is a state of arrival.

The "Mind Like Water" Simile

In karate there is an image that's used to define the position of perfect readiness: "mind like water." Imagine throwing a pebble into a still pond. How does the water respond? The answer is, totally appropriately to the force and mass of the input; then it returns to calm. It doesn't overreact or underreact.

> Your ability to generate power is directly proportional to your ability to relax.

Water is what it is, and does what it does. It can overwhelm, but it's not overwhelmed. It can be still, but it is not impatient. It can be forced to change course, but it is not frustrated. Get it?

The power in a karate punch comes from speed, not muscle; it comes from a focused "pop" at the end of the whip. That's why petite people can learn to break boards and bricks with their hands: it doesn't take calluses or brute strength; just the ability to generate a focused thrust with speed. But a tense muscle is a slow one. So the high levels of training in the martial arts teach and demand balance and relaxation as much as anything else. Clearing the mind to being open and appropriately responsive is the key.

Anything that causes you to overreact or underreact can control you, and often does. Responding inappropriately to your e-mail, your thoughts about what you need to do, your children, or your boss will lead to less effective results than you'd like. Most people give either more or less attention to things than they deserve, simply because they don't operate with a mind like water.

Can You Get into Your "Productive State" When Required?

Think about the last time you felt highly productive. You probably had a sense of being in control, you were not stressed out, you were highly focused on what you were doing, time tended to disappear (lunchtime already?), and you felt you were making noticeable progress toward a meaningful outcome. Would you like to have more such experiences?

> *If your mind is empty, it is always ready for anything; it is open for everything.*
> —*Shunryu Suzuki*

And if you get seriously far out of that state—and start to feel out of control, stressed out, unfocused, bored, and stuck—do you have the ability to get yourself back into it? That's where the methodology of *Getting Things Done* will have the greatest impact on your life, by showing you how to get back to mind like water, with all your resources and faculties functioning at a maximum level. A challenge for many may be the lack of a reference point as to when they fall out of the productive state. Most people have lived in a semistressful experience so consistently, for so long, they don't know that it could be quite different—that there is another and more positive place from which to engage with their world. Hopefully this book will inspire you to raise the bar about how much pressure you will allow yourself to tolerate, knowing you have the techniques to reduce it.

The Principle: Dealing Effectively with Internal Commitments

A basic truism I have discovered over decades of coaching and training thousands of people is that most stress they experience comes from inappropriately managed commitments they make or accept. Even those who are not consciously "stressed out" will invariably experience greater relaxation, better focus, and increased productive energy when they learn more effectively to control the "open loops" of their lives.

You've probably made many more agreements with yourself than you realize, and every single one of them—big or little—is being

Anything that does not belong where it is, the way it is, is an "open loop," which will be pulling on your attention if it's not appropriately managed.

tracked by a less-than-conscious part of you. These are the "incompletes," or "open loops," which I define as anything pulling at your attention that doesn't belong where it is, the way it is. Open loops can include everything from really big to-do items like "End world hunger" to the more modest "Hire new assistant" to the tiniest task such as "Replace porch lightbulb."

In order to deal effectively with all of that, you must first identify and capture all those things that are "ringing your bell" in some way, clarify what, exactly, they mean to you, and then make a decision about how to move on them. That may seem like a simple process, but in reality most people don't do it in a consistent way. They lack the knowledge or the motivation, or both, and most likely because they aren't aware of the prices paid for neglecting that practice.

The Basic Requirements for Managing Commitments

Managing commitments well requires the implementation of some basic activities and behaviors:

• First of all, if it's on your mind, your mind isn't clear. Anything you consider unfinished in any way must be captured in a trusted system outside your mind, or what I call a collection tool, that you know you'll come back to regularly and sort through.

• Second, you must clarify exactly what your commitment is and decide what you have to do, if anything, to make progress toward fulfilling it.

You must *use* your mind to get things *off* your mind.

• Third, once you've decided on all the actions you need to take, you must keep reminders of them organized in a system you review regularly.

An Important Exercise to Test This Model

I suggest that you write down the project or situation that is most on your mind at this moment. What most bugs you, distracts you, or interests you, or in some other way consumes a large part of your conscious attention? It may be a project or problem that is really "in your face," something you are being pressed to handle, or a situation you feel you must deal with sooner rather than later.

Maybe you have a holiday trip coming up that you need to make some major last-minute decisions about. You just read an e-mail about a new and pressing issue in your department. Or perhaps you just inherited six million dollars and you don't know what to do with the cash. Whatever.

Got it? Good. Now, describe, in a single written sentence, your intended successful outcome for this problem or situation. In other words, what would need to happen for you to check this project off as "done"? It could be as simple as "Take the Hawaii vacation," "Handle situation with customer X," "Resolve college situation with Susan," "Clarify new divisional management structure," "Implement new investment strategy," or "Research options for dealing with Manuel's reading issue." All clear? Great.

Now write down the *very next physical action required to move the situation forward.* If you had nothing else to do in your life but get closure on this, what visible action would you take right now? Would you call or text someone? Write an e-mail? Take pen and paper and brainstorm about it? Surf the Web for data? Buy nails at the hardware store? Talk about it face-to-face with your partner, your assistant, your attorney, or your boss? What?

Got the answer to that? Good.

Was there any value for you in those two minutes of thinking? If you're like the vast majority of people who complete that drill in our seminars, you'll be experiencing at least a tiny bit of enhanced control, relaxation, and focus. You'll also be feeling more motivated to actually *do* something about that situation you've merely been thinking about till now. Imagine that motivation magnified a thousandfold, as a way to live and work.

> *Think like a man of action, act like a man of thought.*
> —*Henri Bergson*

If anything at all positive happened for you in this little exercise, think about this: What changed? What happened to create that improved condition within your own experience? The situation itself is no further along, at least in the physical world. It's certainly not finished yet. What probably happened is that you acquired a clearer definition of the outcome desired and the next action required. What did change is the most important element for clarity, focus, and peace of mind: how you are engaged with your world.

But what created that? Not "getting organized" or "setting priorities." The answer is, *thinking*. Not a lot; just enough to solidify your commitment about a discrete pressure or opportunity and the resources required dealing with it. People think a lot, but most of that thinking is *of* a problem, project, or situation—not *about* it. If you actually did this suggested exercise, you were required to structure your thinking toward an outcome and an action, and that does not usually happen without a consciously focused effort. Reacting is automatic, but thinking is not.

The Real Work of Knowledge Work

Welcome to the real-life experience of "knowledge work," and a profound operational principle: you have to think about your stuff more than you realize but not as much as you're afraid you might. As Peter Drucker wrote: "In knowledge work . . . the task is not given; it has to be determined. 'What are the expected results from this work?' is . . . the key question in making knowledge workers productive. And it is a question that demands risky decisions.

> *The ancestor of every action is a thought.*
>
> *—Ralph Waldo Emerson*

There is usually no right answer; there are choices instead. And results have to be clearly specified, if productivity is to be achieved."*

Most people have a resistance to initiating the burst of energy that it will take to clarify the real meaning, for them, of something they have let into their world, and to decide what they need to do

---

*"Knowledge work" may seem an unfamiliar concept to many in this century, simply because so much of our lives now incorporates so many nonphysical and nonobvious things we need to decide, demanding constant thinking and choices. Most of us are in it all the time (the last thing a fish notices is water). But the realization of the thinking process itself that we must be applying is not explicitly realized or exercised yet by most. Knowledge work may seem an idea limited to white-collar professionals. That was the initial population in the past century that dealt with this, but anyone who has moved out of mere survival mode finds himself or herself in this game. Any parent who has ever wondered what class to choose for a child or what digital device to give him or her is in this category.

about it. We're never really taught that we have to think about our work before we can do it; much of our daily activity is already defined for us by the undone and unmoved things staring at us when we come to work, or by the family to be fed, the laundry to be done, or the children to be dressed at home. Thinking in a concentrated manner to define desired outcomes and requisite next actions is something few people feel they have to do (until they *have* to). But in truth, it is the most effective means available for making wishes a reality.

Why Things Are on Your Mind

Most often, the reason something is on your mind is that you want it to be different than it currently is, and yet:

- you haven't clarified exactly what the intended outcome is;
- you haven't decided what the very next physical action step is; and/or
- you haven't put reminders of the outcome and the action required in a system you trust.

> *This consistent, unproductive preoccupation with all the things we have to do is the single largest consumer of time and energy.*
>
> —*Kerry Gleeson*

That's why it's on your mind. Until those thoughts have been clarified and those decisions made, and the resulting data has been stored in a system that you *absolutely* know you will access and think about when you need to, your brain can't give up the job. You can fool everyone else, but you can't fool your own mind. It knows whether or not you've come to the conclusions you need to, and whether you've put the resulting outcomes and action reminders in a place that can be trusted to resurface appropriately within your conscious mind.* If you haven't done those things, it won't quit working overtime. Even if you've already decided on the next step you'll take to resolve a problem, your mind can't let go until and unless you park a reminder in a place it *knows* you will, without fail, look. It will keep pressuring you about that untaken next step, usually when you can't do anything about it, which will just add to your stress.

---

*See Baumeister's validating research, referenced in chapter 14.

Your Mind Doesn't Have a Mind of Its Own

At least a portion of your mind is really kind of stupid, in an interesting way. If it had any innate intelligence and logic, it would remind you of the things you needed to do only when you could do something about them.

Do you have a flashlight somewhere with dead batteries in it? When does your mind tend to remind you that you need more batteries? When you notice the dead ones! That's not very smart. If your mind had any innate intelligence, it would remind you about those dead batteries only when you passed new ones in a store. And ones of the right size, to boot.

Between the time you woke up today and now, did you think of anything you needed to do that you still haven't done? Have you had that thought more than once? Why? It's a waste of time and energy to keep thinking about something that you make no progress on. And it only adds to your anxiety about what you should be doing and aren't.

> *Rule your mind or it will rule you.*
>
> *—Horace*

Most people let their reactive mental process run a lot of the show, especially where the too-much-to-do syndrome is concerned. You've probably given over a lot of your "stuff," a lot of your open loops, to an entity on your inner committee that is incapable of dealing with those things effectively the way they are—your mind. Research has now proven that a significant part of your psyche cannot help but keep track of your open loops, and not (as originally thought) as an intelligent, positive motivator, but as a detractor from anything else you need or want to think about, diminishing your capacity to perform.

The Transformation of "Stuff"

Here's how I define "stuff": anything you have allowed into your psychological or physical world that doesn't belong where it is, but for which you haven't yet determined what, exactly, it means to you, with the desired outcome and the next action step. The reason most organizing systems haven't worked for most people is that they haven't yet transformed all the stuff they're trying to organize.

As long as it's still stuff, it's not control-
lable.

We need to transform all the "stuff" we've attracted and accumulated into a clear inventory of meaningful actions, projects, and usable information.

Almost all of the to-do lists I have seen over the years (when people had them at all!) were merely listings of stuff, not inventories of the resultant real work that needed to be done. They were partial reminders of a lot of things that were unresolved and as yet untranslated into outcomes and actions—that is, the real outlines and details of what the list maker had to do.

Typical things you will see on a to-do list: "Mom" "Bank" "Doctor" "Baby-sitter" "VP Marketing" etc. Looking at these often creates more stress than relief, because, though it is a valuable trigger for something that you've committed to do or decide something about, it still calls out psychologically, "Decide about me!" And if you do not have the energy or focus at the moment to think and decide, it will simply remind you that you are overwhelmed.

Stuff is not inherently a bad thing. Things that command or attract our attention, by their very nature, usually show up as stuff. But once we allow stuff to come into our lives and work, we have an inherent commitment to ourselves to define and clarify its meaning. In the professional world, our jobs require us to think, assess, decide, and execute—minute by minute—whether about an e-mail or our notes from the morning's strategy meeting. That's inherent in your job. If you didn't have to think about those things, you're probably not required to. And personally, we will shortchange ourselves when we allow issues in our daily lifestyle—home, family, health, finances, career, or relationships—to lie fallow in our consciousness because of lack of definition of the specific outcomes desired and actions required.

At the conclusion of one of my seminars, a senior manager of a major biotech firm looked back at the to-do list she had come in with and said, "Boy, that was an amorphous blob of undoability!" That's the best description I have ever heard about what passes for organizing lists in most systems. The vast majority of people have been trying to get organized by rearranging incomplete lists of unclear things; they haven't yet realized how much

Thought is useful when it motivates action and a hindrance when it substitutes for action.

—Bill Raeder

and what they need to organize in order to get the real payoff. They need to gather everything that requires thinking about and then *do* that thinking if their organizational efforts are to be successful.

The Process: Managing Action

You can train yourself, almost like an athlete, to be faster, more responsive, more proactive, and more focused in dealing with all the things you need to deal with. You can think more effectively and manage the results with more ease and control. You can minimize the loose ends across the whole spectrum of your work life and personal life and get a lot more done with less effort. And you can make front-end decision making about all the stuff you collect and create standard operating procedure for living and working in this millennium.

Before you can achieve any of that, though, you'll need to get in the habit of keeping nothing on your mind. And the way to do *that*, as we've seen, is not by managing time, managing information, or managing priorities. After all:

- you don't manage five minutes and wind up with six;
- you don't manage information overload—otherwise you'd walk into a library and die, or the first time you connected to the Web, you'd blow up; and
- you don't manage priorities—you *have* them.

The beginning is half of every action.

—*Greek proverb*

Instead, the key to managing all of your stuff is managing your *actions*.

Managing Action Is the Prime Challenge

What you do with your time, what you do with information, and what you do with your body and your focus relative to your priorities—those are the real options to which you must allocate your limited resources. The substantive issue is how to make appropriate choices about what to do at any point in time. The real work is to manage our actions.

That may sound obvious. However, it might amaze you to discover how many next actions for how many projects and commitments remain undetermined by most people. It's extremely difficult to manage actions you haven't identified or decided on. Most people have dozens of things that they need to do to make progress on many fronts, but they don't yet know what they are. And the common complaint that "I don't have time to ___" (fill in the blank) is understandable because many projects seem overwhelming—and *are* overwhelming because you can't *do* a project at all! You can only do an action related to it. Many actions require only a minute or two, in the appropriate context, to move a project forward.

In training and coaching many thousands of people, I have found that lack of time is not the major issue for them (though they may think it is); the real problem is a lack of clarity and definition about what a project really is, and what associated next-action steps are required. Clarifying things on the front end, when they first appear on the radar, rather than on the back end, after trouble has developed, allows people to reap the benefits of managing action.

> Things rarely get stuck because of lack of time. They get stuck because what "doing" would look like, and where it happens, hasn't been decided.

Getting things done requires two basic components: defining (1) what "done" means (outcome) and (2) what "doing" looks like (action). And these are far from self-evident for most people about most things that have their attention.

The Value of a Bottom-Up Approach

I have discovered over the years the practical value of working on personal productivity improvement from the bottom up, starting with the most mundane, ground-floor level of current activity and commitments. Intellectually, the most appropriate way ought to be to work from the top down, first uncovering personal and organizational purpose and vision, then defining critical objectives, and finally focusing on the details of implementation. The trouble is, however, that most people are so embroiled in commitments on a day-to-day level that their ability to focus successfully on the larger horizon is seriously impaired. Consequently, a bottom-up approach is usually more effective.

Getting current on, and in control of, what's in your in-tray and on your mind right now, and incorporating practices that you can trust will help you *stay* that way, will provide the best means of broadening your horizons. A creative, buoyant energy will be unleashed that will better support your focus on new heights, and your confidence will increase to handle what that creativity produces. An immediate sense of freedom, release, and inspiration naturally comes to people who roll up their sleeves and implement this process.

Vision is not enough; it must be combined with venture. It is not enough to stare up the steps; we must step up the stairs.

—Václav Havel

You'll be better equipped to undertake higher-focused thinking when your tools for handling the resulting actions for implementation are part of your ongoing operational style. There are more meaningful things to think about than your in-tray, but if your management of that level is not as efficient as it could be, it's like trying to swim in baggy clothing.

Many executives I have worked with during the day to clear the decks of their mundane stuff have spent the evening having a stream of ideas and visions about their company and their future lifestyle. This happens as an automatic consequence of unsticking their workflow.

Horizontal and Vertical Action Management

You need to control commitments, projects, and actions in two ways—horizontally and vertically. Horizontal control maintains coherence across all the activities in which you are involved. Imagine your psyche constantly scanning your environment like a police radar; it may land on any of a thousand different items that invite or demand your attention during any twenty-four-hour period: the drugstore, your daughter's boyfriend, the board meeting, your aunt Martha, an incoming text message, the strategic plan, lunch, a wilting plant in the office, an upset customer, shoes that need shining. You need to buy stamps, figure out what to do about the presentation tomorrow, deposit that check, make the hotel reservation, cancel a meeting, and watch a movie tonight. You might be surprised at the volume of things you actually think about and have to deal with just in one day. You need a good system that can keep track of as many of them as possible, supply required information about them on demand, and allow you to shift your focus from one thing to the next quickly and easily.

Vertical control, in contrast, manages thinking, development, and coordination of individual topics and projects. For example, your inner "police radar" lands on your next vacation as you and your life partner talk about it over dinner—where and when you'll go, what you'll do, how to prepare for the trip, and so on. Or you and your boss need to make some decisions about the new departmental reorganization you're about to launch. Or you just need to get your thinking up-to-date on the customer you're about to call. This is "project planning" in the broad sense. It's focusing in on a single endeavor, situation, or person and fleshing out whatever ideas, details, priorities, and sequences of events may be required for you to handle it, at least for the moment.

The goal for managing horizontally and vertically is the same: to get things off your mind and get them done. Appropriate action management lets you feel comfortable and in control as you move through your broad spectrum of work and life, while appropriate project focusing gets you clear about and on track with the specifics needed.

The Major Change: Getting It All Out of Your Head

There is no real way to achieve the kind of relaxed control I'm promising if you keep things only in your head. As you'll discover, the individual behaviors described in this book are things you're already doing. The big difference between what I do and what others do is that I capture and organize 100 percent of my stuff in and with objective tools at hand, not in my mind. And that applies to everything—little or big, personal or professional, urgent or not. Everything.*

> There is usually an inverse relationship between how much something is on your mind and how much it's getting done.

---

*Not exactly everything. Much of the time my mind is simply "grazing"—noticing or thinking about things, and potentially maturing my awareness about something or other. I'm not writing down thousands of thoughts I have during the day. Almost all are complete in themselves. It's the ones that create some open loop in my psyche—a

I'm sure that at some time or other you've gotten to a point in a project, or in your life, where you just *had* to sit down and *make a list*. Subsequently you felt at least slightly more focused and in control. If so, you have a reference point for what I'm talking about. Nothing externally changed in your world, and yet you felt better about it. What did change, significantly, is *how you were engaged with your world*. That always happens when you get potentially meaningful things out of your head. Most people, however, do that kind of list-making drill only when the confusion gets too unbearable and they just *have* to do something about it. They usually, though, only make a list about the specific area that's bugging them. But if you made that kind of externalization and review a characteristic of your on-going life- and work style, and you maintained it across all areas of your life (not just the most "urgent"), you'd be practicing the kind of mind like water management style I'm describing. In my experience this process *always* improves our perspective and our experience. Why wait?

There is no reason to ever have the same thought twice, unless you like having that thought.

I try to make intuitive choices based on my options, instead of trying to think about what those options are. I need to have thought about all of that already and captured the results in a trusted way. I don't want to waste time thinking about things more than once. That's an inefficient use of creative energy and a source of frustration and stress.

And you can't fudge this thinking. Your mind will keep working on anything that's still in that undecided state. But that kind of recursive spinning in your mind has now been proven to reduce your capacity to think and perform, and there's a limit to how much unresolved stuff it can contain before it blows a fuse.

Any "would, could, or should" commitment held only in the psyche creates irrational and unresolvable pressure, 24-7.

The short-term-memory part of your mind—the part that tends to hold all of the incomplete, undecided, and unorganized stuff—functions much like RAM (random-access memory) on a computer. Your conscious mind, like the

---

restaurant I read about I might want to try, an idea for possible content for the revision of this book, something I thought of that I want to do for my wife, a question I have for my accountant, something to get at the hardware store, etc.

computer screen, is a focusing tool, not a storage place. You can think about only two or three things at once. But the incomplete items are still being stored in the short-term-memory space. And as with RAM, there's limited capacity; there's only so much stuff you can store in there and still have that part of your brain function at a high level. Most people walk around with their RAM bursting at the seams. They're constantly distracted, their focus disturbed and performance diminished by their own internal mental overload. Recent research in the cognitive sciences has now validated this conclusion. Studies have demonstrated that our mental processes are hampered by the burden put on the mind to keep track of things we're committed to finish, without a trusted plan or system in place to handle them.*

For example, in the past few minutes, has your mind wandered off into some area that doesn't have anything to do with what you're reading here? Probably. And most likely where your mind went was to some open loop, some incomplete situation that you have an investment in. That situation merely reared up out of the RAM part of your brain and yelled at you internally. And what did you do about it? Unless you wrote it down and put it in a trusted collection tool that you know you'll review appropriately sometime soon, more than likely you worried, or at least reinforced some unresolved tension, about it. Not the most effective behavior: no progress was made, and stress increased.

A big problem is that your mind keeps reminding you of things when you can't do anything about them. It has no sense of past or future. That means as soon as you tell yourself that you might need to do something, and store it only in your head, there's a part of you that thinks you should be doing that something *all the time*. Everything you've told yourself you ought to do, it thinks you should be doing *right now*. Frankly, as soon as you have two things to do stored only in your mind, you've generated personal failure, because you can't do them both at the same time. This produces a pervasive stress factor whose source can't be pinpointed.

> *It is hard to fight an enemy who has outposts in your head.*
> —*Sally Kempton*

---

*An excellent book that covers this topic (and many others) is *Willpower: Rediscovering the Greatest Human Strength*, by Roy Baumeister and John Tierney (Penguin, 2011).

Most people have been in some version of this mental stress state so consistently, for so long, that they don't even know they're in it. Like gravity, it's ever present—so much so that those who experience it usually aren't even aware of the pressure. The only time most of them will realize how much tension they've been under is when they get rid of it and notice how different they feel. It's like the constant buzzing noise in a room you didn't know was there until it stops.

Can you get rid of that kind of stress and noise? You bet. The rest of this book will explain how.

2

Getting Control of Your Life: The Five Steps of Mastering Workflow

THE CORE PROCESS for mastering the art of relaxed and controlled engagement is a five-step method for managing your workflow—the ever-present ingestion and expressions of our experiences. No matter what the setting, there are five discrete stages that we go through as we deal with our life, our work, and their consistent inputs and changes. Getting things under control, whether that's in your kitchen or in your company, will incorporate them. And each of these separate aspects has its own best practices and tools, and must work together with the rest as a whole to produce that wonderfully productive state of being present amid all the complexity. It's not simply about "getting organized" or "setting priorities." Those are good things, but they happen as a result of applying these five steps—not by themselves. These procedures I will describe work together as a whole, and using them to produce results is both easier and more challenging than you may think.

> Don't let life get in your way.

We (1) *capture* what has our attention; (2) *clarify* what each item means and what to do about it; (3) *organize* the results, which presents the options we (4) *reflect* on, which we then choose to (5) *engage* with. This constitutes the management of the horizontal aspect of our lives, incorporating everything that we need to consider at any time, as we move forward moment to moment.

These are not arbitrary or purely theoretical suggestions—they are what we all do, anytime we want to bring

> *A useful definition of liberty is obtained only by seeking the principle of liberty in the main business of human life, that is to say, in the process by which men educate their responses and learn to control their environment.*
>
> *—Walter Lippmann*

something under control and stabilize it for productive action. If you're planning to cook dinner for friends, but you come home and find the kitchen a total mess, how do you get on top of it? First you identify all the stuff that doesn't belong where it is, the way it is (capture); you then determine what to keep and what to throw away (clarify); you put things where they need to go—back in the refrigerator, in the garbage, or in the sink (organize); you then check your recipe book, along with the ingredients and utensils you have (reflect); and you get started by putting butter in the pan to start melting (engage).

The method is straightforward enough in principle, and it is generally how we all go about our work in any case, but in my experience most people can significantly improve their handling of each one of the five steps. The quality of our workflow management is only as good as the weakest link in this five-phase chain, so all the links must be integrated and supported with consistent standards.

Most people have had major inefficiencies in their versions of this control process in the larger contexts of life and work, but the stresses of our new world are blowing out the weak spots. The ubiquity of information access and rapidity of change happening, as you read this, consistently increase the complexity of your life and work. Only having to deal with a messy kitchen would be a relief! Small leaks, with added pressure, become big ones. One missed e-mail, untracked commitment, or decision avoided can have hugely magnified consequences. Because the volume of pertinent content is not diminishing or the input slowing down, avoiding getting a grip on the martial art of workflow mastery will be at your own peril.

Most people have major weaknesses in their (1) *capture* process. Most of their commitments to do something are still in their head. The number of coulds, shoulds, might-want-tos, and ought-tos they generate in their minds are way out beyond what they have recorded anywhere else.

Many have collected lots of things but haven't (2) *clarified* exactly what they represent or decided what action, if any, to take about them. Random lists strewn everywhere, meeting notes, vague to-dos on Post-its on their refrigerator or computer screens or in their Tasks function in a digital tool—all lie not acted on and numbing to the psyche in their effect. Those lists alone often create more stress than they relieve.

Others make good decisions about stuff in the moment but lose the value of that thinking because they don't efficiently (3) *organize* the results. They determined they should talk to their boss about something, but a reminder of that lies only in the dark recesses of their mind, unavailable in the appropriate context, in a trusted format, when they could use it.

Still others have good systems but don't (4) *reflect* on the contents consistently enough to keep them functional. They may have lists, plans, and various checklists available to them (created by capturing, clarifying, and organizing), but they don't keep them current or access them to their advantage. Many people don't look ahead at their own calendars consistently enough to stay current about upcoming events and deadlines, and they consequently become victims of last-minute craziness.

> Ask yourself, "When do I need to see what, in what form, to get it off my mind?" You build a system for function, not just to have a system.

Finally, if any one of these previous links is weak, what someone is likely to choose to (5) *engage* in at any point in time may not be the best option. Most decisions for action and focus are driven by the latest and loudest inputs, and are based on hope instead of trust. People have a constant nagging sense that they're not working on what they should be, that they "don't have time" for potentially critical activities, and that they're missing out on the timeless sense of meaningful doing that is the essence of stress-free productivity.

The dynamics of these five steps need to be understood, and good techniques and tools implemented to facilitate their functioning at an optimal level. I have found it very helpful, if not essential, to separate these stages as I move through my day. There are times when I want only to collect input and not decide what to do with it yet. At other times I may just want to process my notes from a meeting. Or I may have just returned from a big trip and need to distribute and organize what I collected and processed on the road. Then there are times when I want to review the whole inventory of my work, or some portion of it. And obviously a lot of my time is spent merely doing something that I need to get done.

I have discovered that one of the major reasons many people haven't had a lot of success with getting organized is simply that they have tried to do all five steps at one time. Most, when they sit down to make a list, are trying to collect the "most important things" in some order that reflects priorities and sequences, without setting out many (or any) real actions to take. But if you don't decide what needs to be done about your assistant's birthday, because it's "not that important" right now, that open loop will take up energy and prevent you from having a totally effective, clear focus on what's important.

This chapter explains the five steps in detail. Chapters 4 through 8 provide a step-by-step program for implementing an airtight system for each phase, with lots of examples and best practices.

Capture

It's important to know what needs to be captured and how to do that most effectively so you can process it appropriately. In order for your mind to let go of the lower-level task of trying to hang on to everything, you have to know that you have truly captured everything that might represent something you have to do or at least decide about, and that at some point in the near future you will process and review all of it.

Gathering 100 Percent of the "Incompletes"

In order to eliminate "holes in your bucket," you need to collect and gather placeholders for, or representations of, all the things you consider incomplete in your world—that is, anything personal or professional, big or little, of urgent or minor importance, that you think ought to be different than it currently is and that you have any level of internal commitment to changing.

Many of the things you have to do are being collected *for* you as you read this. Mail is coming into your various mailboxes—physical and virtual. You're likely still getting packages and letters at home. Physical stuff is still landing in your in-tray at work, along with e-mail, texts, and voice mails into your digital tools. But at the same time, you've been capturing things in your environment and in your head that don't belong where they are, the way they are, for all eternity. Even though it may not be as obviously "in your face" as your e-mail, the stuff still requires some kind of resolution—a loop to be closed, something to be done. Strategy ideas loitering in a notebook, "dead" gadgets in your desk drawers that need to be fixed or thrown away, and out-of-date magazines on your coffee table all fall into this category of stuff.

As soon as you attach a "should," "need to," or "ought to" to an item, it becomes an incomplete. Decisions you still need to make about whether or not you are going to do something, for example, are already incompletes. This includes all of your I'm-going-tos, in which you've decided to do something but haven't started moving on it yet. And it certainly includes all pending and in-progress items, as well as those things on which you've done everything you're ever going to do except acknowledge that you're finished with them.

> *A task left undone remains undone in two places—at the actual location of the task, and inside your head. Incomplete tasks in your head consume the energy of your attention as they gnaw at your conscience.*
>
> —*Brahma Kumaris*

In order to manage this inventory of open loops appropriately, you need to capture it into "containers" that hold items in abeyance until you have a few moments to decide what they are and what, if anything, you're going to do about them. Then you must empty these containers regularly to ensure that they remain viable capture tools.

Basically, everything potentially meaningful to you is already being collected, in the larger sense. If it's not being directly managed in a trusted external system of yours, then it's resident somewhere in your mental space. The fact that you haven't put an item in your in-tray doesn't mean you haven't got it. But we're talking here about making sure everything you need is collected somewhere other than in your head.

The Capture Tools

There are several types of tools, both low- and high-tech, that can be used to collect your incompletes. The following can all serve as versions of an in-tray, capturing self-generated input as well as information from external sources:

- Physical in-tray
- Paper-based note-taking devices
- Digital/audio note-taking devices
- E-mail and text messaging

The Physical In-Tray

The standard plastic, wood, leather, or wire tray has for years been the most common tool for collecting paper-based and physical materials that need some sort of processing: mail, magazines, meeting notes, corporate reports, tickets, receipts, flash drives, business cards—even flashlights with dead batteries!

Writing Paper and Pads

Loose-leaf and bound notebooks, note cards, and paper pads of all shapes and sizes work fine for collecting random ideas, input, things to do, and so on. Whatever fits your taste and logistical needs.

Digital and Voice Note Taking

Computers, tablets, smartphones, and all kinds of new mobile tech gadgetry emerging daily can be used for capturing notes for later processing, preserving an interim record of things you need to remember to deal with.

E-mail and Texting

If you're wired to the rest of the world through e-mail and texting, your software contains some sort of holding area for incoming messages and files, where they can be stored until they are viewed, read, and processed.

Technology Integration

The evolution of the digital world has made it increasingly possible to integrate these various channels automatically. Written notes from paper and whiteboards can be instantly recorded, recognized, and funneled into software storage. Voice messages can be recorded, digitized, and printed out. You can text an idea to your e-mail from your mobile device.

Whether high-tech or low-tech, all of the tools and functions I've described serve similarly as in-trays, capturing potentially meaningful information, commitments, ideas, and agreements for action.

The Success Factors for Capturing

Unfortunately, merely having an in-tray doesn't make it functional. Most people do have collection devices of some sort, but usually they're more or less out of control or seriously underutilized. Let's examine the three requirements to make the capturing phase work:

1 | Every open loop must be in your capture system and out of your head.
2 | You must have as few capturing buckets as you can get by with.
3 | You must empty them regularly.

Get It All Out of Your Head

If you're still trying to keep track of too many things in your mental space, you likely won't be motivated to use and empty your in-trays with integrity. Most people are relatively careless about these tools because they know they don't represent discrete, whole systems anyway; there's an incomplete set of things in their in-tray and an incomplete set in their mind, and they're not getting a real payoff from either one, so their thinking goes. It's like trying to play pinball on a machine that has big holes in the table, so the balls keep falling out: there's little motivation to keep playing the game.

Get a purge for your brain. It will do better than for your stomach.

—Michel Eyquem de Montaigne

These collection tools should become part of your lifestyle. Keep them close by so no matter where you are you can collect a potentially valuable thought—think of them as being as indispensable as your toothbrush or your driver's license or your glasses. The sense of trust that nothing possibly useful will get lost will give you the freedom to have many more good ideas.

Keep everything *in* your head or *out* of your head. If it's in between, you won't trust either one.

Minimize the Number of Capture Locations

You should have as many in-trays as you need and as few as you can get by with. You need this function to be available to you in every context, since things you'll want to capture may show up almost anywhere. If you have too many collection zones, however, you won't be able to process them easily or consistently.

An excess of collection buckets can easily happen in both the low-tech and hi-tech arenas. There is a real improvement opportunity for most people on the low-tech side, primarily in the areas of note taking and physical in-tray collection. Written notes need to be corralled and processed instead of left lying embedded in stacks, notebooks, and drawers. Paper and physical materials need to be funneled into physical in-trays instead of being scattered over myriad piles in all the available corners of the world. On the high-tech side, potential sources of input for stuff to be assessed and processed have proliferated tremendously, with the advent of social media, multiple connected devices, and the ubiquity of e-mail. People now often have more than one e-mail account, are participating in at least one if not several social media worlds, and operate with numerous digital devices. Paradoxically, the tendency to accumulate a huge backlog of random inputs to deal with, and the number of people troubled with that, have increased dramatically, as the digital revolution has "streamlined" our lives.

Funnel all potentially meaningful inputs through minimal channels, directed to you for easily accessed review and assessment about their nature.

Implementing standard tools and procedures for capturing ideas and input will become more and more critical as your life and work become more sophisticated. As you proceed in your career, for instance, you'll probably notice that your best ideas about work will not come to you *at* work. The ability to leverage that thinking with good collection devices that are always at hand is key to staying on top of your world.

Empty the Capture Tools Regularly

The final success factor for capturing should be obvious: if you don't empty and process the stuff you've collected, your tools aren't serving any function other than the storage of amorphous material. Emptying the contents does not mean that you have to finish what's there; it just means that you have to decide more specifically what it is and what should be done with it, and if it's still unfinished, organize it into your system. You must get it out of the container. You don't leave it or put it back into "in"! Not emptying your in-tray is like having garbage cans and mailboxes that no one ever dumps or deals with—you just have to keep buying new ones to hold an eternally accumulating volume.

In order to get "in" to empty, however, an integrated life-management system must be in place. Too much stuff is left piled in in-trays (physical and digital) because of a lack of effective systems "downstream" from there. It often seems easier to leave things in "in" when you know you have to do something about them but can't do it right then. The in-tray, especially for paper and e-mail, is the best that many people can do in terms of organization—at least they know that *somewhere* in there is a reminder of something they still have to do. Unfortunately, that safety net is lost when the piles get out of control or the inventory of e-mails gets too extensive to be viewed on one screen.

> Blockage in the flow of anything undermines the ability to be present, fresh, and creative in that arena.

When you master the next two steps and know how to process and organize your inputs and incompletes easily and rapidly, "in" can return to its original function. Let's move on to how to get those in-trays and e-mail systems empty without necessarily having to do the work now.

Clarify

Teaching them the item-by-item thinking required to get their collection containers empty is perhaps the most critical improvement I have made for virtually all the people I've worked with. When the head of a major department in a global corporation had finished processing all her open items with me, she sat back in awe and told me that though she had been able to relax about what meetings to go to thanks to her trust in her calendar, she had never felt that same relief about all the many other aspects of her job, which we had just clarified together. The actions and information she needed

It is better to be wrong than to be vague.

—Freeman Dyson

to be reminded of were now identified and entrusted to a concrete system.

What do you need to ask yourself (and answer) about each e-mail, text, voice mail, memo, page of meeting notes, or self-generated idea that comes your way? This is the component of input management that forms the basis for your personal organization. Many people try to get organized but make the mistake of doing it with incomplete batches of stuff. You can't organize what's incoming—you can only capture it and process it. Instead, you organize the actions you'll need to take based on the decisions you've made about what needs to be done. The whole deal—both the *capturing* and *organizing* phases—is represented in the center "trunk" of the decision-tree model shown here.

What Is It?

This is not a dumb question. We've talked about stuff. And we've talked about collection buckets. But we haven't discussed what stuff is and what to do about it. For example, many of the items that tend to leak out of our personal organizing systems are amorphous forms that we receive from the government or from our company—do we actually need to do something about them? And what about that e-mail from human resources, letting us know that blah-blah about the blah-blah is now the policy of blah-blah? I've unearthed piles of messages in stacks and desk drawers that were tossed there because the client didn't take just a few seconds to figure out what, in fact, the communication or document was really about. Which is why the next decision is critical.

Is It Actionable?

There are two possible answers for this: **yes** and **no**.

No Action Required If the answer is **no**, there are three possibilities:

1 | It's trash, no longer needed.
2 | No action is needed now, but something might need to be done later (incubate).
3 | The item is potentially useful information that might be needed for something later (reference).

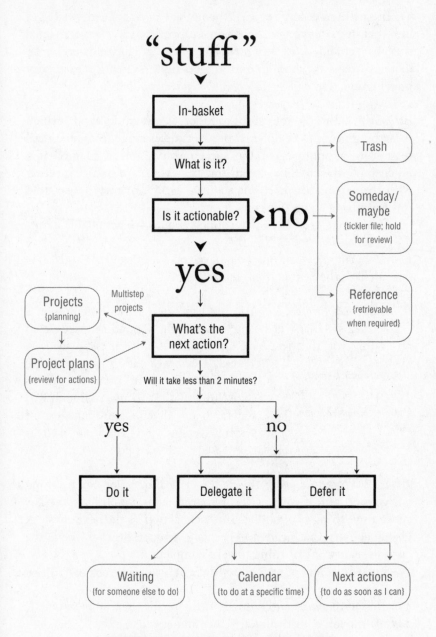

WORKFLOW DIAGRAM—CLARIFYING

These three categories can themselves be managed; we'll get into that in a later chapter. For now, suffice it to say that you need a wastebasket and <Del> key for trash, a "tickler" file or calendar for material that's incubating, and a good filing system for reference information.

Actionable   This is the **yes** group of items, stuff about which something needs to be done. Typical examples range from an e-mail requesting a summary of the speech you've agreed to give at a luncheon to the notes in your in-tray from your face-to-face meeting with the group vice president about a significant new project that involves hiring an outside consultant.

Two things need to be determined about each actionable item:

1 | What "project" or outcome have you committed to? and
2 | What's the next action required?

If It's About a Project . . .   You need to capture that outcome on a "Projects" list. That will be the stake in the ground that will keep reminding you that you have an open loop until it is finished. A Weekly Review of the list (see page 50) will bring this item back to you as something that's still outstanding. It will stay fresh and alive in your management system (versus your head) until it is completed or eliminated.

> *It does not take much strength to do things, but it requires a great deal of strength to decide what to do.*
>
> *—Elbert Hubbard*

What's the Next Action?   This is the critical question for anything you've captured; if you answer it appropriately, you'll have the key substantive thing to organize. The "next action" is the next physical, visible activity that needs to be engaged in, in order to move the current reality of this thing toward completion.

Some examples of next actions might be:

• Call Fred re: name and number of the repair shop he mentioned.
• Draft thoughts for the budget-meeting agenda.
• Talk to Angela about the filing system we need to set up.
• Research Internet for local watercolor classes.

These are all real physical activities that need to happen. Reminders of these will become the primary grist for the mill of your personal productivity-management system.

Do It, Delegate It, or Defer It   Once you've decided on the next action, you have three options:

1. *Do it.* If an action will take less than two minutes, it should be *done* at the moment it is defined.

2. *Delegate it.* If the action will take longer than two minutes, ask yourself, Am I the right person to do this? If the answer is no, *delegate* it to the appropriate entity.

3. *Defer it,* If the action will take longer than two minutes, and you are the right person to do it, you will have to *defer* acting on it until later and track it on one or more "Next Actions" lists.

Organize

The outer ring of the workflow diagram shows the eight discrete categories of reminders and materials that will result from your processing all your stuff. Together they make up a total system for organizing just about everything that's on your plate, or could be added to it, on a daily and weekly basis.

> Being organized means simply that where something is matches what it means to you.

For nonactionable items, the possible categories are *trash*, *incubation*, and *reference*. If no action is needed on something, you toss it, "tickle" it for later reassessment, or file it so you can find the material if you need to refer to it at another time. To manage actionable things, you will need a *list of projects*, *storage or files for project plans and materials*, a *calendar*, a *list of reminders of next actions*, and a *list of reminders of things you're waiting for.*

All of the organizational categories need to be physically contained in some form. When I refer to "lists," I just mean some sort of reviewable set of reminders, which could be lists on notebook paper or in some computer program or even file folders holding separate pieces of paper for each item. For instance, the list of current projects could be kept on a page in a loose-leaf planner; it could be held

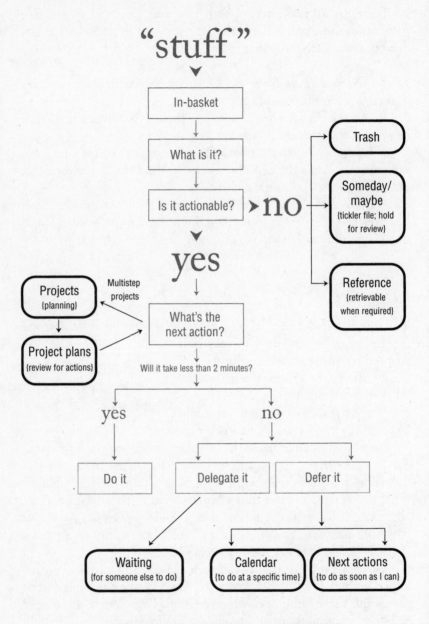

WORKFLOW DIAGRAM—ORGANIZING

in a category within the Tasks function of a software application; or it could be in a simple physical file folder labeled "Projects List." Incubating reminders (such as "After 01 March contact my accountant to set up a meeting") may be stored in a paper-based "tickler" or "bring-forward" file or in a digital calendar application.

Projects

I define a project as any desired result that can be accomplished within a year that requires more than one action step. This means that some rather small things you might not normally call projects are going to be on your Projects list, as well as some big ones. The reasoning behind my definition is that if one step won't complete something, some kind of goalpost needs to be set up to remind you that there's something still left to do. If you don't have a placeholder to remind you about it, it will slip back into your head. The reason for the one-year time frame is that anything you are committed to finish within that scope needs to be reviewed weekly to feel comfortable about its status. Another way to think of this is as a list of open loops, no matter what the size.

A Partial Projects List

Get new staff person on board	Get reprints of HBR article
Take August holiday	Get a publicist
Produce staff off-site retreat	Plant spring garden
Publish book	Research resources for video project
Finalize computer upgrades	Establish next year's conference schedule
Update will	Finalize employment agreements
Finalize budgets	Install new porch lighting
Finalize new product offering	Get a new kitchen table
Learn new CRM software	Enroll Maria in middle school

Projects do not initially need to be listed in any particular order, by size, or by priority. They just need to be on a master list so you can review them regularly enough to ensure that appropriate next actions have been defined for each of them.

You don't actually *do* a project; you can only do action steps *related* to it. When enough of the right action steps have been taken, some situation will have been created that matches your initial picture of the outcome closely enough that you can call it "done." The list of projects is the compilation of finish lines we put before us to keep our next actions moving on all tracks appropriately.

There may be reasons to sort your projects into different subcategories, based upon different areas of your focus, but initially creating a single list of all of them will make it easier to customize your system appropriately as you get more comfortable with its usage.

Project Support Material

For many of your projects, you will accumulate relevant information that you will want to organize by theme or topic or project name. Your Projects list will be merely an index. All of the details, plans, and supporting information that you may need as you work on your various projects should be contained in separate file folders, computer files, notebooks, or binders.

Support Materials and Reference Files Once you have organized your project support material by theme or topic, you will probably find that it is almost identical to your reference material and could be kept in the same reference file system (a Wedding file could be kept in the general-reference files, for instance). The only difference is that in the case of active projects, support material may need to be reviewed on a more consistent basis to ensure that all the necessary action steps are identified.

I usually recommend that people store their support materials out of sight. If you have a good working reference file system close enough at hand, you may find that that's the simplest way to organize them. There will be times, though, when it'll be more convenient to have the materials out and instantly in view and available, especially if you're working on a hot project that you need to check references for several times during the day. File folders in wire standing holders or in stackable trays within easy reach can be practical for this kind of pending paperwork.

The digital world has paradoxically made organizing reference and support materials simultaneously simpler and more complex. It's quick and easy to capture something from somewhere and copy it somewhere else, but deciding where it goes can be daunting, given the plethora of parking places available to us and the myriad ways that we might want the information available to others as well as ourselves. The best practice is to keep your digital reference world as simple as possible, and consistently reviewed and purged.

The Next-Action Categories

As the workflow diagram makes clear, the next-action decision is central. That action needs to be the next physical, visible behavior, without exception, on every open loop.

Any less-than-two-minute actions that you perform, and all other actions that have already been completed, do not, of course, need to be tracked; they're done. What *does* need to be tracked is every action that has to happen at a specific time or on a specific day (enter those on your calendar); those that need to be done as soon as they can (add these to your Next Actions lists); and all those that you are waiting for others to do (put these on a Waiting For list).

Calendar

Reminders of actions you need to take fall into two categories: those about things that have to happen on a specific day or time, and those about things that just need to get done as soon as possible. Your calendar handles the first type of reminder.

Three things go on your calendar:

• time-specific actions;
• day-specific actions; and
• day-specific information

Time-Specific Actions This is a fancy name for appointments. Often the next action to be taken on a project is attending a meeting that has been set up to discuss it. Simply tracking that on the calendar is sufficient.

Day-Specific Actions These are things that you need to do sometime on a certain day, but not necessarily at a specific time. Perhaps you told Mioko you would call her on Friday to check that the report you're sending her is OK. She won't have the report until Thursday, and she's leaving the country on Saturday, so Friday is the time window for taking the action—but anytime Friday will be fine. That should be tracked on the calendar for Friday but not tied to any particular time slot—it should just go on the day. It's useful to have a calendar on which you can note both time-specific and day-specific actions.

Day-Specific Information   The calendar is also the place to keep track of things you want to know about on specific days—not necessarily actions you'll have to take but rather information that may be useful on a certain date. This might include directions for appointments, activities that other people (family or staff) will be involved in then, or events of interest. It's helpful to put short-term tickler information here, too, such as a reminder to call someone after he or she returns from vacation. This is also where you would want to park important reminders about

Blessed are the flexible, for they shall not be bent out of shape.

—Michael McGriffy, M.D.

when something might be due, or when something needs to be started (in case it hasn't been yet), given a determined lead time.

No More "Daily To-Do" Lists on the Calendar   Those three things are what go on the calendar, and nothing else! This might be heresy to past-century time-management training, which almost universally taught that the daily to-do list is key. But such lists embedded on a calendar don't work, for two reasons.

First, constant new input and shifting tactical priorities reconfigure daily work so consistently that it's virtually impossible to nail down to-do items ahead of time. Having a working game plan as a reference point is always useful, but it must be able to be renegotiated at any moment. Trying to keep a list on the calendar, which must then be reentered on another day if items don't get done, is demoralizing and a waste of time. The Next Actions lists I advocate will hold all of those action reminders, even the most time-sensitive ones. And they won't have to be rewritten daily.

Second, if there's something on a daily to-do list that doesn't absolutely *have* to get done that day, it will dilute the emphasis on the things that truly do. If I *have* to call Mioko on Friday because that's the only day I can reach her, but then I add five other, less important or less time-sensitive calls to my to-do list, when the day gets crazy I may never call Mioko. My brain will have to take back the reminder that that's the one phone call I won't get another chance at. That's not utilizing the system appropriately. The way I look at it, the calendar should be sacred territory. If you write something there, it must get done that day or not at all. The only rewriting should be for changed appointments.

That said, there's absolutely nothing wrong with creating a quick, informal, short list of "if I have time, I'd really like to . . ." kinds of things, picked from your Next Actions inventory. It just should not be confused with your "have-tos," and it should be treated lightly enough to discard or change quickly as the inevitable surprises of the day unfold.

The "Next Actions" List(s)

So where do your entire action reminders go? On Next Actions lists, which, along with the calendar, are at the heart of daily action-management organization and orientation.

Any longer-than-two-minute, non-delegatable action you have identified needs to be tracked somewhere. "Call Jim Smith re: budget meeting," "E-mail family update to friends," and "Draft ideas re: the annual sales conference" are all the kinds of action reminders that need to be kept in appropriate lists, to be assessed as options for what we will do at any point in time.

If you have only twenty or thirty of these, it may be fine to keep them all on one list labeled "Next Actions," which you'll review whenever you have any free time. For most of us, however, the number is more likely to be fifty to 150. In that case it makes sense to subdivide your Next Actions list into categories, such as Calls to make when you have a window of time and your phone, or Computer action items to see as options when you're at that device.

> *Everything should be made as simple as possible, but no simpler.*
> *—Albert Einstein*

Nonactionable Items

You need well-organized, discrete systems to handle things that require no action as well as those that do. No-action systems fall into three categories: trash, incubation, and reference.

Trash

Trash should be self-evident. Throw away, shred, or recycle anything that has no potential future action or reference value. If you leave this stuff mixed in with other categories, it will seriously undermine the system and your clarity in the environment.

Incubation

There are two other groups of things besides trash that require no immediate action but that you will want to keep. Here, again, it's critical that you separate nonactionable from actionable items; otherwise you will tend to go numb to your piles, stacks, and lists and not know where to start or what needs to be done.

Say you read something in a newsletter that gives you an idea for a project you might want to do someday, but not now. You'll want to be reminded of it again later so you can reassess the option of doing something about it in the future. Or you get a notice about the upcoming season of your local symphony, and you see that the program that really interests you is still four months away—too distant for you to move on it yet (you're not sure what your travel schedule will be that far out). But if you are in town, you'd like to go. What should you do about that?

There are two kinds of incubation tools that could work for this kind of thing: Someday/Maybe lists and a tickler system.

Someday/Maybe   It can be useful and inspiring to maintain an ongoing list of things you might want to do at some point but not now. This is the "parking lot" for projects that would be impossible to move on at present but that you don't want to forget about entirely. You'd like to be reminded of the possibility at regular intervals.

Typical Partial Someday/Maybe List

Get a sailboat	Set up a foundation for kids
Learn Spanish	Get a piano
Take a watercolor class	Publish my memoir
Renovate the kitchen	Get scuba certification
Build a lap pool	Learn to tango
Take a balloon ride	Learn to throw pottery
Build a wine cellar	Give a neighborhood party
Spend a month in Tuscany	Build a koi pond
Create my own Web page	

These items are of the nature of "projects I might want to do, but not now . . . but I'd like to be reminded of them regularly." You must review this list periodically if you're going to get the most value from it. I suggest you include a scan of the contents in your Weekly Review (see page 50).

You'll probably have some other types of information that are similar to Someday/Maybe but that probably need a review only when you have an urge to engage in a particular kind of activity. These would be lists such as:

• Books to read
• Wines to taste
• Recipes to try
• Movies to rent
• Weekend trips to take
• Things my kids might like to do
• Seminars to take
• Web sites to surf

These kinds of reminders can greatly expand your options for creative exploration. Having an organizational tool that allows you to easily make lists such as these, ad hoc, is quite worthwhile.

Tickler System   A second type of things to incubate are those you don't want or need to be reminded of until some designated time in the future. A most elegant version of holding for review of this nature is the tickler file, sometimes also referred to as a "suspense," "follow-on," or "perpetual" file. This is a system that allows you to almost literally mail something to yourself, for receipt on some designated date in the future.

Your calendar can serve the same function. You might remind yourself on your calendar for March 15, for example, that your taxes are due in a month; or for September 12, that *Swan Lake* will be presented by the Bolshoi at the Civic Auditorium in six weeks.

For further details, refer to chapter 7.

Reference Material

Many things that come your way require no action but have intrinsic value as information. You will want to keep and be able to retrieve these as needed. They can be stored in paper-based or digital form.

Paper-based material—anything from the menu for a local takeout deli to the plans, drawings, and vendor information for a landscape project—is best stored in efficient physical or digital retrieval systems. These can range from pages in a loose-leaf planner or notebook, for a list of favorite restaurants or the phone numbers of members of a school committee, to whole file cabinets dedicated to the due-diligence paperwork for a corporate merger. Though more and more information is showing up in digital form, print versions are at times still an effective way for it to be stored and reviewed.

Electronic storage can include everything from cloud-based data storage to archive folders in your communications software.

The most important thing to remember here is that reference should be exactly that—information that can be *easily* referred to when required. Reference systems generally take two forms: (1) topic- and area-specific storage, and (2) general-reference files. The first types usually define themselves in terms of how they are stored—for example, a file drawer dedicated to contracts, by date; a drawer containing only confidential employee-compensation information; a series of cabinets for closed legal cases that might need to be consulted for future trials; or a customer relations management (CRM) database for client and prospect histories.

General Reference Filing   The second type of reference system is one that everyone needs close at hand for storing ad hoc information that doesn't belong in some predesigned larger category. You need somewhere to keep the instruction manuals for your kitchenware, the handwritten notes from your meeting about the Smith project, and those yen you didn't get to exchange at the end of your most recent trip to Tokyo (and that you can use when you go back there).

The lack of a good general-reference file can be one of the biggest bottlenecks in implementing an efficient personal management system. If filing and storing isn't easy and fast (and even fun!), you'll tend to stack, pile, or digitally accumulate things instead of putting them away appropriately. If your reference material doesn't have nice clean edges to it, the line between actionable and nonactionable items will blur, visually and psychologically, and your mind will go numb to the whole business. Establishing a good working system for this category of material is critical to ensuring stress-free productivity; we will explore it in detail in chapter 7.

Reflect

It's one thing to write down that you need milk; it's another to be at the store and remember it. Likewise, writing down that you need to call a friend to find out how he's doing after a significant event in his life and wish him well is different from remembering it when you're at a phone and have some discretionary time.

You need to be able to step back and review the whole picture of your life and work from a broader perspective as well as drop down "into the weeds" of concrete actions to take, as needed, and at appropriate intervals. For most people the magic of workflow management is realized in the consistent use of the reflection step. This is where, in one important case, you take a look at all your outstanding projects and open loops, at what I call Horizon 1 level (see page 55), on a weekly basis. It's your chance to scan all the defined actions and options before you, thus radically increasing the efficacy of the choices you make about what you're doing at any point in time.

Your life is more complex than any single system can describe or coordinate, but the GTD methodology creates a coherent model for placeholding key elements, which still require attention, being kept current, and being reviewed in a coordinated way. Most people have some simple components of this in various places, but the contents and the utilization of these are elementary, at best.

What to Review When

If you set up a personal organization system structured as I recommend, with a Projects list, a calendar, Next Actions lists, and a Waiting For list, not much will be required to maintain that system.

The item you'll probably review most frequently is your calendar, which will remind you about the "hard landscape" for the day—that is, what things truly *have* to be handled

> Review whatever lists, overviews, and orientation maps you need to, as often as you need to, to get their contents off your mind.

that day. This doesn't mean that the contents there are the most "important" in some grand sense—only that they must get done. At any point in time, knowing what has to get done and when creates a terrain for maneuvering. It's a good habit, as soon as you conclude an action on your calendar (a meeting, a phone call, the final draft of a report that's due), to check and see what else remains to be done.

After checking your calendar, you'll most often turn to your Next Action lists. These hold the inventory of predefined actions that you can take if you have any discretionary time during the day. If you've organized them by context (At Home; At Computer; In Meeting with George) they'll come into play only when those contexts are available.

Projects, Waiting For, and Someday/Maybe lists need to be reviewed only as often as you think they have to be in order to stop you from wondering about them.

Critical Success Factor: The Weekly Review

Everything that might require action must be reviewed on a frequent enough basis to keep your mind from taking back the job of remembering and reminding. In order to

> *The affairs of life embrace a multitude of interest, and he who reasons in any one of them, without consulting the rest, is a visionary unsuited to control the business of the world.*
>
> —*James Fenimore Cooper*

trust the rapid and intuitive judgment calls that you make about actions from moment to moment, you must consistently retrench at some more elevated level. In my experience (with thousands of people), that translates into a behavior critical for success: the Weekly Review.

All of your Projects, active project plans, and Next Actions, Agendas, Waiting For, and even Someday/Maybe lists should be reviewed once a week. This also gives you an opportunity to ensure that your brain is clear and that all the loose strands of the past few days have been captured, clarified, and organized.

If you're like most people, you've found that things can get relatively out of control during the course of a few days of operational intensity. That's to be expected, but it will continue to increase in tandem with the ubiquity of your always-on, connected world. You wouldn't want to distract yourself from too much of the work at hand in an effort to stay totally "squeaky clean" all the time. But in order to afford the luxury of "getting on a roll" with confidence, you'll probably need to clean house and refresh the contents once a week.

The Weekly Review is the time to:

• Gather and process all your stuff.
• Review your system.
• Update your lists.
• Get clean, clear, current, and complete.

Most people don't have a really complete system, and they get no real payoff from reviewing things for just that reason: their overview isn't total. They still have a vague sense that something may be missing. That's why the rewards to be gained from implementing this whole process are exponential: the more complete the system is, the more you'll trust it. And the more you trust it, the more complete you'll be motivated to keep it. The Weekly Review is a master key to maintaining that standard.

> You have to use your mind to get things off your mind.

Most people feel best about their work the week before they go on vacation, but it's not because of the vacation itself. What do you do the last week before you leave on a big trip? You clean up, close up, clarify, organize, and renegotiate all your agreements with yourself and others. You do this so you can relax and be present on the beach, on the golf course, or on the slopes, with nothing else on your mind. I suggest you do this weekly instead of yearly, so you can bring this kind of "being present" to your everyday life.

Engage

The basic purpose of this workflow-management process is to facilitate good choices about what you're doing at any point in time. At 10:33 a.m. Monday, deciding whether to call Sandy, finish the proposal, or clean up your e-mails will always be an intuitive call, but with the proper orientation you can feel much more confident about your choices. You can move from hope to trust in your actions, immediately increasing your energy and effectiveness.

> Every decision to act is an intuitive one. The challenge is to migrate from *hoping* it's the right choice to *trusting* it's the right choice.

Three Models for Making Action Choices

Let's assume for a moment that you're not resisting any of your stuff out of insecurity or procrastination. There will always be a long list of actions that you are not doing at any given moment. So how will you decide what to do and what not to do, and feel good about both?

The answer is, by trusting your intuition. If you have *captured*, *clarified*, *organized*, and *reflected* on all your current commitments, you can galvanize your intuitive judgment with some intelligent and practical thinking about your work and values.

There are three models that will be helpful for you to incorporate in your decision making about what to do. They won't tell you answers—whether you call Mario, e-mail your son at school, or just have an informal conversation with your secretary—but they will assist you in framing your options more intelligently. And that's something that the simple time- and priority-management panaceas can't do.

1. The Four-Criteria Model for Choosing Actions in the Moment

At 3:22 on Wednesday, how do you choose what to do? At that moment there are four criteria you can apply, in this order: context, time available, energy available, and priority.

The first three describe the constraints within which you

continually operate, and the fourth provides the hierarchical values to ascribe to your actions.

Context You are always constrained by what you have the capability to do at this time. A few actions can be done anywhere (such as drafting ideas about a project with pen and paper), but most require a specific location (at home, at your office) or having some productivity tool at hand, such as a phone or a computer. These are the first factors that limit your choices about what you can do in the moment.

Time Available When do you have to do something else? Having a meeting in five minutes would prevent doing any actions that require more time.

> There is always more to do than you can do, and you can do only one thing at a time. The key is to feel as good about what you're *not* doing as about what you *are* doing at that moment.

Energy Available How much energy do you have? Some actions you have to do require a reservoir of fresh, creative mental energy. Others need more physical horsepower. Some need very little of either.

Priority Given your context, time, and energy available, what action remaining of your options will give you the highest payoff? You're in your office with a phone and a computer, you have an hour, and your energy is 7.3 on a scale of 10. Should you call the client back, work on the proposal, process your e-mails, or check in with your spouse to see how his or her day is going?

This is where you need to access your intuition and begin to rely on your judgment call in the moment. To explore that concept further, let's examine two more models for deciding what's most important for you to be doing.

2. The Threefold Model for Identifying Daily Work

When you're getting things done, or "working" in the universal sense, there are three different kinds of activities you can be engaged in:

- Doing predefined work
- Doing work as it shows up
- Defining your work

Doing Predefined Work When you're doing predefined work, you're working from your Next Actions lists and calendar—completing tasks that you have previously determined need to be done, or managing your workflow. You're making the calls you need to make, drafting ideas you want to brainstorm, attending meetings, or preparing a list of things to talk to your attorney about.

Doing Work as It Shows Up Often things come up ad hoc— unsuspected, unforeseen—that you either have to or choose to engage in as they occur. For example, your partner walks into your office and wants to have a conversation about the new product launch, so you talk to her instead of doing all the other things you could be doing. Every day brings surprises—unplanned-for things that just show up—and you'll need to expend at least some time and energy on many of them. When you follow these leads, you're deciding by default that these things are more important than anything else you have to do at those times.

Defining Your Work Defining your work entails clearing up your in-tray, your digital messages, and your meeting notes, and breaking down new projects into actionable steps. As you process your inputs, you'll no doubt be taking care of some less-than-two-minute actions and tossing and filing numerous things (another version of doing work as it shows up). A good portion of this activity will consist of identifying things that need to get done sometime, but not right away. You'll be adding to all of your lists as you go along.

Once you have defined all your work, you can trust that your lists of things to do are complete. And your context, time, and energy available still allow you the option of more than one thing to do. The final thing to consider is the nature of your work, and its goals and standards.

3. The Six-Level Model for Reviewing Your Own Work

Priorities should drive your choices, but most models for determining them are not reliable tools for much of our real work activity. In order to know what your priorities are, you have to know what your work is. And there are at least six different perspectives from which to define that. To use an appropriate analogy, the conversation has a lot do with the horizon, or distance of perception. Looking out from a building, you will notice different things from different floors.

- Horizon 5: Purpose and principles
- Horizon 4: Vision
- Horizon 3: Goals
- Horizon 2: Areas of focus and accountabilities
- Horizon 1: Current projects
- Ground: Current actions

Let's start from the bottom up:

Ground: Current Actions   This is the accumulated list of all the actions you need to take—all the phone calls you have to make, the e-mails you have to respond to, the errands you've got to run, and the agendas you want to communicate to your boss and your life partner. You'd probably have more than a hundred of these items to handle if you stopped the world right now with no more input from yourself or anyone else.

Horizon 1: Current Projects   Generating most of the actions that you currently have in front of you are the thirty to one hundred projects on your plate. These are the relatively short-term outcomes you want to achieve, such as setting up a new home computer, organizing a sales conference, moving to a new headquarters, and getting a dentist.

Horizon 2: Areas of Focus and Accountabilities   You create or accept your projects and actions because of the roles, interests, and accountabilities you have. These are the key areas of your life and work within which you want to achieve results and maintain standards. Your job may entail at least implicit commitments for things like strategic planning, administrative support, staff development, market research, customer service, or asset management. And your personal life has an equal number of such focus arenas:

> *Complete the projects you begin, fulfill the commitments you have made, live up to your promises—then both your subconscious and conscious selves can have success, which leads to a feeling of fulfillment, worthiness and oneness.*
>
> *—John-Roger*

health, family, finances, home environment, spirituality, recreation, etc. These are not things to finish but rather to use as criteria for assessing our experiences and our engagements, to maintain balance and sustainability, as we operate in our work and our world. Listing and reviewing these responsibilities gives a more comprehensive framework for evaluating your inventory of projects.

Horizon 3: Goals   What you want to be experiencing in various areas of your life and work one to two years from now will add another dimension to defining your work. Often meeting the goals and objectives of your job will require a shift in emphasis of your job focus, with new accountabilities emerging. At this horizon personally, too, there probably are things you'd like to accomplish or have in place, which could add importance to certain aspects of your life and diminish others.

Horizon 4: Vision   Projecting three to five years into the future generates thinking about bigger categories: organization strategies, environmental trends, career and lifestyle transition circumstances. Internal factors include longer-term career, family, financial, and quality-of-life aspirations and considerations. Outer-world issues could involve changes affecting your job and organization, such as technology, globalization, market trends, and competition. Decisions at this altitude could easily change what your work might look like on many levels.

Horizon 5: Purpose and Principles   This is the big-picture view. Why does your company exist? Why do *you* exist? What really matters to you, no matter what? The primary purpose for anything provides the core definition of what the work really is. It is the ultimate job description. All goals, visions, objectives, projects, and actions derive from this, and lead toward it.

These horizon analogies are somewhat arbitrary, and in real life the important conversations you will have about your focus and your priorities may not exactly fit one level or another. They can provide a useful framework, however, to remind you of the multilayered nature of your commitments and tasks.

Minute-to-minute and day-to-day you don't have time to think. You need to have already thought.

Obviously many factors must be

considered before you feel comfortable that you have made the best decision about what to do and when. "Setting priorities" in the traditional sense of focusing on your long-term goals and values, though obviously a necessary core focus, does not provide a practical framework for a vast majority of the decisions and tasks you must engage in day to day. Mastering the flow of your work at all the levels you experience that work provides a much more holistic way to get things done and feel good about it.

Part 2 of this book will provide specific coaching about how to use these models for making action choices, and how the best practices for capturing, clarifying, planning, organizing, and reflecting all contribute to your greatest success with them.

3

Getting Projects Creatively Under Way: The Five Phases of Project Planning

THE KEY INGREDIENTS of relaxed control are (1) clearly defined outcomes (projects) and the next actions required to move them toward closure, and (2) reminders placed in a trusted system that is reviewed regularly. This is what I call horizontal focus. Although it may seem simple, the actual application of the process can create profound results.

Enhancing Vertical Focus

Horizontal focus is all you'll need in most situations, most of the time. Sometimes, however, you may need greater rigor and focus to get a project or situation under control, to identify a solution, or to

You've got to think about the big things while you're doing small things, so that all the small things go in the right direction.

—Alvin Toffler

ensure that all the right steps have been determined. This is where vertical focus comes in. Knowing how to think productively in this more vertical way and how to integrate the results into your personal system is the second powerful behavior set needed for knowledge work.

This kind of thinking doesn't have to be elaborate. Most of the thinking you'll need to do is informal, what I call back-of-the-envelope planning—the kind of thing you do literally on the back of an envelope or napkin in a coffee shop with a colleague as you're hashing out the agenda and structure of a sales presentation. In my experience this tends to be the most productive kind of planning you can do in terms of your output relative to the energy you put into it. True, once in a while everyone may need to develop a more formal structure or plan to clarify components, sequences, or priorities. And more detailed outlines will also be necessary to coordinate more complex situations—if teams need to collaborate about various project pieces, for example, or if business plans need to be drafted to convince an investor you know what you're doing. But as a general rule, you can be pretty creative with nothing more than a pen and piece of paper.

The greatest need I've seen in project thinking in the professional world is not for more formal models; usually the people who need those models already have them or can get them as part of an academic or professional curriculum. Instead, I've found the biggest gap to be the lack of a project-focusing model for the rest of us. We need ways to validate and support our thinking, no matter how informal. Formal planning sessions and high-horsepower planning tools (such as project management software) can certainly be useful at times, but too often the participants in a meeting will need to have *another* meeting—a back-of-the-envelope (or whiteboard) session—to actually get a piece of work fleshed out and under control. More formal and structured meetings also tend to skip over at least one critical issue, such as why the project is being done in the first place. Or they don't allow adequate time for brainstorming, the development of a bunch of ideas nobody's ever thought about that would make the project more interesting, more profitable, or just more fun. And finally, very few such meetings bring to bear sufficient rigor in determining action steps and accountabilities for the various aspects of a project plan.

> The goal is to get projects and situations sufficiently clear and under control to get them off your mind, and not to lose any potentially useful ideas.

The good news is, there *is* a productive way to think about projects, situations, and topics that creates maximum value with minimal expenditure of time and effort. It happens to be the way we naturally plan when we consciously try to get a project under control or simply execute for a desired outcome. In my experience, when people do more planning, informally and naturally, they relieve a great deal of stress *and* obtain better results.

The Natural Planning Model

You're already familiar with the most brilliant and creative planner in the world: your brain. You yourself are actually a planning machine.

The most experienced planner in the world is your brain.

You're planning when you get dressed, eat lunch, go to the store, or simply talk. Although the process may seem somewhat random, a quite complex series of steps has to occur before your brain can make anything happen physically. Your mind goes through five steps to accomplish virtually any task:

1 | Defining purpose and principles
2 | Outcome visioning
3 | Brainstorming
4 | Organizing
5 | Identifying next actions

A Simple Example: Planning Dinner Out

The last time you went out to dinner, what initially caused you to think about doing it? It could have been any number of things—the desire to satisfy hunger, socialize with friends, celebrate a special occasion, sign a business deal, or develop a romance. As soon as any of these turned into a real inclination that you wanted to move on, you started planning. Your intention was your **purpose**, and it automatically triggered your internal planning process. Your **principles** created the boundaries of your plan. You probably didn't consciously think about your principles regarding going out to dinner, but you thought within them: standards of food and service, affordability, convenience, and comfort all may have played a part. In any case, your purpose and principles were the defining impetus and boundaries of your planning.

Once you decided to fulfill your purpose, what were your first substantive thoughts? Probably not "Point II.A.3.b. in plan." Your first ideas were more likely things like "Italian food at Giovanni's," or "Sitting at a sidewalk table at the Bistro Café." You probably also imagined some positive picture of what you might experience or how the evening would turn out—maybe the people involved, the atmosphere, and/or the outcome. That was your **outcome visioning**. Whereas your purpose was the *why* of your going out to dinner, your vision was an image of the *what*—of the physical world's looking, sounding, and feeling the ways that best fulfilled your purpose.

Once you'd identified with your vision, what did your mind naturally begin doing? What did it start to think about? "What time should we go?" "Is it open tonight?" "Will it be crowded?" "What's the weather like?" "Should we change clothes?" "Is there gas in the car?" "How hungry are we?" That was **brainstorming**. Those questions were part of the naturally creative process that happens once you commit to some outcome that hasn't happened yet. Your brain noticed a gap between what you were looking toward and where you actually were at the time, and it began to resolve that cognitive dissonance by trying to fill in the blanks. This is the beginning of the *how* phase of natural planning. But it did the thinking in a somewhat random and ad hoc fashion. Lots of different aspects of going to dinner just occurred to you. You almost certainly didn't need to actually write all of them down on a piece of paper, but you did a version of that process in your mind.*

Once you had generated a sufficient number of ideas and details, you couldn't help but start to **organize** them. You may have thought or said, "First we need to find out if the restaurant is open," or "Let's call the Andersons and see if they'd like to go out with us." Once you've generated various thoughts relevant to the outcome, your mind will automatically begin to sort them by components (subprojects), priorities, and/or sequences of events. *Components* would be: "We need to handle logistics, people, and location." *Priorities* would be: "It's critical to find out if the client really would like to go to dinner." *Sequences* would be: "First we need to check whether the restaurant is open, then call the Andersons, then get dressed." This is the section of natural planning that incorporates *challenge*, *comparisons*, and *evaluation*, by its very nature. One thing is better, bigger, or ahead of something else.

> The key to intelligent thought is more intelligent thinking.

Finally (assuming that you're really committed to the project—in

---

*If, however, you were handling the celebration for your best friend's recent triumph, the complexity and detail that might accrue in your head should warrant at least the back of an envelope!

this case, going out to dinner), you focus on the **next action** that you need to take to make the first component actually happen. "Call Café Rouge to see if it's open, and make the reservation."

These five phases of project planning occur naturally for everything you accomplish during the day. It's how you create things—dinner, a relaxing evening, a new product, or a new company. You have an urge to make something happen; you image the outcome; you generate ideas that might be relevant; you sort those into a structure; and you define a physical activity that would begin to make it a reality. And you do all of that naturally, without giving it much thought.

Natural Planning Is Not Necessarily Normal

But is the process described in the previous section the way your committee is planning the retreat? Is it how your IT team is approaching the new system installation? Is it how you're organizing the wedding or thinking through the potential merger?

Have you clarified the primary purpose of the project and communicated it to everyone who ought to know it? And have you agreed on the standards and behaviors you'll need to adhere to in order to make it successful?

Have you envisioned wild success about anything lately?

Have you envisioned success and considered all the innovative things that might result if you achieved it?

Have you gotten all possible ideas out on the table—everything you need to take into consideration that might affect the outcome?

Have you identified the mission-critical components, key milestones, and deliverables?

Have you defined all the aspects of the project that could be moved on right now, what the next action is for each part, and who's responsible for what?

If you're like most people I interact with in a coaching or consulting capacity, the collective answer to these questions is, probably not. There are likely to be at least some components of the natural planning model that you haven't implemented.

In some of my seminars I get participants to actually plan a current strategic project that uses this model. In only a few minutes they walk themselves through all five phases, and usually end up being amazed at how much progress they've made compared with what they have tried to do in the past. One gentleman came up afterward and told me, "I don't know whether I should thank you or be angry. I just finished a business plan I've been telling myself would take months, and now I have no excuses for not doing it!"

You can try it for yourself right now, if you like. Choose one project that is new or stuck or that could simply use some improvement. Think of your purpose. Think of what a successful outcome would look like: where would you be physically, financially, in terms of reputation, or whatever? Brainstorm potential steps. Organize your ideas. Decide on the next actions. Are you any clearer about where you want to go and how to get there?

The Unnatural Planning Model

To emphasize the importance of utilizing the natural planning model for the more complex things we're involved with, let's contrast it with the more "normal" model used in most environments— what I call unnatural planning.

When the "Good" Idea Is a Bad Idea

Have you ever heard a well-intentioned manager or project head start a meeting with the question, "OK, so who's got a good idea about this?"

What's the assumption here? Before any evaluation of what's a good idea can be trusted, the purpose must be clear, the vision must be well defined, and all the relevant data must have been collected (brainstormed) and analyzed (organized). "What's a good idea?" is a good question, but only when you're about 80 percent of the way through your thinking! *Starting* there would probably blow anyone's creative mental fuses.

> If you're waiting to have a good idea before you have any ideas, you won't have many.

Trying to approach any situation from a perspective that is not the natural way your mind operates will be difficult. People do it all the time, but it almost always engenders a lack of clarity and increased stress. In interactions with others, it opens the door for egos, politics, and hidden agendas to take over the discussion (generally speaking, the most verbally aggressive will run the show). And if it's just you, attempting to come up with a good idea before defining your purpose, creating a vision, and collecting lots of initial bad ideas is likely to give you a case of creative constipation.

The Reactive Planning Model

The unnatural model is what most people still consciously think of as "planning," and because it's so often artificial and irrelevant to real work, people just don't plan. At least not on the front end: they resist planning meetings, presentations, and strategic operations until the last minute.

When you find yourself in a hole, stop digging.

—Will Rogers

But what happens if you don't plan ahead of time? In many cases, crisis! ("Didn't you get the tickets?" "I thought you were going to do that!") Then, when the urgency of the last minute is upon you, the reactive planning model ensues.

What's the first level of focus when the stuff hits the fan? **Action!** Work harder! Overtime! More people! Get busier! And a lot of stressed-out people are thrown at the situation.

Then, when having a lot of busy people banging into each other doesn't resolve the situation, someone gets more sophisticated and says, "We need to get **organized**!" (Catching on now?) Then people draw boxes around the problem and label them. Or *redraw* the boxes and *relabel* them.

At some point they realize that just redrawing boxes isn't really doing much to solve the problem. Now someone (much more sophisticated) suggests that more creativity is needed. "Let's **brainstorm**!" With everyone in the room, the boss asks, "So, who's got a *good* idea here?"

Don't just do something. Stand there.

—Rochelle Myer

When not much happens, the boss may surmise that his staff has used up most of its internal creativity. Time to hire a consultant! Of course, if the consultant is worth his salt, at some point he is probably going to ask the big question: "So, what are you really trying to *do* here, anyway?" (**vision, purpose**).

Natural Planning Techniques: The Five Phases

It goes without saying, but still must be said again: thinking in more effective ways about projects and situations can make things happen sooner, better, and more successfully. So if our minds plan naturally anyway, what can we learn from that? How can we use that model to facilitate getting more and better results in our thinking?

Let's examine each of the five phases of natural planning and see how we can leverage these contexts.

Purpose

It never hurts to ask the *why* question. Almost anything you're currently doing can be enhanced and even galvanized by more scrutiny at this top level of focus.

> *Fanaticism consists of redoubling your efforts when you have forgotten your aim.*
>
> —*George Santayana*

Why are you going to your next meeting? What's the purpose of your task? Why are you having friends over for dinner? Why are you hiring a marketing director instead of an agency? Why are you putting up with the situation in your service organization? Why do you have a budget? Ad infinitum.

I admit it: this is nothing but advanced common sense. To know and to be clear about the purpose of any activity are prime directives for appropriate focus, creative development, and cooperation. But it's common sense that's not commonly practiced, simply because it's so easy for us to create things, get caught up in the form of what we've created, and let our connection with our real and primary intentions slip.

I know, based upon thousands of hours spent in many offices with many sophisticated people, that the *why* question cannot be ignored. When people complain to me about having too many meetings, I have to ask, "What is the purpose of the meetings?" When they ask, "Who should I invite to the planning session?" I have to ask, "What's the purpose of the planning session?" When the dilemma is whether to stay connected with work and e-mail on a vacation or not, I have to ask, "What's the primary purpose of the vacation?" Until we have the answer to my questions, there's no possible way to come up with an appropriate response to theirs.

The Value of Thinking About Why

Here are just some of the benefits of asking why:

- It defines success.
- It creates decision-making criteria.
- It aligns resources.
- It motivates.
- It clarifies focus.
- It expands options.

> People love to win. If you're not totally clear about the purpose of what you're doing, you have no game to win.

Let's take a closer look at each of these in turn.

It Defines Success   People are starved for "wins" these days. We love to play games, and we like to win, or at least be in a position where we could win. And if you're not totally clear about the purpose of what you're doing, you have no chance of winning. Purpose defines success. It's the primal reference point for any investment of time and energy, from deciding to run for elective office to designing a form.

Ultimately you can't feel good about a staff meeting unless you know what the purpose of the meeting was. And if you want to sleep well, you'd better have a good answer when your board asks why you fired your head of marketing or hired that hotshot MBA as your new finance director. You won't really know whether or not your business plan is any good until you hold it up against the success criterion that you define by answering the question, "Why do we need a business plan?"

It Creates Decision-Making Criteria   How do you decide whether to spend the money for a five-color brochure or just go with a two-color? How do you know whether it's worth hiring a major Web design firm to handle your new Web site? How do you know if you should send your daughter to private school?

> Often the only way to make a hard decision is to come back to the purpose of what you're doing.

It all comes down to purpose. Given what you're trying to accomplish, are these investments required? There's no way to know until the purpose is defined.

It Aligns Resources   How should we spend our staffing allocation in the corporate budget? How do we best use the cash flow right now to maximize our viability as a retailer over the next year? Should we spend more money on the luncheon or on the speakers for the monthly association meeting?

In each case, the answer depends on what we're really trying to accomplish—the *why*.

It Motivates   Let's face it: if there's no good reason to be doing something, it's not worth doing. I'm often stunned by how many people have forgotten why they're doing what they're doing—and by how quickly a simple question like, "Why are you doing that?" can get them back on track.

> If you're not sure why you're doing something, you can never do enough of it.

It Clarifies Focus   When you land on the real purpose for anything you're doing, it makes things clearer. Just taking two minutes and writing out your primary reason for doing something invariably creates an increased sharpness of vision, much like bringing a telescope into focus. Frequently, projects and situations that have begun to feel scattered and blurred grow clearer when someone brings it back home by asking, "What are we really trying to accomplish here?"

It Expands Options   Paradoxically, even as purpose brings things into pinpoint focus, it opens up creative thinking about wider possibilities. When you really know the underlying *why*—for the conference, for the staff party, for your vacation, for the elimination of the management position, or for the merger—it expands your thinking about how to make the desired result happen. When people write out their purpose for a project in my seminars, they often claim it's like a fresh breeze blowing through their mind, clarifying their vision of what they're doing.

Is your purpose clear and specific enough? If you're truly experiencing the benefits of a purpose focus—motivation, clarity, decision-making criteria, alignment, and creativity—then your purpose probably *is* specific enough. But many purpose statements are too vague to produce such results. "To have a good team," for example, might be too broad or vague a goal. After all, what constitutes a "good team"? Is it a group of people who are highly motivated, collaborating in healthy ways, and taking initiative? Or is it a team that comes in under budget? In other words, if you don't really know when you've met your purpose or when you're off track, you don't have a viable directive. The question, "How will I know when this is off purpose?" must have a clear answer.

Principles

Of equal value as prime criteria for driving and directing a project are the standards and values you hold. Although people seldom think about these consciously, they are always there. And if they are violated, the result will inevitably be unproductive distraction and stress.

Simple, clear purpose and principles give rise to complex and intelligent behavior. Complex rules and regulations give rise to simple and stupid behavior.

—Dee Hock

A great way to think about what your principles are is to complete this sentence: "I would give others totally free rein to do this as long as they . . ."

As long as they what? What policies, stated or unstated, will apply to your group's activities? "As long as they stayed within budget"? "satisfied the client"? "ensured a healthy team"? "promoted a positive image"?

It can be a major source of stress when others engage in or allow behavior that's outside your standards. If you never have to deal with this issue, you're truly graced. If you do, some constructive conversation about, and clarification of, principles could align the energy and prevent unnecessary conflict. You may want to begin by asking yourself, "What behavior might undermine what I'm doing, and how can I prevent it?" That will give you a good starting point for defining your standards.

Another great reason for focusing on principles is the clarity and reference point they provide for positive conduct. How do you want or need to work with others on this project to ensure its success? What behaviors are in- and out-of-bounds for your kids on the family vacation? You and others are at your best when you're acting how?

Whereas purpose provides the juice and the direction, principles define the parameters of action and the criteria for excellence of conduct.

Vision/Outcome

In order to most productively access the conscious and unconscious resources available to you, you must have a clear picture in your mind of what success would look, sound, and feel like. Purpose and principles furnish the impetus and the monitoring, but vision provides the actual blueprint of the final result. This is the *what* instead of the *why*. What will this project or situation really be like when it successfully appears in the world?

For example, graduates of your seminar are demonstrating consistently applied knowledge of the subject matter. Market share has increased 2 percent within the northeastern region over the last fiscal year. Your daughter is clear about your guidelines and support for her first semester in college.

The Power of Focus

Since the 1960s thousands of books have expounded on the value of appropriate positive imagery and focus. Forward-looking focus has even been a key element in Olympic-level sports training, with athletes imagining the physical effort, the positive energy, and the successful result to ensure the highest level of unconscious support for their performance.

Imagination is more important than knowledge.

—*Albert Einstein*

We know that the focus we hold in our minds affects what we perceive and how we perform. This is as true on the golf course as it is in a staff meeting or during a serious conversation with a life partner. My interest here lies in providing a model for focus that is dynamic in a practical way, especially in project thinking.

When you focus on something—the vacation you're going to take, the meeting you're about to go into, the project you want to launch—that focus instantly creates ideas and thought patterns you wouldn't have had otherwise. Even your physiology will respond to an image in your head as if it were reality.

The Reticular Activating System The May 1957 issue of *Scientific American* magazine contains an article describing the discovery of the reticular formation at the base of the brain. The reticular formation is basically the gateway to your conscious awareness; it's the switch that turns on your perception of ideas and data, the thing that keeps you asleep even when music's playing but wakes you if a special little baby cries in another room.

Just like a computer, your brain has a search function—but it's even more phenomenal than a computer's. It seems to be programmed by what we focus on and, more primarily, what we identify with. It's the seat of what many people have referred to as the paradigms we maintain. We notice only what matches our internal belief systems and identified contexts. If you're an optometrist, for example, you'll tend to notice people wearing eyeglasses across a crowded room; if you're a building contractor, you may notice the room's physical details. If you focus on the color red right now and then just glance around your environment, if there is any red at all, you'll see even the tiniest bits of it.

The implications of how this filtering works—how we are unconsciously made conscious of information—could fill a weeklong seminar, if not the rest of

> *Your automatic creative mechanism is teleological. That is, it operates in terms of goals and end results. Once you give it a definite goal to achieve, you can depend upon its automatic guidance system to take you to that goal much better than "you" ever could by conscious thought. "You" supply the goal by thinking in terms of end results. Your automatic mechanism then supplies the means whereby.*
>
> *—Maxwell Maltz*

your life! Suffice it to say that something automatic and extraordinary happens in your mind when you create and focus on a clear picture of what you want.

Clarifying Outcomes

There is a simple but profound principle that emerges from understanding the way your perceptive filters work: you won't see how to do it until you see yourself doing it.

It's easy to envision something happening if it has happened before or you have had experience with similar successes. It can be quite a challenge, however, to identify with images of success if they represent new and foreign territory—

that is, if you have few reference points about what an event might actually look like and little experience of your own ability to make it happen.

> You often need to make it up in your mind before you can make it happen in your life.

Many of us hold ourselves back from imagining a desired outcome unless someone can show us *how to get there*. Unfortunately, that's backward in terms of how our minds work to generate and recognize solutions and methods.

One of the most powerful life skills, and one of the most important to hone and develop for both professional and personal success, is creating clear outcomes. This is not as self-evident as it may sound. We need to constantly define (and redefine) what we're trying to accomplish on many different levels, and consistently reallocate resources toward getting these tasks complete as effectively and efficiently as possible.

> *I always wanted to be somebody.*
> *I should have been more specific.*
> —*Lily Tomlin*

What will this project look like when it's done? How do you want the client to feel, and what do you want him to know and do after the presentation? Where will you be in your career three years from now? How would the ideal head of finance do his job? What would your Web site really look like and have as capabilities if it could be the way you wanted it? What would your relationship with your son feel like if this conversation you need to have with him were successful?

Outcome/vision can range from a simple statement of the project, such as "Finalize computer-system implementation," to a completely scripted movie depicting the future scene in all its glorious detail.

When I am able to get people to focus on a successful scenario of their project, they usually experience heightened enthusiasm and think of something unique and positive about it that didn't occur to them before. "Wouldn't it be great if . . ." is not a bad way to start thinking about a situation, at least for long enough to have the option of getting an answer.

Brainstorming

The best way to get a good idea is to get lots of ideas.

—Linus Pauling

Once you know what you want to happen and why, the *how* mechanism is brought into play. When you identify with some picture in your mind that is different from your current reality, you automatically start filling in the gaps, or brainstorming. Ideas begin to pop into your head in somewhat random order—little ones, big ones, not-so-good ones, good ones. This process usually goes on internally for most people about most things, and that's often sufficient. For example, you think about what you want to say to your boss as you're walking down the hall to speak to her. But there are many other instances

Your mind wants to figure out how to get from here to there, but initially in somewhat random order.

when writing things down, or capturing them in some external way, can give a tremendous boost to productive output and thinking.

Capturing Your Ideas

Over the past several decades, a number of graphics-oriented brainstorming techniques have been introduced to help develop creative thinking about projects and topics. They've been been given names such as mind mapping, clustering, patterning, webbing, and fish boning. Although the authors of these various processes may portray them as being different from one another, for most of us end users the basic premise remains the same: give yourself permission to capture and express any idea, and then later on figure out how it fits in and what to do with it. If nothing else (and there is plenty of "else"), this practice adds to your efficiency—when you have the idea, you grab it, which means you won't have to have the idea again.

The most popular of these concepts and techniques is called mind mapping, a name coined by Tony Buzan, a British researcher in brain functioning, to label this process of brainstorming ideas into a graphic format. In mind mapping, the core idea is presented in the center, with associated ideas growing out in a somewhat free-form fashion around it. For instance, if I found out that I had to move my office, I might think about computers, changing my business cards, all the connections I'd have to change, new furniture, moving the phones, purging and packing, and so on. If I capture these thoughts graphically it might start to look something like this:

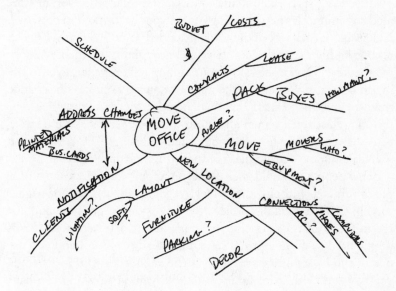

You could do this kind of mind mapping on Post-its that could be stuck on a whiteboard, or you could input ideas into a word processing program, outlining program, or one of the many mind-mapping software applications on the market.

Distributed Cognition

The great thing about external brainstorming is that in addition to capturing your original ideas, it can help generate many new ones that might not have occurred to you if you didn't have a mechanism to hold your thoughts and continually reflect them back to you. It's as if your mind were to say, "Look, I'm only going to give you as many ideas as you feel you can effectively use. If you're not collecting them in some trusted way, I won't give you that many. But if you're actually doing something with the ideas—even if it's just recording them for later evaluation—then here, have a bunch! And, oh wow! That reminds me of another one, and another," etc.

Nothing is more dangerous than an idea when it is the only one you have.

—Emile Chartier

Psychologists have now labeled this and similar processes "distributed cognition." It's getting things out of your head and into objective, reviewable formats—building an "extended mind." But my English teacher in high school didn't have to know about the theory to give me the key: "David," he said, "you're going to college, and you're going to be writing papers. Write all your notes and quotes on separate three-by-five-inch cards. Then, when you get ready to organize your thinking, just spread them all out on the floor, see the natural structure that emerges, and figure out what's missing. Mr. Edmundson was teaching me a major piece of the natural planning model!

Few people can hold their focus on a topic for more than a couple of minutes without some objective structure and tool or trigger to help them. Pick a big project you have going right now and just try to think of nothing else for more than thirty seconds. This is pretty hard to do unless you have a pen and paper in hand and use one of those "cognitive artifacts" as the anchor for your ideas. Then you can stay with it for hours. That's why good thinking can happen while you're working on a computer document about a project, mind mapping it on a notepad, doodling about it on a paper tablecloth, or just having a meeting about it with other people in a room that allows you to hold the context (a whiteboard with nice wet markers really helps there, too).

Only he who handles his ideas lightly is master of his ideas, and only he who is master of his ideas is not enslaved by them.

—Lin Yutang

Brainstorming Keys

Many techniques can be used to facilitate brainstorming and out-of-the-box thinking. The basic principles, however, can be summed up as follows:

• Don't judge, challenge, evaluate, or criticize.
• Go for quantity, not quality.
• Put analysis and organization in the background.

Don't Judge, Challenge, Evaluate, or Criticize   It's easy for the unnatural planning model to rear its ugly head in brainstorming, making people jump to premature evaluations and critiques of ideas. If you care even slightly about what a critic thinks, you'll censor your expressive process as you look for the "right" thing to say. There's a very subtle distinction between keeping brainstorming on target with the topic and stifling the creative process. It's also important that brainstorming be put into the overall context of the planning process, because if you think you're doing it just for its own sake, it can seem trite and inappropriately off course. If you can understand it instead as something you're doing right now, for a certain period, before you move toward a resolution at the end, you'll feel more comfortable giving this part of the process its due.

> Determining what might go most wrong in a situation is at times the best way to generate the best ideas about how to make it successful.

This is not to suggest that you should shut off critical thinking, though—everything ought to be fair game at this stage. "Here's what might be wrong with that approach" needs to be on the table, if it's present. Often it's the most challenging and critical ideas that have the germ of the best ones. It's just wise to understand what kinds of thoughts you're having and to park them for use in the most appropriate way. The primary criteria must be inclusion and expansion, not constriction and contraction.

Go for Quantity, Not Quality   Going for quantity keeps your thinking expansive. Often you won't know what's a good idea until you have it. And sometimes you'll realize it's a good idea, or the germ of one, only later on. You know how shopping at a big store with lots of options lets you feel comfortable about your choice? The same holds true for project thinking. The greater the volume of thoughts you have to work with, the better the context you can create for developing options and trusting your choices.

Put Analysis and Organization in the Background Analysis and evaluation and organization of your thoughts should be given as free a rein as creative, out-of-the-box thinking. But in the brainstorming phase, this critical activity should not be the driver.

Making a list can be a creative thing to do; it's a way to consider the people who should be on your team, the customer requirements for the software, or the components of the business plan. Just make sure to grab all that and keep going until you get into the weeding and organizing of focus that make up the next stage.

Organizing

If you've done a thorough job of emptying your head of all the things that came up in the brainstorming phase, you'll notice that a natural organization is emerging. As my high school English teacher suggested, once you get all the ideas out of your head and in front of your eyes, you'll automatically notice natural relationships and structure. This is what most people are referring to when they talk about organizing a project.

A project plan identifies the smaller outcomes, which can then be naturally planned.

Organizing usually happens when you identify components and subcomponents, sequences of events, and/or priorities. What are the things that must occur to create the final result? In what order must they occur? What is the most important element to ensure the success of the project?

This is the stage in which you can make good use of structuring tools ranging from informal bullet points scribbled on the back of an envelope to heavy-horsepower project-planning software. When a project calls for substantial objective control, you'll need some type of hierarchical outline with components and subcomponents, and/or a Gantt-type chart showing stages of the project laid out over time, with independent and dependent parts and milestones identified in relationship to the whole.

Creative thinking doesn't stop here; it just takes another form. Once you perceive a basic structure, your mind will start trying to fill in the blanks. Identifying the three key things that you need to handle on the project, for example, may cause you to think of a fourth and a fifth when you see them all lined up.

The Basics of Organizing

The key steps here are:

- Identify the significant pieces
- Sort by (one or more):
  - components
  - sequences
  - priorities
- Detail to the required degree

I have never seen any two projects that needed to have exactly the same amount of structure and detail developed in order to get things off people's minds and moving successfully. But almost all projects can use some form of creative thinking from the sequential part of the brain, along the lines of "What's the plan?"

Next Actions

The final stage of planning comes down to decisions about the allocation and reallocation of physical resources to actually get the project moving. The question to ask here is, "What's the next action?"

As we noted in the previous chapter, this kind of grounded, reality-based thinking, combined with clarification of the desired outcome, forms the critical component for defining and clarifying what our real work is. In my experience, creating a list of what your real projects are and consistently managing your next action for each one will constitute 90 percent of what is generally thought of as project planning. This ground-floor approach will make you honest about all kinds of things. Are you really serious about doing this? Who's responsible? Have you thought things through enough?

At some point, if the project is an actionable one, this next-action-thinking decision must be made.* Answering the question about what, specifically, you would do about something physically if you had nothing else to do will test the maturity of your thinking about the project. If you're not yet ready to answer that question, you have more to flesh out at some prior level in the natural planning sequence.

The Basics

• Decide on next actions for each of the current "moving parts" of the project.
• Decide on the next action in the planning process, if necessary.

Activating the Moving Parts   A project is sufficiently planned for implementation when every next-action step has been decided on every front that can actually be moved on without some other component's having to be completed first. If the project has multiple components, each of them should be assessed appropriately by asking, "Is there something that anyone could be doing on this right now?" You could be coordinating speakers for the conference, for instance, at the same time that you're finding the appropriate site.

In some cases there will be only one aspect that can be activated, and everything else will depend on the results of that. So there may be only one next action, which will be the linchpin for all the rest.

More to Plan?   What if there's still more planning to be done before you can feel comfortable with what's next? There's still an action step—it is just a process action. What's the next step in the continuation of planning? Drafting more ideas. E-mailing Ana Maria and Sean to get their input. Telling your assistant to set up a planning meeting with the product team.

The habit of clarifying the next action on projects, no matter what the situation, is fundamental to you staying in relaxed control.

---

*You can also plan nonactionable projects and *not* need a next action—for example, designing your dream house. The lack of a next action by default makes it a "someday/maybe" project . . . and that's fine for anything of that nature.

When the Next Action Is Someone Else's . . . If the next action is not yours, you must nevertheless clarify whose it is (this is a primary use of the Waiting For action list). In a group-planning situation, it isn't necessary for everyone to know what the next step is on every part of the project. Often all that's required is to allocate responsibility for parts of the project to the appropriate persons and leave it up to them to identify next actions on their particular pieces.

This next-action conversation forces organizational clarity. Issues and details emerge that don't show up until someone holds everyone's feet to the fire about the physical-level reality of resource allocation. It's a simple practical discussion to foster, and one that can significantly stir the pot and identify weak links.

How Much Planning Do You Really Need to Do?

How much of this planning model do you really need to flesh out, and to what degree of detail? The simple answer is, as much as you need to get the project off your mind.

In general, the reason things are on your mind is that the outcome and action step(s) have not been appropriately defined, and/or reminders of them have not been put in places where you can be trusted to look for them appropriately. Additionally, you may not have developed the details, perspectives, and solutions sufficiently to trust the efficacy of your blueprint.

Most projects, given my definition of a project as an outcome requiring more than one action, need no more than a listing of their outcome and next action for you to get them off your mind. You need a new stockbroker? You just have to call a friend for a recommendation. You want to set up a new printer at home? You just need to surf the Web to check out different models and prices. I estimate that 80 percent of projects are of that nature. You'll still be doing the full planning model on all of them, but only in your head, and just enough to figure out next actions and keep them going until they're complete.

| If the project is still on your mind, there's more thinking required.

Another 15 percent or so of projects might require at least some external form of brainstorming—maybe a mind map or a few notes in a word processing or presentation program. That might be sufficient for planning meeting agendas, your vacation, or a speech to the local chamber of commerce.

A final 5 percent of projects might need the deliberate application of one or more of the five phases of the natural planning model. The model provides a practical recipe for unsticking things, resolving them, and moving them forward productively. Are you aware of a need for greater clarity, or great action, on any of your projects? If so, using the model can often be the key to making effective progress.

Need More Clarity?

If greater clarity is what you need, shift your thinking up the natural planning scale. People are often very busy (action) but nonetheless experience confusion and a lack of clear direction. They need to pull out the plan or create one (organize). If there's a lack of clarity at the planning level, there's probably a need for more brainstorming to generate a sufficient inventory of current ideas and data to create trust in the plan. If the brainstorming session gets bogged down with fuzzy thinking, the focus should shift back to the vision of the outcome, ensuring that the reticular filter in the brain will open up to deliver the how-to thinking. If the outcome/vision is unclear, you must return to a clean analysis of why you're engaged in the situation in the first place (purpose).

Need More to Be Happening?

If more action is what's needed, you need to move down the model. There may be enthusiasm about the purpose of a project but at the same time some resistance to actually fleshing out what fulfilling it in the real world might look like. These days, the task of improving quality of work life may be on the radar for a manager, but often he won't yet have defined a clear picture of the desired result. The thinking must go to the specifics of the vision. Again, ask yourself, "What would the outcome look like?"

If you've formulated an answer to that question, but things are still stuck, it's probably time for you to grapple with some of the *how* issues and the operational details and perspectives (brainstorming). I often have clients who have inherited a relatively clearly articulated project, such as "Implement the new performance-review system," but who aren't moving forward because they haven't yet taken a few minutes to dump some ideas out about what that might entail.

If brainstorming gets hung up (and very often it does for the more "blue sky" types), rigor may be required to do some evaluation of and decision making about mission-critical deliverables that have to be handled (organizing). This is sometimes the case when an informal back-and-forth meeting that has generated lots of ideas ends without producing any decision about what actually needs to happen next on the project.

And if there *is* a plan, but the rubber still isn't hitting the road like it should, someone needs to assess each component with the focus of "What's the next action, and who's got it?" One manager, who had taken over responsibility many months in advance for organizing a major annual conference, asked me how to prevent the crisis all-nighters her team had experienced near the deadline of the previous year. When she produced an outline of the various pieces of the project she'd inherited, I asked, "Which pieces could actually be moved on right now?" After identifying half a dozen, we clarified the next action on each one. It was off and running, in time to prevent a repeat of the previous year's last-minute chaos.

In the prior two chapters, I covered the basic models of how to stay maximally productive and in control, with minimal effort, at the two most basic levels of our life and work: the actions we take and the projects we enter into that generate many of those actions.

> You need no new skills to increase your productivity and reduce your stress—just an enhanced set of systematic behaviors with which to apply them.

The fundamentals remain true—you must be responsible for collecting all your open loops, applying a front-end thought process to each of them, and managing the results with organization, review, and action.

For all those situations that you have any level of commitment to complete, there is a natural planning process that occurs to get you from here to there. Leveraging that five-phase model can often make the evolution easier, faster, and more productive.

> *Plans get you into things but you've got to work your way out.*
> —*Will Rogers*

These models are simple to understand and easy to implement. Applying them creates remarkable results. You need essentially no new skills—you already know how to write things down, clarify outcomes, decide next actions, put things into categories, review it all, and make intuitive choices. *Right now* you have the ability to focus on successful results, brainstorm, organize your thinking, and get moving on your next steps.

But just knowing how to do all of those things does not produce results. Merely having the ability to be highly productive, relaxed, and in control doesn't make you that way. If you're like most people, you could use a coach—someone to walk you step-by-step through the experience and provide some guideposts and handy tricks along the way, until your new operational style is elegantly embedded.

You'll find that in part 2.

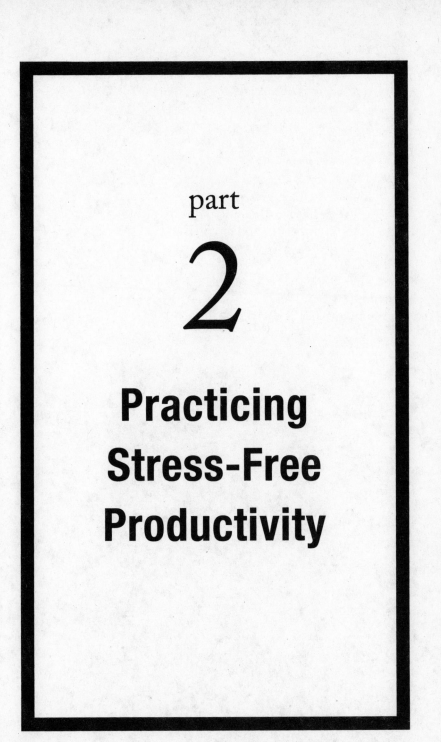

part

2

**Practicing
Stress-Free
Productivity**

4

Getting Started: Setting Up the Time, Space, and Tools

IN PART 2 we'll move from a conceptual framework and limited application of workflow mastery to full-scale implementation and best practices. Going through this program often gives people a level of relaxed control they may never have experienced before, but it usually requires the catalyst of step-by-step procedures to get there. To that end, I'll provide a logical sequence of things to do, to make it as easy as possible for you to get on board and glean the most value from these techniques.

Much of the detail in this section can easily seem more than you can digest or implement on a first read. It's included to provide a blow-by-blow instruction manual for you if you've decided to do a full-scale implementation of the model, which could take at least two full, uninterrupted days to implement. It is information and suggestions you will very likely want to revisit at some point, to glean a new level of application, as you get started down the GTD path.

Implementation—Whether All-Out or Casual—Is a Lot About "Tricks"

If you're not sure you're committed to an all-out implementation of these methods, let me assure you that much of the value people get from this material is good tricks. Sometimes just one good trick can make it worthwhile to range through this information: I've had people tell me, for example, that the best thing they got from our seminars was simply the two-minute rule. Tricks are for the not-so-smart, not-so-conscious part of us. To a great degree, the

It is easier to act yourself into a better way of feeling than to feel yourself into a better way of action.

—*O. H. Mowrer*

highest-performing people I know are those who have installed the best tricks in their lives. I know that's true of me. The smart part of us sets up things for us to do that the not-so-smart part responds to almost automatically, creating behavior that produces high-performance results. We trick ourselves into doing what we ought to be doing.

For instance, if you're a semi-regular exerciser like I am, you probably have your own little tricks to get yourself to exercise. My best trick is *costume*—the clothing I put on or take off. If I put on exercise gear, I'll start to feel like exercising; if I don't I'm very likely to feel like doing something else.

Let's look at an example of a real productivity trick. You've probably taken work home that you had to bring back the next day, right? It was mission-critical that you not forget it the next morning. So where did you put it the night before? Did you put it in front of the door, or on your keys, so you'd be sure to take it with you? For this you get an education? What a sophisticated piece of self-management technology you've installed in your life! But actually that's just what it is. The smart part of you the night before knows that the not-so-smart part of you first thing in the morning may barely be conscious. "What's this in front of the door? Oh, that's right, I've got to take this with me!"

What a class act. But really, it is. It's a trick I call Put It in Front of the Door. For our purposes the "door" is going to be the door of your mind, not your house. But it's the same idea.

If you were to take out your calendar right now and look closely at every single item for the next fourteen days, you'd probably come up with *at least* one "Oh, that reminds me, I need to _____." If you then captured that value-added thought into some place that would trigger you to act, you'd feel better already, have a clearer head, and get more positive things done. It's not rocket science, just a good trick.

If you take out a clean sheet of paper right now, along with your favorite writing instrument, and for three minutes focus solely on the most awesome project on your mind, I guarantee you'll have at least one "Oh, yeah, I need to consider _____." Then capture what shows up in your head on the piece of paper and put it where you might actually use the idea or information. You won't be one ounce smarter than you were ten minutes ago, but you'll have added value to your work and life.

> The big secret to efficient creative and productive thinking and action is to put the right things in your focus at the right time.

Much of learning how to manage workflow in a masterful way is about laying out the gear and practicing the moves so that the requisite thinking happens more automatically and it's a lot easier to get engaged in the game. The suggestions that follow about getting time, space, and tools in place are all trusted methods for making things happen at a terrific new level.

If you're sincere about making a major leap forward in your personal management systems, I recommend that you pay close attention to the details and follow through on the suggestions provided next in their entirety. The whole will be greater than the sum of the parts. You'll also discover that the execution of this program will produce real progress on real things that are going on in your life right now. We'll get lots done that you want to get done, in new and efficient ways that may amaze you.

Setting Aside the Time

I recommend that you create a block of time to initialize this process and prepare a workstation with the appropriate space, furniture, and tools. If your space is properly set up and streamlined, it can reduce your unconscious resistance to dealing with your stuff and even make it attractive for you to sit down and crank through your input and your work. An ideal time frame for most people is two whole days, back to back. (Don't be put off by that if you don't have that long to spend, though: doing any of the activities I suggest will be useful, no matter how much or how little time you devote to them. Two days are not required to benefit from these techniques and principles—they will start to pay off almost instantly.) Implementing the full capturing process can take up to six hours or more, and clarifying and deciding on actions for all the input you'll want to externalize and capture in your system can easily take another eight hours. Of course, you can also collect

> *Don't be afraid to take a big step if one is indicated. You can't cross a chasm in two small jumps.*
> —David L. George

and process your stuff in chunks, but it'll be much easier if you can tackle that front-end portion in one fell swoop.

The ideal time for me to work with someone in implementing this methodology is on a weekend or holiday, because the chance of outside disturbance is minimal then. If I work with someone on a typical workday, we first make sure that no meetings are scheduled and only emergency interruptions are allowed; phone calls are routed to voice mail or logged by assistants for review and handling during a break. I don't recommend using after-hours for this work. It usually means seriously reduced horsepower and a big tendency to get caught up in "rabbit trails."*

For many of the executives I work with, holding the world back for two contiguous days is the hardest part of the whole process—the perceived necessity to be constantly available for meetings and communications when they're at work is difficult for them to let go of. That's why we often resort to weekends. If you work in an open cubicle or office, it will be even more of a challenge to isolate sufficient time blocks on a regular workday during office hours.

> Dedicate two days to this process, and it will be worth many times that in terms of your productivity and mental health.

It's not that the procedure itself is so sacred; it's just that it takes a lot of mental energy to capture and make decisions about such a large inventory of open loops, especially when they've been open, undecided, or stuck for way too long. Interruptions can double the time it takes to get through everything. If you can get to ground zero in one contained time period, it gives you a huge sense of control and accomplishment and frees up a reservoir of energy and creativity. Later on you can maintain your system in shorter spurts "between the lines" of your regular day.

Setting Up the Space

You'll need to choose a physical location to serve as as your central cockpit of control. If you already have a desk and office space set up

---

*After-hours is actually a good time to crank through a group of similar tasks that you wouldn't normally do in the course of your typical workday, like filing a big backlog of papers, cleaning a desk drawer, surfing the Web about your upcoming vacation, or processing expense receipts.

where you work, that's probably the best place to start. If you work from a home office, obviously that will be your prime location. If you already have both, you'll want to establish identical, even inter-changeable systems in both places, though one will probably be primary. If you feel that you don't have either—you really don't have any central physical spot you would call home for dealing with your stuff—it's imperative that you create one. Even if you have a mobile, high-tech life that is primarily virtual, you'll still require a private setting as a base camp from which to operate. You will want to implement this program wherever you might actually do work and process input, but starting with a primary location is optimal.

The basics for a workspace are just a writing surface and room for an in-tray, and probably (for most people) space for core digital tools as well. Some, such as a foreman in a machine shop, an intake nurse on a hospital floor, or your children's nanny, won't need much more than that. Most homemakers won't necessarily need a large area to manage their workflow, but having enough of a discrete space dedi-cated to the processing of notes, mail, home and family projects and activities, finances, and the like is critical. Usually this business-of-life stuff is scattered helter-skelter in the kitchen, in the hallway, on the dining table, on book and media shelves, etc., with a numbing effect.

The writing surface will of course expand for most profession-als, to include a phone (and charger), a computer, stacking trays, working file drawers, reference shelves. Some may feel the need for a printer, whiteboards, and/or multimedia conferencing equip-ment. The seriously self-contained will also want gear for exercise, leisure, and hobbies.

A functional workspace is critical. If you don't already have a dedicated workspace and in-tray, get them now. That goes for students, home-makers, and retirees, too. Everyone must have a physical locus of control from which to deal with everything else.

> You must have a dedicated, individual, self-contained workspace—at home, at work, and even in transit.

If I had to set up an emergency workstation in just a few min-utes, I would buy an unfinished door, place it on top of two two-drawer filing cabinets (one at each end), place three stack trays on it, and add a paper, pad, and pen. That would be my home base. (If I had time to sit down, I'd also buy a stool!) Believe it or not, I've been in several executive offices that wouldn't be as functional.

If You Go to an Office, You'll Still Need a Space at Home

Don't skimp on workspace at home. As you'll discover through this process, it's critical that you have at least a satellite home system identical to the one in your office. Many people I've worked with have been somewhat embarrassed by the degree of chaos that reigns in their homes, in contrast to their offices at work; they've gotten tremendous value from giving themselves permission to establish the same setup in both places. If you're like many of them, you'll find that a weekend spent setting up a home workstation can make a revolutionary change in your ability to organize your life.

An Office Space in Transit

If you move around much, as a business traveler or just as a person with a mobile lifestyle, you'll also want to set up an efficiently organized micro-office-in-transit. More than likely this will consist of a briefcase, pack, or satchel with appropriate folders and portable workstation supplies.

Many people lose opportunities to be productive because they're not equipped to take advantage of the odd moments and windows of time that open up as they move from one place to another, or when they're in off-site environments. The combination of a good processing style, the right tools, and good interconnected systems at home and at work can make traveling a highly leveraged way to get certain kinds of work done. As technology continues to deliver both more powerful mobile hardware and fast global access to most of us, the ability to virtually manage your life increases. But the problem inherent with that is the confusion of managing the traffic that ensues with all the options available on your mobile device(s). Without a good capturing, clarifying, and organizing methodology in place, with the appropriate applications and tools structured to handle it as it happens, the new world of global mobile access will be underutilized, if not a source of unproductive distraction and stress itself.

Don't Share Space!

It is imperative that you have your own workspace—or at least your own in-tray and a place in which to process paper and physical material. Too many couples I've worked with have tried to work out of a single desk at home, and it always makes light-years of difference when they expand to two workstations. Far from being the "separation" they expect, the move in fact relieves them of a subtle stress in their relationship about managing the stuff of their shared lives. One couple even decided to set up an additional mini-workstation in the kitchen for the stay-at-home mom, so she could process work while keeping an eye on their infant in the family room.

Some organizations are interested in the concept of "hotel-ing"— that is, having people create totally self-contained and mobile workstation capabilities so they can "plug in" anywhere in the company, at any time, and work from there. That can provide savings in office space requirements, as companies operate more virtually with a workforce that can function independently from the "mother ship." But that presupposes that each worker involved has a locus of control on his or her own. Experiments have failed in this scheme, because they disrupted the stable workstation. There must be zero resistance to using the systems we have. Having to continually reinvent our in-tray, our filing system, and how and where we process our stuff ("Where's a darn Post-it, and a stapler?!") can only be a source of incessant distraction.

> You need to *use* your system—not continually have to re-create it.

You can work virtually anywhere if you have a clean, compact system and know how to process your stuff rapidly and portably. But you'll still need a home base with a well-grooved set of tools and sufficient space for all the reference and support material that you'll want somewhere close at hand when you land. Most people I work with need at least two file drawers for their general-reference and project-support types of paper-based materials. Given digital scanners and the continual technology advances in this regard, it is conceivable that one day all that support material can be in the cloud and retrievable as needed, anywhere. But it will still be a while before you don't need your physical passport, EU cash you brought back from your trip to Milan, and temporary paper-based documentation of all sorts that remains the optimum way to handle some data. Big or small, that inventory of reference and collateral items needs a home, with easy access to it.

Getting the Tools You'll Need

If you're committed to a full implementation of this workflow process, there are some basic supplies and equipment that you'll need to get you started. As you go along, you're likely to dance between using what you're used to and evaluating any possibilities for new and different gear to work with.

Note that good tools don't necessarily have to be expensive. Often, on the low-tech side, the more "executive" something looks, the more dysfunctional it really is.

The Basic Processing Tools

Let's assume you're starting from scratch. In addition to a desktop workspace, you'll need:

- Paper-holding trays (at least three)
- A stack of plain letter-size paper
- A pen/pencil
- Post-its (3×3"s)
- Paper clips
- A stapler and staples
- Scotch tape
- Rubber bands
- An automatic labeler
- File folders
- A calendar
- Wastebasket/recycling bins
- Current tools being used for data capture, organizing, and to-do lists, including mobile devices, personal computers, and paper-based planners and notebooks (if any)

Paper-Holding Trays

These will serve as your in-tray and out-tray, with one or two others for work-in-progress support papers and/or your read-and-review stack. The most functional trays are the side-facing letter- or legal-sized stackable kinds, which have no "lip" on them to keep you from sliding out a single piece of paper.

Plain Paper

You'll use plain paper for the initial collection process. Believe it or not, putting one thought on one full-size sheet of paper can have enormous value. Most people will wind up processing their notes into some sort of list organizer, but by having initial thoughts separated into discrete placeholders (versus on one amorphous list), it makes it easier to wrestle it to closure later, in the processing and organizing steps. In any case, it's important to have plenty of letter-size writing paper or tablets around to make capturing ad hoc input easy.

Post-its, Clips, Stapler, Etc.

Post-its, clips, stapler, tape, and rubber bands will come in handy for routing and storing paper-based materials. Though their use is diminishing, we're not finished with paper and other physical materials yet (if you haven't noticed!), and the simple tools for managing them are essential.

> Moment-to-moment collecting, thinking, processing, and organizing are challenging enough; always ensure that you have the tools to make them as easy as possible.

Labeler

The labeler is a surprisingly useful tool in this process. Thousands of people we have worked with now have their own automatic labelers, and our archives are full of their comments, like "Incredible—I wouldn't have believed what a difference it makes!" The labeler will be used to label file folders, binder spines, and numerous other things.

I prefer a stand-alone tool or a simple plug-and-play labeler for the computer that can make single labels in the moment, reducing any friction to filing something when it shows up.

File Folders

You'll need plenty of file folders. You may also need an equal number of file-folder hangers, if your filing system requires them. Plain-colored folders are fine—color-coding is a level of complexity that's hardly ever worth the effort. Your general-reference filing system should just be a simple library.*

Calendar

Although you may not need a calendar just to collect your incomplete items, you'll certainly come up with actions that need to be put there, nonetheless. As I noted earlier, the calendar should be used not to hold action lists but to track the "hard landscape" of things that have to get done on a specific day or at a specific time.

Most professionals these days already have some sort of working calendar system in place, ranging from loose-leaf organizers to mobile devices to shared enterprise software applications.

The calendar has often been the central tool that people rely on to be "organized." It's certainly a critical component in managing particular kinds of data and reminders of the commitments and information that relate to specific times and days. There are many reminders and some data that you will want a calendar for, but you won't be stopping there: your calendar will need to be integrated with a much more comprehensive system that will emerge as you apply this method.

You may wonder what kind of calendar would be best to use, and I'll discuss that in more detail in the next chapter. For now, just keep using the one you've got. After you develop a feel for the whole systematic approach, you'll have a better reference point for deciding about graduating to a different tool.

Wastebasket/Recycling Bins

If you're like most people, when you implement this process you're going to toss a lot more stuff than you expect, so get ready to create

---

*In many countries it is difficult to find simple, inexpensive folders for the elementary but necessary general-reference system I advocate. You may have to improvise to find something workable.

a good bit of trash. Some executives I have coached have found it extremely useful to arrange for a large trash bin to be parked immediately outside their offices the day we work together!

Do You Need an Organizer?

Whether or not you need an organizer tool, and if so, what kind, will depend on a number of factors. Are you already committed to using something for managing lists and at-hand reference information? How do you want to see your reminders of actions, agendas, and projects? Where and how often do you need to review them? Because your head is not the place in which to hold things, you'll obviously need something to manage your triggers and orient yourself externally. You could maintain everything in a purely low-tech fashion, by keeping pieces of paper in folders. Or you could even use a paper-based notebook or planner, or a digital version thereof. Or you could employ some combination of these.

> Once you know how to process your stuff and what to organize, you really just need to create and manage lists.

All of the low-tech gear listed in the previous section is used for various aspects of collecting, processing, and organizing. You'll use a tray and random paper for collecting. As you process your in-tray, you'll complete many less-than-two-minute actions that will require Post-its, a stapler, and paper clips. The magazines, articles, and paper reports and documents that are your longer-than-two-minute reading will go in another of the trays. And you'll probably have quite a bit just to file away. What's left—maintaining a project inventory, logging calendar items and action and agenda reminders, and tracking the things you're waiting for—will require some form of lists, or reviewable groupings of similar items.

Lists can be managed in a low-tech way, as pieces of paper kept in a file folder (e.g., separate sheets/notes for each person you need to call in a Calls file, or bills to pay in a To Pay folder or tray), or they can be arranged in a more mid-tech fashion, in loose-leaf notebooks or planners (a page titled Calls with the names listed down the sheet). Or they can be high-tech, digital versions (such as a Calls category in the Tasks or To-Do section of a software application).

In addition to holding portable reference material (e.g., contact info) most organizing tools are designed for managing lists. (Your calendar is actually a form of a list, with time- and day-specific action reminders listed chronologically.)

One of the best tricks for enhancing your productivity is having organizing tools you love to use.

Probably thousands of types of organizers have been on the market since the latter twentieth century, from the early Day-Timers and Filofaxes, to the more sophisticated planners like Time/system and FranklinCovey, to the retro use of a simple Moleskine notebook, to the current flood of task-management software applications.*

Should you implement the *Getting Things Done* process in what you're currently using, or should you install something new? The answer is, do whichever one will actually help you change your behavior so you'll use the tools appropriately. There are efficiency factors to consider here, too. Do you get a lot of digital information that would be easier to track with a digital tool? Do you need a paper-based calendar for all the appointments you have to make and change rapidly on the run? Where and how is the easiest way for you to be reminded of calls you need to make when you're moving fast? And so on. There are also the aesthetic and enjoyment factors. I've done some of my best planning and updating for myself when I simply wanted some excuse to use (i.e., play with) my smartphone while waiting for dinner alone in a restaurant!

If your reference system is not under control, it creates a blockage in your workflow that causes amorphous content to back up into your world.

Keep in mind, though, that the tool you use will not give you stress-free productivity. That is something *you* create by implementing the GTD method. The structure you incorporate *will* be extremely important in how you express and implement the process, but it is not a substitute for it. A great hammer doesn't make a great carpenter; but a great carpenter will always want to have a great hammer.

When considering whether to get and use any organizing tool, and if so, which one, keep in mind that all you really need to do is manage lists. You've got to be able to create a list on the run and

---

*Since the original publication of *Getting Things Done*, scores of software programs have emerged using the core GTD methodology as a basis for their models. Most are simply digital and mobile to-do and task list managers, with a variety of enhancements, connections, and graphic views.

review it easily and as regularly as you need to. Once you know what to put on the lists and how to use them, the medium really doesn't matter. Just go for simplicity, speed, and fun.

The Critical Factor of a Filing System

A simple and highly functional personal reference system is critical to this process. The filing system at hand is one of the first things I assess before beginning the workflow process in anyone's office. As I noted in chapter 2, the lack of a good general-reference system can be one of the greatest obstacles to implementing a personal management system, and for most of the executives I have coached, it represents one of the biggest opportunities for improvement. It's not because the content is so important or strategic—it's rather that, unmanaged, it inordinately clouds physical and mental space. Random nonactionable but potentially relevant material, unprocessed and unorganized, produces a debilitating psychological noise. More important, it produces a block in the "flow" part of workflow, and things tend to back up into the area like we see with clogged plumbing. Many times I have driven to the local office-supply store with a client and bought a filing cabinet, a big stack of file folders, and a labeler, just so we could create an appropriate place in which to put two-thirds of the stuff lying around his or her desk and office. The transformation in clarity and focus regarding work was inevitably dramatic.

> You will resist the whole process of capturing information if your reference systems are not fast, functional, and fun.

We're concerned here mostly with general-reference filing—as distinct from discrete filing systems devoted to contracts, financial information, patient records, or other categories of data that deserve their own place and indexing. General-reference files should hold articles, brochures, pieces of paper, notes, printouts, documents, and even physical things like tickets, keys, buyers-club membership cards, and flash drives—basically anything that you want to keep for its interesting or useful data or purpose and that doesn't fit into your specialized filing systems and won't stand up by itself on a shelf (as will large software manuals and seminar binders).

If you are a digitally oriented person, you may think there's no longer any need for file folders for physical stuff. At some point in the future, I may not need a physical passport, birth certificate, older kitchen appliance instructions, medical records, keys for seldom-used boxes, or paper currency from countries I will revisit. But until then, I need a coordinated physical place to park them.

> *To capture what you experience and sort it out . . . you must set up a file. . . . Whenever you feel strongly about events or ideas you must try not to let them pass from your mind, but instead to formulate them for your files and in so doing draw out their implications, show yourself how foolish these feelings or ideas are, or how they might be articulated into productive shape.*
>
> —C. Wright Mills

If you have a trusted secretary or assistant who maintains that system for you, so you can put a "File as X" Post-it on the document and send it out to him or her, great. But ask yourself if you have some potentially interesting, confidential, or useful support material that should be accessible at any moment, even when your assistant isn't around. If so, you'll still need your own system in your desk or somewhere near it.

The same dynamic holds true, whether reference is in paper or digital form. As more and more information is coming to us virtually, the need to have general-reference locations for ad hoc data on your computer or mobile device is critical. Many people are still using their e-mail in-tray area as an amorphous general-reference storage place ("I need to keep this e-mail because it has information about my son's school event schedule"), but they resist making an electronic folder named "Robert" or "School schedules" in their e-mail application in which to drag and store it, or copying and pasting it in a good reference storage program or database. Software is now available that allows capturing and categorizing this kind of information (and synchronizing it with multiple devices), but it does require some thought about how to structure it, as well as some directed behavior to flow this kind of stuff into appropriate places instead of complicating and confusing your digital environment. When I instituted a new general-reference filing application on my computer, it required a good three months of my experimentation to find the optimal way to organize it, and another three months to get it on "cruise control," so now I'm just *using* it instead of thinking so much *about* it.

Success Factors for Filing

I strongly suggest that you maintain a personal, at-hand filing system—both physical and digital. It should take you less than one minute to pick something up out of your in-tray or print it from e-mail, decide it needs no next action but has some potential future value, and finish storing it in a trusted system. The same is true for scanning and storing documents or copying and pasting information in the computer. You may have a preponderance of digital over paper-based reference material (or vice versa), but without a streamlined system for both, you will resist keeping potentially valuable information, or what you do keep will accumulate in inappropriate places. If it takes longer than a minute to file something in an easily retrievable format, you'll likely stack it or stuff it somewhere instead. Besides being fast, the system needs to be fun and easy, current and complete. Otherwise you'll unconsciously resist emptying your in-tray because you know there's likely to be something in there that ought to get filed, and you won't even want to look at the papers or your clogged e-mail. Take heart: I've seen people go from resisting to actually enjoying sorting through their piles and digital world once their personal filing system is set up and humming.

You must feel equally comfortable about filing a single piece of paper on a new topic—even a scribbled note—in its own file as you would about filing a more formal, larger document. Because it requires so much work to make and organize files, people either don't keep them or have junked-up cabinets and drawers full of all sorts of one-of-a-kind items, like menus for the local takeout café or the current train schedule. If you trust that all that kind of information is instantly and virtually available through the Web and you would never need to access hard copies, then make sure you're not duplicating systems unnecessarily, and that what you choose and how you use it is seamless.

Whatever you need to do to get your reference system to that quick and easy standard for everything it has to hold, do it. My system works wonderfully for me and for many others who try it, and I highly recommend that you consider incorporating all of the following guidelines to really make reference filing automatic.

Keep Your General-Reference Files Immediately at Hand   Filing has to be instantaneous and easy. If you have to get up every time you have some ad hoc piece of paper you want to file, or you have to search multiple places on your computer for an appropriate location for a piece of information you want to keep, you'll tend to stack it or leave it in its original place instead of filing it. You're also likely to resist the whole in-tray process (because you know there's stuff in there that might need filing!). Many people I have coached have redesigned their office space so they have plenty of general-reference file drawers literally within swivel distance, instead of across the room.

One Alpha System   I have one A–Z alphabetical physical filing system for general reference, not multiple ones. My e-mail reference folders are also organized this way. People have a tendency to want to use their files as a personal management system, and therefore they attempt to organize them in groupings by projects or areas of focus. This magnifies geometrically the number of places something *isn't* when you forget where you filed it. Once you have filtered all the reminders for actions into your next-action lists, this kind of data is simply the content of your personal library. You should have the freedom to be as much of a pack rat as you wish. The only issue you need to deal with is how much room you have for storage, and how accessible the information is when you need it. One simple alpha system files everything by topic, person, project, or company, so it can be in only three or four places if you forget exactly where you put it. You can usually put at least one subset of topics on each label, like "Gardening—pots" and "Gardening—ideas." These would be filed under G.

> Using an effectively simple and easily accessible general-reference filing system gives you the freedom to keep as much information as you want.

The digital world provides the advantage of the search function across a wide swath of your data, and the ability to tag content with key words adds even more capability for retrieval. However, with so many options and locations for data storage, that power also can easily add complexity and confusion. Most people I know who are even moderately busy won't take the time and effort to use these tools to catalog all their stuff within all their possible applications. So, though the computer gives us great power and flexibility and opportunity for a great reference library, it creates an even greater challenge to design your own simple and effective formats for referential information. Even digitally, it is very helpful to have a visual map sorted in ways that make sense—either by indexes or data groups organized effectively, usually in an alpha format. To find restaurants in London that I like, I go my current general-reference application, where I find "Locales," then "London," then "Restaurants"—all alphabetized within each level of abstraction.

The biggest issue for digitally oriented people is that the ease of capturing and storing has generated a write-only syndrome: all they're doing is capturing information—not actually accessing and using it intelligently. Some consciousness needs to be applied to keep one's potentially huge digital library functional, versus a black hole of data easily dumped in there with a couple of keystrokes. "I don't need to organize my stuff, because the search feature can find it sufficiently" is, from what I've experienced, quite suboptimal as an approach. We need to have a way to overview our mass of collected information with some form of effective categorization.

Every once in a while someone has such a huge amount of reference material on one topic or project that it should be put in its own discrete drawer, cabinet, or digital directory. But if the physical material is less than half a file drawer's worth, I recommend including it in the single general alphabetical system. And if it is a digital grouping, it perhaps deserves its own place as a subdirectory.

Make It Easy to Create a New Folder   I keep a large supply of new file folders instantly at hand and reachable from where I sit to process my in-tray. Nothing is worse than having something to file and not having plenty of folders to grab from to make the process easy. Always ensure a supply within reach. The virtual version of this is getting comfortable with how to instantly create a new directory in your data-storage software as needed.

Make Sure You Have Plenty of Space for Easy Storage   Always try to keep your physical file drawers less than three-quarters full. If they're stuffed, you'll unconsciously resist putting things in there, and reference materials will tend to stack up instead. If a drawer is starting to get tight, I may purge it while I'm on hold on the phone.

If you have any attention on the storage room in your digital devices, it's a good time to review and purge.

I know almost no one who doesn't have overstuffed file drawers. If you value your cuticles, and if you want to get rid of your unconscious resistance to filing, then you must keep the drawers loose enough that you can insert and retrieve files without effort. The digital version of this is having any concern about space on the computer or in the cloud. A judgment call you consistently have to make is how much room to give yourself so that the content remains meaningfully and easily accessible, without creating a black hole of an inordinate amount of information amorphously organized. At times when I'm on hold on the phone, I'm purging my e-mail folders and old document directories.

Some people's reaction to this is, "I'd have to buy more file cabinets!" or "I'd have to get a larger hard drive!" as if that were something horrible. But if the stuff is worth keeping, it's worth keeping so that it's easily accessible, right? And if it's not, then why are you keeping it? If we're in the Information Age, and you're doing *anything* that hinders your usage of it . . . not smart.

You may need to create another tier of reference storage to give yourself sufficient working room with your general-reference files at hand. Material such as finished project notes and "dead" client files may still need to be kept, but they can be stored off-site, on storage drives, in the cloud, or at least out of your workspace.

Label Your File Folders with an Auto Labeler   No matter how small your inventory of physical reference materials is, you need to stay positively engaged with it. Typeset labels change the nature of your physical files and your relationship to them. Labeled files feel comfortable on a boardroom table; everyone can identify them; you can easily see what they are from a distance and in your briefcase; and when you open your file drawers, you get to see what looks almost like a printed index of your files in alphabetical order. It makes it fun to open the drawer to find or insert things.

> Things you name, you own. Collected but unnamed stuff owns you.

Perhaps later in this new millennium the brain scientists will give us some esoteric and complex neurological explanation for why labeled files work so effectively. Until then, trust me. Get a labeler. And get your own. To make the whole system work without a hitch, you'll need to have it at hand all the time, so you can file something whenever you want. And don't share! If you have something to file and your labeler's not there, you'll just stack the material instead of filing it. The labeler should be as basic a tool as your stapler.

> In the fire zone of real work, if it takes longer than sixty seconds to file something where it belongs, you won't file, you'll "stack."

Purge Your Files at Least Once a Year   Cleaning house in your files regularly keeps them from going stale and seeming like a black hole, and it also gives you the freedom to keep anything on a whim "in case you might need it." You know everything will be reassessed within a few months anyway, and you can redecide then what's worth keeping and what isn't. This applies equally to digital as well as paper-based reference information. As I said, I purge my files while I'm on hold on the phone (or marking time on a conference call that's dragging on and on!).

I recommend that all organizations (if they don't have one already) establish a "purge day," when all employees get to come to work in jeans, put their phone on do-not-disturb, and get current with all their stored stuff.* Large trash bins, recycle containers, and "to shred" boxes are available, and everyone has permission to spend the whole day in purge mode—around their office and on their computer. A personal purge day is an ideal thing to put into your tickler file, either during the holidays, at year's end, or around early spring tax-preparation time, when you might want to tie it in with archiving the previous year's financial files.

Filing as a Success Factor Itself

Reference and support materials seldom are associated with urgency, nor are they strategic, in the grand scheme of things. Hence their management is very often relegated to a low priority, if dealt with at all. The problem, however, is that your mental and physical workspaces become cluttered with nonactionable but potentially relevant

---

*A great time to do this is Christmas Eve day, or some similar near-holiday that falls on a workday. Most people are in "party mode" anyway, so it's an ideal opportunity to get funky and clean house.

Wherever items of different character or meaning are piled into the same location, it's too much work to continually think about the nature of the contents, so your brain will go numb to the pile.

and useful stuff. "What is this?" "Why is this here?" "What should I do with this?" and "Where is what I need to access right now?" become subliminal voices plaguing the consciousness if this aspect of your world is not rigorously set up and maintained.

Reference materials need to be contained and organized within their own discrete boundaries—physically and digitally—so that they don't cloud other categories in your system, are available for a specific purpose, and can be accessed efficiently. Because they can be so voluminous, it is critical that they be easily managed for capturing, sorting, and accessing what you need, when you need it, and that they don't get in the way of the more action-oriented components of your system. I have spent countless hours with some of the most sophisticated professionals in the world, assisting them in cleaning up and setting up a simple and functional reference system, and the results have often been phenomenal in freeing up their attention for the bigger things.

One Final Thing to Prepare . . .

You've blocked off some time, you've gotten a work area set up, and you've got the basic tools to start implementing the methodology. Now what?

If you've decided to commit a certain amount of time to setting up your workflow system, there's one more thing that you'll need to do to make it maximally effective: you must clear the decks of any other commitments for the duration of the session.

If there's someone you absolutely need to call, or something your secretary has to handle for you or you have to check with your life partner about, do it *now*. Or make an agreement with yourself about when you *will* do it, and then put some reminder of that where you won't miss it. It's critical that your full attention be available for the work at hand.

Almost without exception, when I sit down to begin coaching people, even though they've blocked out time and committed significant money to utilize me as a resource for that time, they still have things they're going to have to do before we quit for the day, and they haven't arranged for them yet in their own systems. "Oh, yeah, I've got to call this client back sometime today," they'll say, or "I have to check in with my spouse to see if he's gotten the tickets for tonight." It bespeaks a certain lack of awareness and maturity in our culture, I think, that so many sophisticated people are ignoring those levels of responsibility to their own consciousness, on an ongoing operational basis.

So have you handled all that? Good. Now it's time to gather representatives of all of your open loops into one place.

5

Capturing: Corralling Your "Stuff"

IN CHAPTER 2 I described the basic procedures for capturing your potential work and meaningful input. This chapter will lead you in more detail through the process of getting all your incompletes, all your "stuff," into one place—into "in." That's the critical first step in getting to the state of "mind like water." Just gathering a few more things than you currently have will probably create a positive feeling for you. But if you can hang in there and really do the whole capturing process, 100 percent, it will change your experience dramatically and give you an important new reference point for being on top of your work and your world.

When I coach a client through this process, the capture phase usually takes between one and six hours, though it did take an entire twenty hours with one person (finally I told him, "You get the idea"). It can take longer than you think if you are committed to a full-blown collection that will include everything at work and everywhere else. That means going through every storage area, including your computers, and every nook and cranny in every location, including cars, boats, and other garages and homes, if you have them.

Be assured that if you give yourself at least a couple of hours to tackle this part, you can grab the major portion of things outstanding. And you can even capture the rest by creating relevant placeholding notes—for example, "Purge and process boat storage shed" and "Deal with hall closet."

> Until you've captured *everything* that has your attention, some part of you will still not totally trust that you're working with the whole picture of your world.

In the real world, you probably won't be able to keep your stuff 100 percent collected all the time. If you're like most people, you'll move too fast and be engaged in too many things during the course of a week to get all your ideas and commitments captured outside your head. But it should become an ideal standard that keeps you motivated to consistently clean house of all the things about your work and life that have your attention.

Ready, Set . . .

There are very practical reasons to gather everything before you start clarifying it:

1 | it's helpful to have a sense of the volume of stuff you have to deal with;
2 | it lets you know where the "end of the tunnel" is; and
3 | when you're *clarifying* and *organizing*, you don't want to be distracted psychologically by an amorphous mass of stuff that might still be "somewhere." Once you have all the things that require your attention gathered in one place, you'll automatically be operating from a state of enhanced focus and control.

It can be daunting to capture in one location, at one time, all the things that don't belong where they are. It may even seem a little counterintuitive, because for the most part, most of that stuff was not, and is not, "that important"; that's why it's still lying around. It wasn't an urgent thing when it first showed up, and probably nothing's blown up yet because it hasn't been dealt with. It's the business card you put in your wallet of somebody you thought you might want to contact sometime. It's the little piece of techno-gear in the bottom desk drawer that you're missing a part for, or haven't had the time to install properly. It's the printer that you keep telling yourself you're going to move to a better location in your office. These are the kinds of things that nag at you but that you haven't decided either to deal with or to drop entirely from your list of open loops. But because you think there still *could* be something important in there, that stuff is controlling you and taking up more of your energy than it deserves.

> You can only feel good about what you're not doing when you *know* everything you're not doing.

So it's time to begin. Grab your in-tray and half-inch stack of plain paper for your notes, and let's . . .

. . . Go!

Physical Gathering

The first activity is to search your physical environment for any-thing that doesn't permanently belong where it is, the way it is, and put it into your in-tray. You'll be gathering things that are incom-plete, things that have some decision about potential action tied to them. They all go into "in," so they'll be available for later pro-cessing.

What Stays Where It Is

The best way to create a clean decision about whether something should go into the in-tray is to understand clearly what *shouldn't* go in. Here are the four categories of things that can remain where they are, the way they are, with no action tied to them:

- Supplies
- Reference Material
- Decoration
- Equipment

Supplies . . . include anything you need to keep because you use it regularly. Stationery, business cards, stamps, staples, Post-it pads, paper clips, ballpoint refills, batteries, forms you need to fill out from time to time, rubber bands—all of these qualify. Many people also have a "personal supplies" drawer at work containing dental floss, Kleenex, breath mints, and so on.

Reference Material . . . is anything you simply keep for information as needed, such as manuals for your software, the local takeout deli menu, your kid's sports team schedule, or your list of internal phone extensions. This category includes all your telephone and address information, any material relevant to projects, themes, and topics, and sources such as dictionaries, encyclopedias, almanacs, and bound archives of corporate records. It also includes books and magazines that you may be keeping as a library.

Decoration . . . means pictures of family, artwork, and fun and inspiring things pinned to your bulletin board. You also might have plaques, mementos, and/or plants.

Equipment . . . is obviously your phone, computer, printer, scanner, wastebasket, furniture, clock, chargers, pens, and notepads.

You no doubt have a lot of things that fall into these four categories—basically all your tools and your gear, which have no actions tied to them. Everything else goes into "in." But many of the things you might initially interpret as supplies, reference, decoration, or equipment could also have action associated with them because they still aren't exactly the way they need to be.

For instance, most people have, in their desk drawers, on their shelves and bulletin boards, and tucked away in computer files a lot of materials and information that either are out of date or need to be organized somewhere else. Those should go into "in." Likewise, if your supplies drawer is out of control, full of lots of dead or unorganized stuff, that's an incomplete that needs to be captured. Are the photos of your kids current ones? Is the artwork what you want on the wall? Are the mementos really something you still want to keep? Is the furniture precisely the way it should be? Is the computer set up the way you want it? Are the plants in your office alive? In other words, supplies, reference materials, decoration, and equipment may need to be tossed into the in-tray if they're not just where they should be, the way they should be.

Issues About Capturing

As you engage in the capturing step, you may run into one or more of the following:

- you've got a lot more than will fit into one in-tray;
- you're likely to get derailed into purging and organizing;
- you may have some form of stuff already collected and organized; and/or
- you're likely to run across some critical things that you want to keep in front of you.

What If an Item Is Too Big to Go in the In-Tray? If you can't physically put something in the in-tray, then write a note on a piece of letter-size plain paper to represent it. For instance, if you have a poster or other piece of artwork behind the door to your office, just write "Artwork behind door" on a letter-size piece of paper and put the paper in the in-tray.

Be sure to date it, too. This has a couple of benefits. If your organization system winds up containing some of these pieces of paper representing something else, it'll be useful to know when the note was created. It's also just a great habit to date everything you handwrite, from Post-it notes for your assistant, to voice mails you transfer onto a pad, to the note you take on a phone call with a client. If you are using a digital tool that has a date-stamp function, it's great to use that for the same reason. The 3 percent of the time that this little piece of information will be extremely useful makes it worth developing the simple habit.

What If the Pile Is Too Big to Fit into the In-Tray? If you're like 98 percent of the people we work with individually, your initial gathering activity will collect much more than can be comfortably stacked in an in-tray. If that's the case, just create stacks around the in-tray, and maybe even on the floor below it. Ultimately you'll be eliminating the stacks, as you process and organize everything. In the meantime, though, make sure that there's some obvious visual distinction between the stacks that are "in" and everything else.

Instant Dumping If it's immediately evident that something is trash, go ahead and toss it when you see it. For some of my clients, this marks the first time they have ever cleaned their center desk drawer!

If you're not sure what something is or whether it's worth keeping, go ahead and put it into "in." You'll be able to decide about it later, when you process the in-tray. What you *don't* want to do is to let yourself get wrapped up in things piece-by-piece, trying to decide this or that. Clarifying requires a very different mind-set than capturing; it's best to do them separately. You'll process your stuff later anyway if it's in "in," and it's easier to make those kinds of choices when you're in that decision-making mode. The objective for the capturing process is to get everything into "in" *as quickly as possible* so you're appropriately retrenched and have "drawn the battle lines."

Be Careful of the Purge-and-Organize Bug! Many people get hit with the purge-and-organize virus as they're going through various areas of their office (and their home). If that happens to you, it's OK, so long as you have a major open window of time to get through the whole process (at least a whole week). Otherwise you'll need to break it up into chunks and capture them as little projects or actions to do, with reminders in your system, like "Purge four-drawer cabinet" or "Clean office closet."

> *No person who can read is ever successful at cleaning out an attic.*
> —*Ann Landers*

What you *don't* want to do is let yourself get caught running down a rabbit trail cleaning up some piece of your work and then not be able to get through the whole action-management implementation process. It may take longer than you think, and you want to go for the gold and finish processing all your stuff and setting up your system as soon as possible.

What About Things That Are Already on Lists and in Organizers? You may already have some lists and some sort of organization system in place. But unless you're thoroughly familiar with this workflow-processing model and have implemented it previously, I recommend that you treat those lists as items still to be processed, like everything else in "in." You'll want your system to be consistent, and it'll be necessary to evaluate everything from the same viewpoint to get it that way.*

"But I Can't Lose That Thing . . . !" Often in the capturing process someone will run across a piece of paper or a document that causes her to say, "Oh, my God! I forgot about that! I've got to deal with that!" It could be a note about a call she was supposed to handle two days before, or some meeting notes that remind her of an action she was supposed to take weeks ago. She doesn't want to put whatever it is in the huge stack of other stuff in her in-tray because she's afraid she might lose track of it again.

---

*If you have previously implemented some version of the GTD methodology and have action and project lists set up, but the contents are not current and sufficiently active, you are usually better off printing them out, putting them back in your in-tray to use as raw input again, and starting anew. You don't want to be refreshing a new version of your system with outdated material inside.

If that happens to you, first ask yourself if it's something that really *has* to be handled before you get through this initial implementation time. If so, best deal with it immediately so you get it off your mind. If not, go ahead and put it into "in." You're going to get all that processed and emptied soon anyway, so it won't be lost.

If you can't deal with the action in the moment, and you still just *have* to have the reminder right in front of you, go ahead and create an "emergency" stack somewhere close at hand. It's not an ideal solution, but it'll do. Keep in mind that some potential anxiousness is going to surface as you make your stuff more conscious to you than it's been. Create whatever supports you need.

Start with Your Desktop

Ready now? OK. Start piling those things on your desk into "in." Often there'll be numerous things right at hand that need to go in there. Many people use their whole desktop as "in"; if you're one of them, you'll have several stacks around you to begin your collection with. Start at one end of your workspace and move around, dealing with everything you come across. Typical items will be:

- Stacks of mail, memos, reports, reading materials
- Post-it notes
- Collected business cards
- Receipts
- Meeting notes

Resist the urge to say, as almost everyone does initially, "Well, I know what's in that stack, and that's where I want to leave it." That's exactly what hasn't worked before, and it all needs to go into the in-tray. I have never had anyone who gave in and actually put their familiar stacks through this system who didn't feel a ton of relief when they did.

> It's easy to resist and avoid picking up anything in your world that you know requires some thinking.

As you go around your desktop, ask yourself if you have any intention of changing any of the tools or equipment there. Are your mobile devices and phone system OK? Your computer? The desk itself? If anything needs changing, write a note about it and toss it into "in."

Desk Drawers

Next tackle the desk drawers, if you have them, one at a time. Any attention on anything in there? Any actionable items? Is there anything that doesn't belong there? If the answer to any of these questions is yes, put the actionable item into "in" or write a note about it. Again, whether you use this opportunity to clean and organize the drawers or simply make a note to do it later will depend on how much time you have and how much stuff is in there.

Countertops

Continue working your way around your office, collecting everything sitting on the tops of cabinets or tables or counters that doesn't belong there permanently. Often there will be stacks of reading material, mail, reports, and miscellaneous folders and support material for action and projects. Collect it all.

Maybe there is reference material that you've already used and just left out. If that's so, and if you can return it to the file cabinet or the bookshelf in just a second, go ahead and do that. Be careful to check with yourself, though, about whether there is some potential action tied to the material before you put it away. If there is, put it into "in" so you can deal with it later in the process.

Inside the Cabinets

Now look inside the cabinets. What's in there? These are perfect areas for stashing large supplies and reference materials, and equally seductive for holding deeper levels of stuff. Any broken or out-of-date things in there? Often I'll find collectibles and nostalgia that aren't meaningful to the person any longer. One general manager of an insurance office, for example, wound up tossing out at least three dozen recognition awards he had accumulated over the years.

> Consider whether your collectible and nostalgia items are still meaningful to you.

Again, if some of these areas are out of control and need purging and organizing, write that on a note and toss it into "in."

Floors, Walls, and Shelves

Anything on bulletin boards that needs action? Anything tacked onto the walls that doesn't belong there? Any attention on your pictures, artwork, plaques, or decorations? How about the open shelves? Any books that need to be read or donated? Any catalogs, manuals, or binders that are out of date or have some potential action associated with them? Any piles or stacks of things on the floor? Just scoot them over next to your in-tray to add to the inventory.

Equipment, Furniture, and Fixtures

Is there anything you want to do to or change about any of your office equipment or furniture or the physical space itself? Does everything work? Do you have all the lighting you need? If there are actionable items, you know what to do: make a note and put it in "in."

Other Locations

Depending on the scope of what you're addressing in this process, you may want to do some version of the same kind of gathering anywhere else you keep stuff. As I mentioned in the previous chapter, if you're determined to get to a really empty head, it's imperative you do it everywhere.

> Don't let things to be handled that you have considered "not so important" gnaw away at your energy and focus.

Some people I work with find it immensely valuable to take me home with them, or to a second office location, and have me walk them through this process there as well. Often they've allowed the "not so important" trap to ensnare them in their home life and secondary workspaces, and it has gnawed away at their energy.

This Is Not About Throwing Things Away That You Might Want

People often mistake my advice as an advocacy for radical minimalism. On the contrary, if throwing something away is uncomfortable for you, you *should* keep it.* Otherwise you would have attention on the fact that you now don't have something you might want or need. My counsel is how to assess and organize whatever you keep in your ecosystem so that it doesn't pull on your focus unnecessarily. In many areas I'm a confirmed pack rat (such as with digital photos). The issues are simply how much room you have, and that you have made the appropriate distinctions that don't leave embedded projects and actions submerged in what you're keeping. You like having and keeping your twelve boxes of old journals and notes from college? You like keeping all kinds of nutty toys and artwork and gadgets around your office to spur creative thinking? No problem, as long as they are where you want them to be, in the form they're in, and you have anything you want or need to do about that captured and processed in your system.

Mental Gathering: The Mind Sweep

Once you feel you've collected all the physical things in your environment that need processing, you'll want to collect anything else that may be residing in your mental RAM space. What has your attention that isn't represented by something already in your in-tray?

This is where the stack of plain paper really comes into play. I recommend that you write out each thought, each idea, each project or thing that has your attention, on a *separate sheet of paper*. You could make one long list on a pad, or in some digital application, but given how you will later be processing each item individually, it's actually more effective on separate sheets. There is a discipline required initially to stay focused on one item at a time, as you process it. So giving each thought its own placeholder, as trivial as it might seem, makes it that much easier. And your first captured thought will seldom be the final content you'll want to track about it (the desired outcome and next action for it will be). You will likely not keep these pieces of paper, but it'll be handy to have them as discrete items to deal with as you're processing.†

---

*Obsessive-compulsive hoarding is another matter, and a condition to be dealt with outside the scope of this methodology and my expertise.

†Many people (even those who are high-tech oriented), once they experience the value of writing a single thought on a single piece of paper, have made it part of their ongoing self-management practice. It's great to give your potentially meaningful thoughts their due!

It will probably take you between twenty minutes and an hour to clear your head onto separate notes, *after* you've gathered everything else. You'll find that things will tend to occur to you in somewhat random fashion—little things, big things, personal things, professional things, in no particular order.

In this instance, go for quantity. It's much better to overdo this process than to risk missing something. You can always toss the junk later. Your first idea may be "Implement global climate change," and then you'll think, "I need cat food!" Grab them all. Don't be surprised if you discover you've created quite a stack of paper in "in" during this procedure.

Triggers List

To assist in clearing your head, you may want to review the following Incompletion Triggers list, item by item, to see if you've forgotten anything. Often you'll just need a jog to unearth something lurking in the back of your mind. Remember, when something occurs to you, write it on a piece of paper and toss it into "in."

Incompletion Triggers

Professional

Projects started, not completed
Projects that need to be started
"Look into . . ." projects
Commitments/promises to others
  Boss/partners
  Colleagues
  Subordinates
  Others in organization
  "Outside" people
    Customers
    Other organizations
    Professionals
    Vendors
Communications to make/get
  Internal/external
    Initiate or respond to:

Phone calls
Voice mails
E-mails
Text messages
Letters
  Social media postings
Other writing to finish/submit
  Reports
  Evaluations/reviews
  Proposals
  Articles
  Marketing materials
  Manuals/instructions
  Summaries
  Rewrites and edits
  Status reporting

Conversation and communication
    tracking
Meetings that need to be set/requested
Who needs to know about what
    decisions?
Significant read/review
Financial
    Cash
    Budgets
    Forecasts/projections
    Profit and loss
    Balance sheet
    Forecasting
    Credit line
    Banks
    Receivables
    Payables
    Petty cash
    Investors
    Asset management
Planning/organizing
    Formal planning (goals, targets,
        objectives)
    Current projects (next stages)
    Business plans
    Marketing plans
    Financial plans
    Organizational initiatives
    Upcoming events
    Meetings
    Presentations
    Conferences
    Organizational structuring
    Changes in facilities
    Installation of new systems/
        equipment
    Travel
    Vacation
    Business trips

Organization Development
    Organization chart
    Restructuring
    Roles
    Job descriptions
    Facilities
    New systems
    Leadership
    Change initiatives
    Succession planning
    Organization culture
Marketing/promotion
    Campaigns
    Materials
    Public relations
Administration
    Legal
    Insurance
    Personnel
    Staffing
    Policies/procedures
    Training
Staff
    Hiring/firing/promoting
    Reviews
    Communication
    Staff development
    Compensation
    Feedback
    Morale
Sales
    Customers
    Prospects
    Leads
    Sales process
    Training
    Relationship building
    Reporting
    Relationship tracking

Customer service
Systems
  Mobile devices
  Phones
  Computers
  Software
  Databases
  Telecommunications
  Internet
  Filing and reference
  Inventories
  Storage
Office/site
  Space/arrangements
  Furniture
  Equipment
  Decorations
  Utilities
  Supplies
  Maintenance/cleaning
  Security
Meetings
  Upcoming
  Needing to be set/requested
  Need debriefing
Professional development
  Training/seminars
  Things to learn

Things to find out
Skills to practice/develop
Books to read/study
Research
Formal education
  (licensing, degrees)
Career research
Résumé
Performance objectives
Professional wardrobe
Waiting for . . .
  Information
  Delegated tasks/projects
  Completions critical to projects
  Answers to questions
  Replies to:
    E-mails
    Letters
    Proposals
    Calls
    Invitations
  Requisitions
  Reimbursements
  Insurance claims
  Ordered items
  Repairs
  Tickets
  Decisions of others

Personal

Projects started, not completed
Projects that need to be started
Projects—other organizations
  Service
  Community
  Volunteer
  Spiritual organization
Commitments/promises to others

Partner/spouse
Children
Parents
Family
Friends
Professionals
Returnable items
Debts

Communications to make/get
  Calls
  E-mails
  Cards and letters
  Thank-yous
  Texts
  Social media postings
Upcoming events
  Birthdays
  Anniversaries
  Weddings
  Graduations
  Receptions
  Outings
  Holidays
  Vacation
  Travel
  Dinners
  Parties
  Cultural events
  Sporting events
Administration
  Home office supplies
  Equipment
  Phones
  Mobile devices
  Audio/video media
  Voice mail
  Computers
  Software
  Internet
  Filing and records
  Data storage/backup
Leisure
  Books
  Music
  Video
  Travel

Places to visit
People to visit
Web browsing
Photography
Sports equipment
Hobbies
Cooking
Recreation
Financial
  Bills
  Banks
  Investments
  Loans
  Taxes
  Budget
  Insurance
  Mortgage
  Bookkeeping
  Accountants
Pets
  Health
  Training
  Supplies
Legal
  Wills
  Trusts
  Estate
  Legal affairs
Family projects/activities
  Partner/spouse
  Children
  Parents
  Relatives
Home/household
  Real estate
  Repairs
  Construction
  Remodeling

Landlords
  Heating and air conditioning
  Plumbing
  Utilities
  Roof
  Landscaping
  Driveway
  Garage
  Walls
  Floors
  Ceilings
  Decor
  Furniture
  Appliances
  Lights and wiring
  Kitchen supplies/equipment
  Laundry
  Purging, organizing, cleaning
  Storage
  Service providers
Health
  Doctors
  Dentist
  Optometrist
  Healthcare specialists
  Checkups
  Diet
  Food
  Exercise
Personal development
  Classes
  Seminars
  Education
  Coaching/counseling
  Career
  Creative expressions
Transportation
  Motor vehicles
  Bicycles

Maintenance
Repair
Commuting
Clothes
  Professional
  Casual
  Formal
  Sports
  Accessories
  Luggage
  Repairs
  Tailoring
Errands
  Shopping
  Stores
  Hardware
  Supplies
  Groceries
  Gifts
  Pharmacy
  Bank
  Cleaners
  Repairs
Community
  Neighborhood
  Neighbors
  Service
  Schools
  Civic involvement
  Voting
Waiting for
  Product orders
  Repairs
  Reimbursements
  Loaned items
  Information
  RSVPs
  Projects/tasks completed by family/
    friends

The "In" Inventory

If your head is empty of everything, personally and professionally, then your in-tray is probably quite full and likely spilling over. In addition to the paper-based and physical items in your in-tray, your inventory of "in" should include any resident voice mails and all the e-mails that are currently staged in the "in" area of your communication software. It should also include any items on your organizer lists for which you have not yet determined next actions.

> Capturing is complete when you can easily see the outer edges to the inventory of everything that still has some of your attention in any way.

I usually recommend that people transfer their voice mails onto paper notes and put those into their in-trays, along with any organizer notebooks they may have used, the contents of which often need significant reassessment. If you've been using a digital application for anything other than calendar and contact information, I suggest you print out any task and to-do lists and put them, too, into your in-tray. E-mails are best left where they are, because of their volume and the efficiency factor of dealing with them within their own subsystem.

But "In" Doesn't Stay in "In"

When you've done all that, you're ready to take the next step. You don't want to leave anything in "in" for an indefinite period of time, because then it would without fail creep back into your consciousness, since your mind would know you weren't dealing with it. Of course, one of the main factors in people's resistance to collecting stuff into "in" is the lack of a good processing and organizing methodology to handle it.

That brings us to the next chapter: "Getting 'In' to Empty."

6

Clarifying: Getting "In" to Empty

ASSUMING THAT YOU have collected everything that has your attention, your job now is to actually get to the bottom of "in." Getting "in" to empty doesn't mean actually doing all the actions and projects that you've captured. It just means identifying each item and deciding what it is, what it means, and what you're going to do with it.

To get an overview of this process, you may find it useful here to refer to the Workflow Diagram on page 123. The center column illustrates all the steps involved in processing and deciding your next actions.

This chapter focuses on the components in the diagram's center column, the steps from "in" to next action. You'll immediately see the natural organization that results from following this process for each of your open loops. For instance, if you pick up something from "in" and realize, "I've got to call Andrea about that, but I've got to do it on Monday, when she's in her office," then you'll defer that action immediately and enter it on your calendar for Monday.

I recommend that you read through this chapter and the next one, on organizing your actions, before you actually start processing what you've captured in "in." It may save you some steps. When I coach people through this process, it invariably becomes a dance back and forth between the simple decision-making stage of *processing* the open loops and the trickier task of figuring out the best way to enter these decisions in their particular *organization* systems.

Many of the people we work with, for example, are eager to get set up on a mobile device that might synchronize with the enterprise application that their company is using for e-mail and scheduling. The first thing we would have to do (after we've collected the in-tray) is make sure all their hardware and software are working. Then we clean up (print out and erase, usually) everything they have previously tried to organize in their task lists and put it all into

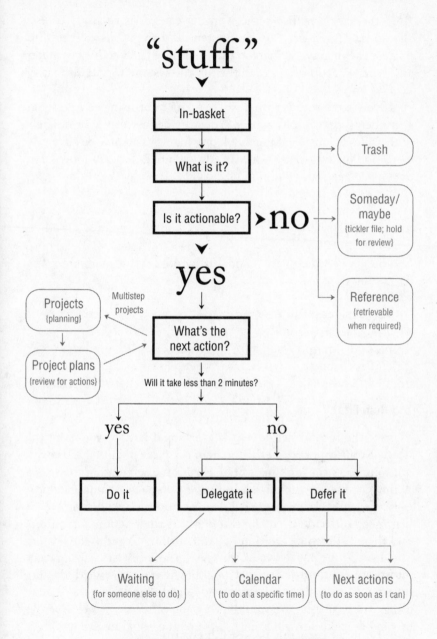

WORKFLOW DIAGRAM—CLARIFYING

"in." Then we establish some working categories such as "Calls," "Errands," "Agendas," "At Computer," and so on. As we begin to process the in-tray, the person can go immediately to his computer and type his action steps directly into the system he will ultimately depend on.

If you're not sure yet what you're going to be using as a personal reminder system, don't worry. You can begin very appropriately with a simple loose-leaf notebook or whatever you may be currently using for making lists. You can always upgrade your tools later, once you have your system in place.

Processing Guidelines

The best way to learn this model is by doing. But there are a few basic rules to follow:

- Process the top item first.
- Process one item at a time.
- Never put anything back into "in."

Top Item First

Even if the second item down is a personal note to you from the head of your country and the top item is a piece of junk mail, you've got to process the junk mail first! That's an exaggeration to make a point, but the principle is an important one: everything gets processed equally. The verb *process* does not mean "spend time on." It just means "decide what the thing is and what action is required, and then dispatch it accordingly." You're going to get to the bottom of the tray as soon as you can anyway, and you don't want to avoid dealing with *anything* in there.

Process does not mean "spend time on."

Emergency Scanning Is Not Clarifying

Most people get to their in-tray or their e-mail and look for the most urgent, most fun, easiest, or most interesting stuff to deal with first.

"Emergency scanning" is fine and necessary sometimes (I do it regularly, too). Maybe you've just come back from an off-site meeting and have to be on a long conference call in fifteen minutes. So you check to make sure there are no land mines about to explode and to see if your client has e-mailed back to you OK'ing the big proposal.

But that's not processing your in-tray; it's emergency scanning. When you're in processing mode, you must get into the habit of starting at one end and just cranking through items one at a time, in order. As soon as you break that rule and process only what you feel like processing, in whatever order, you'll invariably begin to leave things unprocessed. Then you will no longer have a functioning funnel, and it will back up all over your desk and office and e-mail "in" repositories. Many people live in this emergency-scanning mode, always distracted by what's coming into "in," and not feeling comfortable if they're not constantly skimming the contents on their computer or mobile devices. Were they to trust "in" would be totally dealt with every day or two, they wouldn't be so driven by this need for incessant checking.

LIFO or FIFO?

Theoretically you should flip your in-tray upside down and process first the first thing that came in. As long as you go from one end clear through to the other within a reasonable period of time, though, it won't make much difference. You're going to see it all in short order anyway. And if you're going to attempt to clear up a big backlog of e-mails staged in "in," you'll actually discover it's more efficient to process the last-in first because of all the discussion threads that accumulate on top of one another, and you don't want to respond to something prematurely before you've seen the whole discussion.

> The in-tray is a processing station, not a storage bin.

One Item at a Time

You may find you have a tendency, while processing your in-tray, to pick something up, not know exactly what you want to do about it, and then let your eyes wander to another item farther down the stack and get engaged with *it*. That item may be more attractive to you because you know right away what to do with it—and you don't feel like thinking about what's in your hand. This is dangerous territory. What's in your hand is likely to land on a "hmph" stack on the side of your desk because you become distracted by something easier, more important, or more interesting below it.

Thinking about the stuff you've accumulated usually does not happen naturally, of its own accord. You must apply conscious effort to get yourself to think, like getting yourself to exercise or clean house.

Most people also want to take a whole stack of things out of the in-tray at once, put it right in front of them, and try to crank through it all, immediately. Although I empathize with the desire to deal with a big chunk, I constantly remind people to put back everything but the one item on top. The focus on just one thing forces the requisite attention and decision making to get through all your stuff. And if you get interrupted (which is likely), you won't have countless parts of "in" scattered around outside the tray and out of control again.

The Multitasking Exception

There's a subtle exception to the one-item-at-a-time rule. Some personality types really need to shift their focus away from something for at least a minute in order to make a decision about it. When I see this going on with someone, I let him take two or sometimes three things out at once as he's processing. It's then easier and faster for him to make a choice about the action required.

Remember, multitasking is an exception—and it works only if you hold to the discipline of working through every item in short order, and never avoid any decision for longer than a minute or two.

Nothing Goes Back into "In"

There's a one-way path out of "in." This is actually what was meant by the old admonition to "handle things once," though handling things just once is in fact a bad idea. If you did that, you'd never have a list, because you would finish everything as soon as you saw it. You'd also be highly ineffective and inefficient, since most things you deal with are *not* to be acted upon the first time you become aware of them. Where the advice does hold is in eliminating the bad habit of continually picking things up out of "in," not deciding what they mean or what you're going to do about them, and then just leaving them there. A better admonition would be, "The first time you pick something up from your in-tray, decide what to do about it and where it goes. Never put it back in 'in.'"

The cognitive scientists have now proven the reality of "decision fatigue"—that every decision you make, little or big, diminishes a limited amount of your brain power. Deciding to "not decide" about an e-mail or anything else is another one of those decisions, which drains your psychological fuel tank.

The Key Processing Question: "What's the Next Action?"

You've got the message. You're going to deal with one item at a time. And you're going to make a firm next-action decision about each one. This may sound easy—and it is—but it requires you to do some fast, hard thinking. Much of the time the action will not be self-evident; it will need to be determined.

I am rather like a mosquito in a nudist camp; I know what I want to do, but I don't know where to begin.

—Stephen Bayne

On that first item, for example, do you need to call someone? Fill something out? Get information from the Web? Buy something at the store? Talk to your assistant? E-mail your boss? What? If there's an action, its specific nature will determine the next set of options. But what if you say, "There's really nothing to do with this"?

What If There Is No Action?

It's likely that a portion of your in-tray will require no action. There will be three types of things in this category:

• Trash
• Items to incubate
• Reference material

Trash

If you've been following my suggestions, you'll no doubt already have tossed out a big pile of stuff. It's also likely that you will have put stacks of material into "in" that include things you don't need anymore. So don't be surprised if there's still a lot more to throw away as you process your stuff.

Processing all the things in your world will make you more conscious of what you are going to do and what you should *not* be doing. One director of a foundation I worked with discovered that he had allowed way too many e-mails (thousands!) to accumulate—e-mails that in fact he wasn't ever going to respond to anyway. He told me that using my method forced him to "go on a healthy diet" about what he would allow to hang around his world as an incompletion.

It's likely that at some point you'll come up against the question of whether or not to keep something for future reference. I have two ways of dealing with that:

• When in doubt, throw it out.
• When in doubt, keep it.

Take your pick. I think either approach is fine. You just need to trust your intuition and be realistic about your space. Most people have some angst about all of this because their systems have never really been totally functional and clear-edged before. If you make a clean distinction between what's reference and supplies and what requires action, and if your reference system is simple and workable, you can easily keep as much material as you can accommodate. Since no action is required on it, it's just a matter of physical space and logistics. How big would you like your reference library and toolbox to be?

Filing experts can offer you more detailed guidelines about all this, and your accountant can provide record-retention timetables that will tell you how long you should keep what kinds of financial documentation. My suggestion is that you discriminate about whether something is actionable or not. Once it's clear that no

> Too much information creates the same result as too little: you don't have what you need, when and in the way you need it.

action is needed, there's room for lots of options, given your personal preferences and storage and access capabilities.

The digital world offers additional opportunities and challenges around the what-to-keep vs. what-to-throw-away decision. Because computer and cloud storage spaces seem continually to grow exponentially, the good news is that we are forever getting much more room to store much more stuff. Additional good news is the powerful search functionality that has grown along with it. The bad news is that it can easily foster indiscriminate filing and a lot of numbness to the volume and confusion about where things are, even as good as search functions might be. Because digital storage, without much forethought, has become almost automatic, it is very possible to create an environment of constant input but no utilization. You are creating a library so big and overwhelming, you have limited your capacity to make it functional for the work that's important for you to do. The key here is the regular reviewing and purging of outdated information, as I suggested in a previous chapter, as well as more conscious filtering on the front end, as you're processing your input: "Is this really necessary or useful for me to keep, or can I trust that I can access it from the Internet or other sources if I need it?"

Incubate

There will probably be things in your in-tray about which you will say to yourself, "There's nothing to do on this now, but there might be later." Examples of this would be:

- An e-mail announcing a chamber of commerce breakfast with a guest speaker you might want to hear, but it's two weeks away, and you're not sure yet if you'll be at home then or out of town on a business trip.
- An agenda for a board meeting you've been invited to attend in three weeks. No action is required on it, other than your briefing yourself a day ahead of the meeting by reading the agenda.
- An advertisement for the next software upgrade for one of your favorite applications. Do you really need this next version? You don't know; you'd rather sleep on it for another week.
- An idea you had about something you might want to do for next year's annual sales meeting. There's nothing to do on this now, but

you'd like to be reminded when the time comes to start planning for it.

• A note to yourself about taking a watercolor class, which you have zero time for right now.

What do you do with these kinds of things? There are two options that could work:

• Write them on a Someday/Maybe list.
• Put a reminder of them on your calendar or in a tickler file.

The point of all of these incubation procedures is that they give you a way to get the items off your mind *right now* and let you feel confident that some reminder of the possible action will resurface at an appropriate time. I'll elaborate on these in more detail in the next chapter, on organizing. For now, just put a Post-it on such items, and label them "maybe" or "remind on October 17," and set them aside in a Pending category you will be accumulating for later sorting.*

It's fine to decide not to decide about something. You just need a decide-not-to-decide system to get it off your mind.

Reference

Many of the things you will uncover in "in" will need no action but may have value as potentially useful information about projects and topics. Ideally, you have already set up a workable filing system (as described in chapter 4) for your reference and support information. As you come across material in your in-tray and that you e-mail (and attachments and Web links therein) that you'd like to keep for archival or support purposes, file it.

You'll probably discover that there are lots of miscellaneous kinds of things that you want to keep but have piled up in stacks or stuffed into drawers because your reference system was too formal

---

*One of your extra stack trays is ideal for this purpose. Use it temporarily during this initial processing to gather things to organize later. Afterward you can use it to hold pending work-in-progress papers and physical reminders of next actions.

or just plain nonexistent. Let me remind you here that a less-than-sixty-second, fun-to-use general-reference filing system within reach of where you sit is a mission-critical component of full implementation of this methodology. In the fast lane of real life, if it's not easy, quick, and fun to file something away, you'll stack or simply accumulate it in "in" instead of organizing. And then it will become much more difficult to keep things processed.

Whenever you come across something you want to keep, make a label for it, put it in a file folder, and tuck that into your filing drawer. Or put a Post-it on it instructing your assistant to do the same. Or appropriately tag or categorize it digitally. In my early days of coaching I used to give my clients permission to keep a To File pile. No longer. I discovered that if you can't get it into your system immediately, you're probably not ever going to. If you won't do it now, you likely won't do it later, either.

For digital inputs that you want to keep for reference, a plethora of options present themselves. If it's simply an e-mail that you want to keep so you can retrieve it later, I suggest using the storage folders that are usually available in e-mail applications—often in the navigator column on the side of the user window. Many people leave these nonactionable e-mails in their "in" section as a sort of amorphous filing cabinet, which seriously clogs the system. You should feel free to instantly create a new reference file for a new topic, theme, person, or project, and drag or insert the e-mail into it right away.

For documents, attachments, text, and graphics in e-mail that you might want to keep, you will have to develop your own filing procedures. These days there are very effective document storage applications in the cloud, as well as note-making and organizing programs accessible from multiple devices. The power, variety, and rapid evolvement of this enabling technology belie a recommendation for any one universal best practice. It behooves each of us to experiment, customize, and modify our digital libraries for what works best. The key to keeping it effective will be regular revisiting of our data and how we're organizing it; and keeping it current and usable.

Again, the key driver should be: Do I still have attention on my reference content or system? If so, create a project and next action to unpack that, to get this significant area for you on cruise control.

And If There Is an Action . . . What Is It?

This is perhaps the most fundamental practice of this methodology. If there's something that needs to be done about the item in "in," then you need to decide what, exactly, that next action is. "Next action," again, means the next physical, visible activity that would be required to move the situation toward closure.

Doing a straightforward, clear-cut task that has a beginning and an end balances out the complexity-without-end that often vexes the rest of my life. Sacred simplicity.

—Robert Fulghum

This is both easier and more difficult than it sounds.

The next action *should* be easy to figure out, but there are often some quick analyses and several planning steps that haven't occurred yet in your mind, and these have to happen before you can determine precisely what has to happen to complete the item, even if it's a fairly simple one.

Let's look at a sample list of the things that a person might typically have his or her attention on.

- Clean the garage
- Do my taxes
- Conference I'm going to
- Bobby's birthday
- Press release
- Performance reviews
- Management changes

Although each of these items may seem relatively clear as a task or project, determining the next action on each one will take some thought.

- Clean the garage

. . . *Well, I just have to get in there and start. No, wait a minute, there's a big refrigerator in there that I need to get rid of first. I should find out if John Patrick wants it for his camp. I should . . .*

- Call John re: refrigerator in garage.

What about . . .

• Do my taxes

   . . . *but I actually can't start on them until I have my last investment income documents back. Can't do anything until then. So I'm . . .*

• Waiting for documents from Acme Trust

   And for the . . .

• Conference I'm going to

   . . . *I need to find out whether Sandra is going to prepare a press kit for us. I guess I need to . . .*

• E-mail Sandra re: press kits for the conference.

   . . . and so forth. The action steps—"Call John," "Waiting for documents," "E-mail Sandra"—are what need to be decided about everything that is actionable in your in-tray.

The Action Step Needs to Be the Absolute Next Physical Thing to Do

Remember that these are physical, visible activities. Many people think they've determined the next action when they get it down to "set meeting." But that's not the next action, because it's not descriptive of physical behavior. How do you set a meeting? Well, it could be with a phone call or an e-mail, but to whom? Decide. If you don't decide now, you'll still have to decide at some other point, and what this process is designed to do is actually get you to finish the thinking exercise about this item. If you haven't identified the next physical action required to kick-start it, there will be a psychological gap every time you think about it even vaguely. You'll tend to resist noticing it, which leads to procrastination.

   When you get to a phone or to your

> Until you know what the next physical action is, there's still more thinking required before anything can happen—before you're appropriately engaged.

computer, you want to have all your thinking completed so you can use the tools you have and the location you're in to more easily get things done, having already defined what there is to do.

What if you say to yourself, "Well, the next thing I need to do is decide what to do about this"? That's a tricky one. Deciding isn't really an action, because actions take time, and deciding doesn't. There's always some physical activity that can be done to facilitate your decision making. Ninety-nine percent of the time you just need more information before you can make a decision. That additional information can come from external sources ("Call Susan to get her input on the proposal") or from internal thinking ("Draft ideas about new reorganization"). Either

Determine what physical activity needs to happen to get you to decide.

way, there's still a next action to be determined in order to move the project forward.

Once You Decide What the Action Step Is

You have three options once you decide what the next action really is:

- *Do it* (if the action takes less than two minutes).
- *Delegate it* (if you're not the most appropriate person to do the action).
- *Defer it* into your organization system as an option for work to do later.

Do It

If the next action can be done in two minutes or less, do it when you first pick the item up. If the e-mail requires just a thirty-second reading and then a quick yes/no/other response back to the sender, do it now. If you can browse the catalog in just a minute or two to see if there might be anything of interest in it, browse away, and then toss it, route it, or reference it as required. If the next action on something is to leave a quick message on someone's voice mail, make the call now.

Even if the item is not a high-priority one, do it now if you're ever going to do it at all. The rationale for the two-minute rule is that it's more or less the point where it starts taking longer to store and track an item than to deal with it the first time it's in your hands—in other words, it's the efficiency cutoff. If the thing's not important enough to be done, *throw it away*. If it is, and if you're going to do it sometime, the efficiency factor should come into play.

Many people find that getting into the habit of following the two-minute rule creates a dramatic improvement in their productivity. One vice president of a large software company told me that it gave him an additional hour a day of quality discretionary time! He was one of those three-hundred-e-mail-a-day high-tech executives, highly focused for most of the workday on three key initiatives. Many of those e-mails were from people who reported to him—and they needed his eyes on something, his comments and OKs, in order to move forward. But because they were not on a topic in his rifle sights, he would just stage the e-mails in "in," to get to "later." After several thousand of them piled up, he would have to go in to work and spend whole weekends trying to catch up. That would have been OK if he were twenty-six, when everything's an adrenaline rush anyway, but he was in his thirties and had young kids. Working all weekend was no longer acceptable behavior. When I coached him he went through all eight-hundred-plus e-mails he currently had in "in." It turned out that a lot could be dumped, quite a few needed to be filed as reference, and many others required less-than-two-minute replies that he whipped through. I checked with him a year later, and he was still current! He never let his e-mails mount up beyond a screenful anymore. He said it had changed the nature of his division because of the dramatic decrease in his own response time. His staff thought he was now made of Teflon!

| The two-minute rule is magic.

That's a rather dramatic testimonial, but it's an indication of just how critical some of these simple processing behaviors can be, especially as the volume and speed of the input increase for you personally.

Two minutes is in fact just a guideline. If you have a long open window of time in which to process your in-tray, you can extend the cutoff for each item to five or ten minutes. If you've got to get to the bottom of all your input rapidly, in order to figure out how best to use your afternoon, then you may want to shorten the time to

You'll be surprised how many two-minute actions you can perform even on your most critical projects.

one minute, or even thirty seconds, so you can get through everything a little faster.

It's not a bad idea to time yourself for a few of these while you're becoming familiar with the process. Most people I work with have difficulty estimating how long two minutes actually is, and they greatly underestimate how long certain actions are likely to take. For instance, if your action is to leave someone a message, and you get the real person instead of his or her voice-mail, the call will usually take quite a bit longer than two minutes.

There's nothing you really need to track about your two-minute actions—you just do them. If, however, you take an action and don't finish the project with that one action, you'll need to clarify what's next on it, and manage that according to the same criteria. For instance, if you act to replace a cartridge in your printer and discover that you're now out of extra cartridges, you'll want to decide on the next action about getting them ("Order printer cartridge refills online") and *do*, *delegate*, or *defer* it appropriately.

The world can only be grasped by action, not by contemplation. The hand is more important than the eye. . . . The hand is the cutting edge of the mind.

—*J. Bronowski*

Adhere to the two-minute rule and see how much you get done in the process of clearing out your "in" stacks. Many people are amazed by how many two-minute actions are possible, often on some of their most critical current projects. They are also delighted with applying this approach to small incompletions that have been lying around and nagging at them much too long.

The two-minute rule has become a salvation for many in getting control of their huge e-mail volume. In an active e-mail environment, it is likely that at least 30 percent of your actionable e-mails will require less than two minutes to respond and dispatch (assuming you have decent keyboard skills). If you're engaging with your e-mail, holding to this suggestion quite significantly improves responsiveness and productivity in your ecosystem. When I spend time with someone cleaning up his or her e-mail inventory, invariably there are dozens of quick actions generated that "move the needle" on multiple fronts, unsticking significant backlog.

That said, you shouldn't become a slave to spending your day doing two-minute actions. This rule should be applied primarily when you are engaging with new input; for example, processing your in-tray, interacting with someone in your office or home, or simply dealing with some random intersection in the hallway. But if you don't do it when it shows up, and you do still need to do it, you will have to take the time and energy to capture, clarify, and track it, to prevent its encroachment into your head.

Delegate It

If the next action is going to take longer than two minutes, ask yourself, "Am I the best person to be doing it?" If not, hand it off to the appropriate party, in a systematic format.

Delegation is not always downstream. You may decide, "This has got to get over to Customer Service," or "My boss needs to put her eyes on this next," or "I need my partner's point of view on this."

A systematic format could be any of the following:

• Send the appropriate party an e-mail.
• Write a note or an over-note on paper and route the item out to that person.
• Send him or her a text or leave a voice mail.
• Add it as an agenda item on a list for your next real-time conversation with that person.
• Talk to him or her directly, either face-to-face or by phone, text, or instant message.

Although any of these options can work, I would (with some exceptions) recommend them in the above order, top to bottom. E-mail is usually the fastest mode in the system; it provides an electronic record; and the receiver gets to deal with it at his or her convenience. Written notes are next because they, too, can get into the system immediately, and the recipient then has a physical particle to use as an organizational reminder. If you're passing on paper-based material as part of the handoff, a written communication is obviously the way to go; as with e-mail, the person you hand it off to can then deal with it on his or her own schedule. Voice mail and texting can be efficient, and many professionals live by it; the downside is that tracking becomes an additional requirement for both you and the recipient, what you say is not always what gets heard, and texts are infamously cryptic. Next would be saving the communication on an agenda list or in a folder for your next regular meeting with the person. At times this is necessary because of the sensitive or detailed nature of the topic, but it then must wait to get moving until that meeting occurs. The least preferable option would be to interrupt what both you and the person are doing in the moment to talk about the item. This is immediate, but it hampers workflow for both of you and has the same downside as voice mail: no written record.

Tracking the Handoff   If you do delegate an action to someone else, and if you care at all whether something happens as a result, you'll need to track it. As I walk you through in the next chapter, about organizing, you'll see that a significant category to manage is Waiting For.

As you develop your own customized system, what you eventually hand off and then track could look like a list in a planner, a file folder holding separate papers for each item, and/or a list categorized as Waiting For in your software. For now, if you don't have a trusted system set up already, just put a note on a piece of paper—"W/F: reply from Bob"—and put that into a Pending stack of notes in a separate pile or tray that may result from your processing.

What If the Ball Is Already in Someone Else's Court?   In the example cited previously about waiting for some documents to arrive so you can do your taxes, the next action is currently on someone else's plate. In such situations you will also want to track the action as a delegated item, or as a Waiting For. On the paper that says "Do my taxes," write something like "Waiting for tax documents from Acme Trust" and put that into your Pending stack.

It's important that you record the date on everything that you hand off to others. This, of all the categories in your personal system, is the most crucial one to keep tabs on. The few times you will actually want to refer to that information ("But I called and ordered that on March 12") will make it worth establishing this as a life-long habit.

Defer It

It's likely that most of the next actions you determine for things in "in" will be yours to do and will take longer than two minutes to complete. A call you need to make to a customer; an e-mail to your team that you need to spend a little time thinking about and drafting; a gift you need to buy for your brother at the sporting goods store; a software application you need to download from the Web and try out; a conversation you must have with your life partner about the school you're thinking of sending your daughter to—all of these fit that description.

These actions will have to be written down somewhere and then organized in the appropriate categories so you can access them when you need to. For the moment, go ahead and put Post-its on the pieces of paper in "in," with the action written on them, and add these to the Pending stack of papers that have been processed.

The Pending Things That Are Left

If you follow the instructions in this chapter, you'll dump a mess of things, file a bunch, do a lot of two-minute actions, and hand off a number of items to other people. You'll also wind up with a stack of items that have actions associated with them that you still need to do—soon, someday, or on a specific date—and reminders of things you're waiting on from other people. This Pending group is made up of the actions you've delegated or deferred. It is what still needs to be organized in some fashion in your personal system, a topic I'll cover in step-by-step detail in the next chapter.

Identifying the *Projects* You Have

This last step in getting to the bottom of "in" requires a shift in perspective from the single-action details to the larger picture—your projects.

Again, I define a project as any outcome you're committed to achieving that will take more than one action step to complete. If you look through an inventory of actions that you have already been generating—"Call Frank about the car alarm"; "E-mail Bernadette re: conference materials"—you'll no doubt recognize a number of things that are larger than the single action you've defined. There's still going to be something to do about the car alarm after the call to Frank, and there will still be something to handle about the conference after the e-mail to Bernadette.

I hope you're able to see the very practical reason for defining projects as broadly as I do: if the action step you've identified will not complete the commitment, then you'll need some stake in the ground to keep reminding you of actions you have pending until you have closure. You need to make a list of projects. A "Projects" list may include anything from "Give holiday party" to "Divest the software product line" to "Finalize compensation package." The purpose of this list is not to reflect your priorities but just to ensure that you've got placeholders for all those open loops.

> Right now you probably have between thirty and a hundred projects.

Whether you draw up your Projects list while you're initially processing your in-tray or after you've set up your action lists doesn't really matter. It just needs to be done at *some* point, and it must be maintained, as it's the key driver for reviewing where you are and where you want to be, and to maintain a sense of week-to-week control of your life.

For now, let's make sure your organizing setup is "all systems go."

7

Organizing: Setting Up the Right Buckets

HAVING A TOTAL and seamless system of organization in place gives you tremendous power because it allows your mind to let go of lower-level thinking and graduate to intuitive focusing, undistracted by matters that haven't been dealt with appropriately. But your physical organization system must be better than your mental one in order for that to happen.

> Airtight organization is required for your focus to remain on the broader horizon and eliminate the constant pressure to remember or be reminded.

Being organized means nothing more or less than where something is matches what it means to you. If you decide you want to keep something as reference and you put it where your reference material needs to be, that's organized. If you think you need a reminder about a call you need to make, as long as you put that reminder where you want reminders of phone calls to make, you're organized. As simple as that sounds, it begs a very big question: What does something *mean* to you? It turns out that much of what people are trying to organize has not been clarified, as per the previous chapter. And even once it has, there are more refined distinctions that are possible, which will add greater creativity and control for you. I will expand on some of those in this chapter, as I'll lead you through the organizing steps and tools that will be required as you process your in-tray. As you initially process "in," you'll create lists and groupings of things you want to organize and you'll invariably think of additional items to include. In other words, your organization system is not something that you'll necessarily create all at once, in a vacuum. It will evolve as you process your stuff and test out whether you have put everything in the best place for *you*. It should and will evolve, as you do. The core distinctions of what things mean to you will be true forever, but the best structure for you to manage them a year from now may look different than what you come up with dealing with your world today.

I must Create a System or be enslav'd by another Man's.

—*William Blake*

The outer ring of the Workflow Diagram (opposite) shows the main groupings into which things will go as you decide what they are and what needs to be done about them.

The Basic Categories

There are seven primary types of things that you'll want to keep track of and manage from an organizational and operational perspective:

• A Projects list
• Project support material
• Calendar actions and information
• Next Actions lists
• A Waiting For list
• Reference material ·
• A Someday/Maybe list

The Importance of Hard Edges

It's critical that all of these categories be kept pristinely distinct from one another. They each represent a discrete type of agreement we make with ourselves, to be reminded of at a specific time and in a specific way, and if they lose their edges and begin to blend, much of the value of organizing will be lost.

That's why capturing and clarifying what your relationship to them is, specifically, is primary to getting organized. Most people try to create more control in their world by just "getting organized," and they wind up rearranging incomplete inventories of still unclear things. Once you've gone through my previously suggested processes, however, you will have very clear contents of what you need

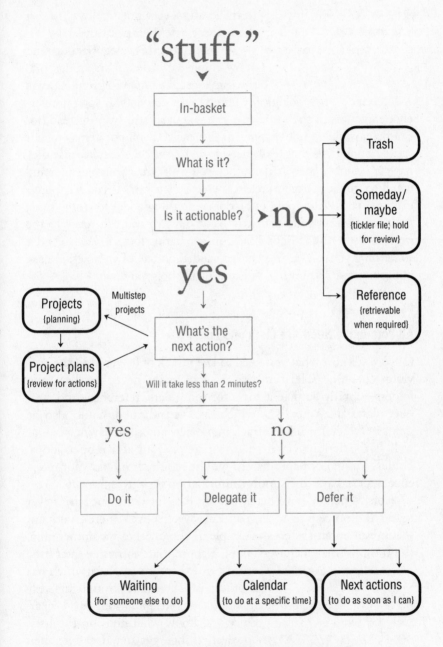

WORKFLOW DIAGRAM—ORGANIZING

The categories must be kept visually, physically, and psychologically separate, to promote clarity.

to track, and a very practical way to sort them and create their descriptors.

If you neglect this categorization, and allow things of different meanings into the same visual or mental grouping, you will tend to go psychologically numb to the contents. If you put reference materials in the same pile as things you still want to read, for example, you'll go unconscious to the stack. If you put items on your Next Actions lists that really need to go on the calendar, because they have to occur on specific days, then you won't trust your calendar and you'll continually have to reassess your action lists. If you have projects that you're not going to be doing anything about for some time, they must go on your Someday/Maybe list so you can relate to the Projects list with the rigorous action-generating focus it needs. And if something you're Waiting For is included on one of your action lists, nonproductive rethinking will continually bog you down.

All You Really Need Are Lists and Folders

Once you know what you need to keep track of (covered in the previous chapter, "Clarifying"), all you really need are lists and folders—totally sufficient tools for reminders, reference, and support materials. Your lists (which, as I've indicated, could also be items in folders) will keep track of projects and someday/maybes, as well as the actions you'll need to take on your active open loops. Folders (digital or paper based) will be required to hold your reference material and the support information for active projects.

Lots of people have been making lists for years but have never found the procedure to be particularly effective. There's rampant skepticism about systems as simple as the one I'm recommending. But most list makers haven't put the appropriate things *on* their lists,

I would not give a fig for the simplicity on this side of complexity, but I would give my life for the simplicity on the other side of complexity.

—Oliver Wendell Holmes

or have left them incomplete, which has kept the lists themselves from being very functional for keeping your head clear. Once you know what goes on the lists, however, things get much easier; then you just need a way to manage them.

As I've said, you shouldn't bother to

create some external structuring of the priorities on your lists that you'll then have to rearrange or rewrite as things change. Attempting to impose such scaffolding has been a big source of frustration in many people's organizing. You'll be prioritizing more intuitively as you see the whole list against quite a number of shifting variables. The list is just a way for you to keep track of the total inventory of active things to which you have made a commitment, and to have that inventory available for review.

When I refer to a "list," keep in mind that I mean nothing more than a grouping of items with some similar characteristic. A list could look like one of at least three things: (1) a file folder or container with separate paper notes for the items within the category; (2) an actual list on a titled piece of paper (often within a loose-leaf organizer or planner); or (3) an inventory of items on a list in a software program or in a digital mobile device.

Organizing Action Reminders

If you've emptied your in-tray, you'll undoubtedly have created a stack of Pending reminders for yourself, representing longer-than-two-minute actions that cannot be delegated to someone else. You'll probably have anywhere from twenty to sixty or seventy or more such items. You'll also have accumulated reminders of things that you've handed off to other people, and perhaps some things that need to be placed on your calendar or in a Someday/Maybe holder.

You'll want to sort all of this into groupings that make sense to you so you can review them as options for work to do when you have time. You'll also want to divide them in the most appropriate way physically to organize those groups, whether as items in folders or on lists, either paper based or digital.

The Actions That Go on Your Calendar

For the purposes of organization, as I've said, there are two basic kinds of actions: those that must be done on a certain day and/or at a particular time, and those that just need to be done as soon as you can get to them, around your other calendar items (some perhaps with a final due date). Calendared action items can be either time specific (e.g., "10:00–11:00 meet with Jim") or day specific ("Call

The calendar should show only the "hard landscape" around which you do the rest of your actions.

Rachel Tuesday to see if she got the proposal").

As you were processing your in-tray, you probably came across things that you put right into your calendar as they showed up. You may have realized that the next action on getting a medical checkup, for example, was to call and make the appointment, and so (since the action required two minutes or less) you actually did it when it occurred to you. Writing the appointment on your calendar as you made it would then have been common sense.

What many want to do, however, based on perhaps old habits of writing daily to-do lists, is put actions on the calendar that they think they'd really *like* to get done next Monday, say, but that actually might not, and that might then have to be moved to following days. *Resist this impulse.* You need to trust your calendar as sacred territory, reflecting the exact hard edges of your day's commitments, which should be noticeable at a glance while you're on the run. That'll be much easier if the only things in there are those that you absolutely *have* to get done, or know about, on that day. When the calendar is relegated to its proper role in organizing, the majority of the actions that you need to do are left in the category of "as soon as possible, against all the other things I have to do."

Organizing As-Soon-As-Possible Actions by Context

Over many years I have discovered that the best way to be reminded of an "as soon as I can" action is by the particular *context* required for that action—that is, either the tool or the location or the situation needed to complete it. For instance, if the action requires a computer, it should go on an At Computer list. If your action demands that you be out and moving around in the world (such as stopping by the bank or going to the hardware store), the Errands list would be the appropriate place to track it. If the next step is to talk about something face-to-face with your partner, Emily, putting it into an "Emily" folder or list makes the most sense.

How discrete these categories will need to be will depend on (1)

how many actions you actually have to track; and (2) how often you change the contexts within which to do them.

If you are that rare person who has only twenty-five next actions, a single Next Actions list might suffice. It could include items as diverse as "Buy nails," "Talk to boss about staff changes," and "Draft ideas about committee meeting." If, however, you have fifty or a hundred next actions pending, keeping all of those on one big list would make it too difficult to see what you need to see; each time you got any window of time to do something, you'd have to do unproductive re-sorting. If you happened to be on a short break at a conference, during which you might be able to make some calls, you'd have to identify the calls among a big batch of unrelated items. When you went out to do odds and ends, you'd probably want to pick out your errands and make another list.

Another productivity factor that this kind of organization supports is leveraging your energy when you're in a certain mode. When you're in "phone mode," it helps to make a lot of phone calls—just crank down your Calls list. When your computer is up and running and you're cruising along digitally, it's useful to get as much done online as you can without having to shift into another kind of activity. It takes more energy than most people realize to unhook out of one set of behaviors and get into another kind of rhythm and tool set. And obviously, when a key person is sitting in front of you in your office, you'd be wise to have all the things you need to talk about with him or her immediately at hand.

The Most Common Categories of Action Reminders

You'll probably find that at least a few of the following common list headings for next actions will make sense for you:

- Calls
- At Computer
- Errands
- At Office (miscellaneous)
- At Home
- Anywhere
- Agendas (for people and meetings)
- Read/Review

Calls   This is the list of all the phone calls you need to make; you can work off it as long as you have a phone available. The more mobile you are, the more useful you'll find it to have one single list of all your calls: those strange little windows of time that you wind up with when you're off-site, out and about, traveling, on a break, or waiting for a plane or for your kid to come out from school offer a perfect opportunity to make use of that list. Having a discrete Calls category makes it much easier to focus and intuitively pick the best one to make in the moment.

I suggest that you take the time to record the phone number alongside each item. There are many situations in which you would probably make the call if the number was already there in front of you but not if you had to look it up, and if you're using a mobile device then only a tap is required to engage.

At Computer   If you work with a computer—particularly if you move around with a laptop/tablet or have a computer at work and another at home—it can be helpful to group all those actions that you need to do when it's on and running. This will allow you to see all your options for computer work to do, reminding you of the e-mails you need to send, the documents you need to draft or edit, and so on.

Because I fly a lot, I maintain an Online action list, separate from my At Computer one. When I'm on a plane without a Wi-Fi service I can't connect to the Web or my servers, as many actions require. So instead of having to rethink what I can and can't do whenever I look at my At Computer list, I can trust that none of my At Computer actions require that I be connected, which frees my mind to make choices based on other criteria.

> Think carefully about *where* and *when* and *under what circumstances* you can do which actions, and organize your lists accordingly.

If you only do at-computer work at your office, or at your home, you could incorporate those actions on those location-specific lists, though you might still find it functional to see reminders of computer work grouped together when you're sitting in that context. On the other hand, if your work and activities are primarily mobile-centric, and you could be taking actions equally on a laptop, tablet, or smartphone, then parking those reminders on a single Digital context list or folding them into the Anywhere category might work best.

Errands It makes a lot of sense to group together in one place reminders of all the things you need to do when you're out and about. When you know you need to go somewhere, it's great to be able to look at that list to allow for the option of handling numerous things along the way, in one trip. Actions like "Get stock certificates from bank deposit box," "Pick up suit at the tailor," and "Buy flowers for Robyn at the florist" would all go here.

This list could, of course, be nothing more elaborate than a Post-it that you keep in your planner or on your refrigerator door, or in an Errands category in some digital task manager.

> *We must strive to reach that simplicity that lies beyond sophistication.*
>
> *—John Gardner*

It's often helpful to track sublists within individual Errands items. For instance, as soon as you realize you need something from the hardware store, you might want to make "hardware store" the list item and then append a sublist of all the things you want to pick up there, as you think of them. On the low-tech end, you could create a "hardware store" Post-it; on the high-tech side, if you were using a digital list, you could attach a "note" to "hardware store" on your list and input the details there.*

At Office If you work in an office, there will be certain things that you can do only there, and a list of those things will be useful to have in front of you then—though obviously, if you have a phone and a computer in your office, and you have "Calls" and "At Computer" as separate lists, they'll be in play as well. I'd use an "Office Actions" or "At Office" list for anything that required me being physically present there to take the action, such as purging

> Simplifying your focus on actions will ensure that more of them get done.

---

*One thrust in personal productivity technology (to some degree precipitated by the popularity of this GTD methodology) is the development of location-based reminders. Your mobile device will sense (given your GPS reading) that you are at a hardware store, or at home, or downtown, and it will then alert you to actions tied to that physical environment. This makes sense in principle, but in practice, with all the variables involved and the desirability to overview our total inventory of actions from multiple angles, these will only be useful as a nice option to add to a rigorously managed list, as part of a totally reviewed and integrated system. Assuming this will keep your head clear and not miss something you'd want to see is still quite overoptimistic about that technology and its usage.

an office filing cabinet or printing and reviewing a large document with a staff person.

A major trend now is for organizations to become more open, flexible, and virtual. "Hotel-ing" (i.e. not having a permanent office, but rather "plugging in" in any available location) is on the rise. Consequently, At Office could mean simply an action that requires being at any of several company locations. Or, for some people, it's useful to have both an At Office "A" and an At Office "B" list, for those things that are still discretely tied to one physical location or another.

At Home   Many actions can be done only at home, and it makes sense to keep a list specific to that context. I'm sure you've got numerous personal and around-the-house projects, and often the next thing to do on them is just to do them. "Hang new watercolor print," "Organize travel accessories," and "Switch closets to winter clothes" would be typical items for this grouping.

If you have an office at home, as I do, anything that can be done only there goes on the At Home list. (If you work *only* at home and don't go to another office, you won't need an At Office list at all—the At Home list could suffice.)

Similar to people who work at various locations, many people have multiple personal work environments, such as vacation homes, boats, and even the local gourmet coffee shop or café. "At Starbucks" can be a fine categorization for an action list!

*Agendas**   Invariably you'll find that many of your next actions need to either occur in a real-time interaction with someone or be brought up in a committee, team, or staff meeting. You have to talk to your partner about an idea for next year; you want to check with your life partner about his schedule for the spring; you need to delegate a task to your assistant that's too complicated to explain in an e-mail. And you must make an announcement at the Monday staff meeting about the change in expense-report policies.

> Standing meetings and people you deal with on an ongoing basis often need their own Agenda list.

---

*I use Agenda in the U.S./American meaning—items to cover with someone or in a meeting (vs. "calendar," "schedule," or "diary" in other cultures).

These next actions should be put on separate Agenda lists for each of those people and for that meeting (assuming you attend it regularly). Professionals who keep a file folder to hold all the things they need to go over with their boss already use a version of this method. If you're conscientious about determining all your next actions, though, you may find that you'll need somewhere between three and fifteen of these kinds of lists. I recommend that separate lists be kept for bosses, partners, assistants, and children. You should also keep the same kind of list for your attorney, financial adviser, accountant, and/or computer consultant, as well as for anyone else with whom you might have more than one thing to go over the next time you talk on the phone or in person.

> The broader your responsibilities, and the more senior your organizational roles, the more you will get things done through your communications and transactions with other people.

If you participate in standing meetings—staff meetings, project meetings, board meetings, committee meetings, parent/teacher meetings, whatever—they, too, deserve their own lists, in which you collect things that will need to be addressed on those occasions.

Often you'll want to keep a running list of things to go over with someone you'll be interacting with only for a limited period of time. For instance, if you have a contractor doing a significant piece of work on your house or property, you can create a list for him for the duration of the project. As you're walking around the site after he's left for the day, you may notice several things you need to talk with him about, and you'll want that list to be easy to capture and to access as needed.

Given the usefulness of this type of list, your system should allow you to add Agendas ad hoc, as needed quickly and simply. For example, inserting a page or a list for a person or a meeting within an Agenda section of a loose-leaf notebook planner takes only seconds, as does adding a dedicated "note" within an Agenda category in your digital tools.

Read/Review   You will no doubt have discovered in your in-tray a number of things for which your next action is to read. I hope you have held to the two-minute rule and dispatched many of those quick-skim items already—tossing, filing, or routing them forward as appropriate.

To-read printed items that you know will demand more than two minutes of your time are usually best managed in a separate physical stack tray labeled "Read/Review." This is still a "list" by my definition, but one that's more efficiently dealt with by grouping the documents and magazines themselves in a tray and/or portable folder.

Those who make the worst use of their time are the first to complain of its shortness.

—Jean de La Bruyère

For many people, the Read/Review stack can get quite large. That's why it's critical that the pile be reserved only for those longer-than-two-minute things that you actually *want* to read when you have time. That can be daunting enough in itself, but things get seriously out of control and psychologically numbing when the edges of this category are not clearly defined. A pristine delineation will at least make you conscious of the inventory, and if you're like most people, having some type of self-regulating mechanism will help you become more aware of what you want to keep and what you should just get rid of.

Some professionals (e.g., attorneys) still work with significant printed materials, and although most of their documents may be generated and maintained in digital form, working with the document in physical form still remains the optimal way to deal with it. In those cases it often makes sense, in addition to a Read/Review box or tray, to have a Review/Respond category for the more rigorous reading that requires a different kind of focus.

It's practical to have organized reading material at hand when you're on your way to a meeting that may be starting late, a seminar that may have a window of time when nothing is going on, a dentist appointment that may keep you waiting, or, of course, if you're going to have some time on a train or plane. Those are all great opportunities to browse and work through that kind of reading. People who don't have their Read/Review material organized can waste a lot of time, since life is full of weird little windows when it could be used.

Given the amount of digital input we're getting that includes data to read and view, much of which is not really critical to our work or life but is potentially interesting or fun, it can be useful to create an organizational bucket within that world for such things. A Review/Watch file in your e-mail folder system or a Surf Web action list could be a good place to hold e-mails with links to recommended videos, blogs, or online articles.

Organizing "Waiting For"

Like reminders of the actions you need to do, reminders of all the things that you're waiting to get back from or get done by others have to be sorted and grouped. You won't necessarily be tracking discrete action steps here, but more often final deliverables or projects that others are responsible for, such as the tickets you've ordered from the theater, the scanner that's coming for the office, the OK on the proposal from your client, and so on. When the next action on something is up to someone else, you don't need an *action* reminder, just a trigger about what you're waiting for and from whom. Your role is to review that list as often as you need to and assess whether you ought to be taking an action, such as checking the status or lighting a fire in some way under the project.

> Manage the commitments of others before their avoidance creates a crisis.

For many people, especially those in managerial or supervisory positions, getting this inventory of unfulfilled commitments that we care about from others captured, current, complete, and reviewed creates tremendous relief and improved focus going forward.

You'll probably find that it works best to keep this Waiting For list close at hand, in the same system as your Next Actions reminder lists. The responsibility for the next step may bounce back and forth many times before a project is finished. For example, you may need to make a call to a vendor to request a proposal (which then goes to your Waiting For list). When the proposal comes in, you have to review it (it lands in your Read/Review tray or on your At Computer list). Once you've gone over it, you send it to your boss for her approval (now it's back on your Waiting For list). And so on.*

---

*Digital list managers (as well as low-tech papers in separate folders) have an advantage here because they let you easily move an item from one category to another as the action changes, without your having to rewrite or rethink anything.

It's also very useful to have your Waiting For list available when you are meeting with or talking to anyone who might be responsible for any of those deliverables. It is much more elegant to broach a conversation early on, such as "Oh yeah, how's it going with the Gonzalez proposal?" than to wait until it's overdue and the situation is in a stress mode.

It's important for this category in particular to include the date that each item is requested for each entry, as well as any agreed-upon due date. Follow-up is much more meaningful when you can say, "But I placed the order March twentieth" or "You've had the proposal now for three weeks." In my experience, just this one tactical detail is worth its weight in gold.

You'll get a great feeling when you know that your Waiting For list is the complete inventory of everything you care about that other people are supposed to be doing.

Using the Original Item as Its Own Action Reminder

The most efficient way to track your action reminders is to add them to lists or folders as they occur to you. The originating trigger won't be needed after you have processed it. You might take notes in the meeting with your boss, but you can toss those after you've pulled out any projects and actions associated with them. While some people try to archive texts or voice mails that they still need to do something about, that's not the most effective way to manage the reminders embedded in them.

Keep actionable e-mails and paper separated from all the rest.

There are some exceptions to this rule, however. Certain kinds of input will most efficiently serve as their own reminders of required actions, rather than your having to write something about them on a list. This is particularly true for some paper-based materials and some e-mail.

Managing Paper-Based Workflow

Some things are their own best reminders of work to be done. The category of Read/Review articles, publications, and documents is a good example. It would obviously be overkill to write "Review

Vogue magazine" on some action list when you could just as easily toss the magazine itself into your Read/Review tray to act as the trigger.

Another example: if you are still doing paper-based bill paying, you'll probably find it easier to deal with the bills by paying them all at one time, so you keep them in a folder or stack tray labeled "Bills to Pay" (or, more generically, "Financial to Process"). Similarly, receipts for expense reporting should be either dealt with at the time they're generated or kept in their own Receipts to Process envelope or folder.*

The specific nature of your work, your input, and your workstation may make it more efficient to organize other categories using only the original document itself. A customer-service professional, for instance, may deal with numerous requests that show up in some standard form, and in that case maintaining a tray or file (paper or digital) containing only those actionable items is the best way to manage them. An attorney or accountant may deal with documents they need to spend time reviewing to determine actions, which could be stacked in a tray on the desk with items of that specific nature.

Whether it makes more sense to write reminders on a list or to use the originating documents in a tray or folder or digital directory will depend to a great extent on logistics. Could you use those reminders somewhere other than at your desk? If so, the portability of the material should be considered. If you couldn't possibly do that work anywhere but at your desk, then managing reminders of it solely at your workstation is the better choice.

> The primary reason for organizing is to reduce cognitive load—i.e. to eliminate the need to constantly be thinking, "What do I need to do about this?"

Whichever option you select, the reminders should be in visibly discrete categories based upon the next action required. If the next action on a service order is to make a call, it should be in a Calls group; if the action step is to review information and input it into the computer, it should be labeled "At Computer." Most

---

*This approach can be dangerous, however, if you don't put those "Bills to Pay" or "Receipts to Process" in front of your face as consistently as you should. Just having them "organized" isn't sufficient to get them off your mind—you've also got to trust that you will appropriately review and deal with them.

undermining of the effectiveness of many workflow systems I see is the fact that all the documents of one type (e.g. service requests) are kept in a single tray or file, even though different kinds of actions may be required on each one. One request needs a phone call, another needs data reviewed, and still another is waiting for someone to get back with some information—but they're all sorted together. This arrangement can cause a person's mind to go numb to the stack because of all the decisions that are still pending about the next-action level of doing.

My personal system is highly portable, with almost everything kept on lists, but I still maintain a Read/Review stack tray in my office and the traveling version as a plastic folder with the same title. Though I store and read some magazines digitally, it's still both logistically functional and aesthetically pleasing to me to have the physical version at hand.

Managing E-mail-Based Workflow

Like some paper-based materials, e-mails that need action are sometimes best as their own reminders—in this case within the e-mail system itself. This is especially true if you get a lot of e-mail and spend a lot of your work time with your e-mail software active at hand. E-mails that you need to act on may then be stored within the system instead of having their embedded actions written out or distributed on another list.

Many people have found it helpful to set up two or three unique folders on their e-mail navigator bars. True, most folders in e-mail should be used for reference or archived materials, but it's also possible to set up a workable system that will keep your actionable messages discretely organized outside the "in" area itself (which is where most people tend to keep them).*

If you choose this route, I recommend that you create one folder for any longer-than-two-minute e-mails that you need to act on (again, you should be able to dispatch many messages right off the bat by following the two-minute rule). The folder name should

---

*If you happen to have a lifestyle that seldom has more than one screenful of un-dealt-with e-mails at any one time, simply keeping them there as a reminder of your work at hand would probably suffice. As soon as the volume expands to something you can't see at a glance, then organizing them outside your "in" area makes much more sense.

begin with a prefix letter or symbol so that (1) it looks different from your reference folders and (2) it sits at the top of your folders in the navigator bar. Use something like the @ sign or the hyphen, whichever will sort into your system at the top. Your resulting @ACTION folder will hold those e-mails that you need to do something about.

Next you can create a folder titled "@WAITING FOR," which will show up in the same place as the @ACTION folder. Then, as you receive e-mails that indicate that someone is going to do something you care about tracking, you can drag them over into the @WAITING FOR file. It can also hold reminders for anything that you delegate via e-mail: when you forward something, or use e-mail to make a request or delegate an action, just save a cc: or bcc: copy into your @WAITING FOR file.*

Some applications allow you to file a copy of an e-mail into one of your folders as you send it (with a "Send and File" button). Others will simultaneously save only into your universal "Sent Mail" folder. In the latter case, what seems to work best for many is to copy ("cc" or "bcc") themselves when they delegate via e-mail, and then to put that copy into their "@WAITING FOR" folder.

> It takes much less energy to maintain e-mail backlog at zero than at a thousand.

Getting E-mail "In" to Empty The method detailed above will enable you to actually get everything out of your e-mail in-tray, which will be a huge boon to your clarity about, and control of, your day-to-day work. You'll reclaim "in" as "in," so anything residing there will be like a new message in your voice mail or an unread text on your mobile device—clues that you need to process something. Most people use their e-mail "in" for staging still-undecided actionable things, reference, and even trash, a practice that rapidly numbs the mind: they know they've got to reassess everything every time they glance at the screen.

Again, getting "in" empty doesn't mean you've handled everything. It means that you've *deleted* what you could, *filed* what you

---

*Some e-mail applications allow you to move or connect your e-mails into a Task list or area, which can work equally well. It will require, however, getting sufficiently familiar with that function within the software to make it easy and seamless.

wanted to keep but don't need to act on, *done* the less-than-two-minute responses, and moved into your reminder folders all the things you're waiting for and all your actionable e-mails. *Now* you can open the @ACTION file and review the e-mails that you've determined you need to spend time on. Isn't that process easier to relate to than fumbling through multiple screens, fearing all the while that you may miss something that'll blow up on you?

A Caution About Dispersing Reminders of Your Actions

There's an obvious danger in putting reminders of things you need to do somewhere out of sight. The function of an organization system is primarily to supply the reminders you need to see when you need to see them, so you can trust your choices about what you're doing (and what you're not doing). Before you leave your office for the day, or before you decide to spend a big part of your day doing something previously unplanned, those actionable e-mails that you still have pending must be reviewed individually, just like your Calls and At Computer lists. In essence, @ACTION is an extension of your At Computer list and should be handled in exactly the same fashion. Your paper-based Pending workflow must likewise be assessed like a list if the paper materials are being used as your only reminders.

> Paper-based data is sometimes easier to trust for utility than digital versions.

Distributing action triggers in a folder, on lists, and/or in an e-mail system is perfectly OK, *as long as you review all of the categories to which you've entrusted your triggers equally, as required.* You don't want things lurking in the recesses of your systems and not being used for their intended purpose: reminding you. The digital world can be dangerous in this regard, because as soon as data is offscreen, it can tend to disappear as a viable prompt. This has caused many computer-savvy people to revert to a paper planner—its physicality and visual obviousness can create much more trust that their reminders will actually remind them!

In order to hang out with friends or take a long, aimless walk and truly have nothing on your mind, you've got to know where all your actionable items are located, what they are, and that they will wait. And you need to be able to do that in a few seconds, not days.

Organizing Project Reminders

Creating and maintaining one list of all your projects (that is, again, every commitment or desired outcome that may require more than one action step to complete) can be a profound experience! You probably have more of them than you think. If you haven't done so already, I recommend that initially you make a Projects list in a very simple format, similar to the ones you've used for your lists of actions; it can be a category in a digital organizer, a page in a loose-leaf planner, or even a single file folder labeled "Projects," with either a master list or separate sheets of paper for each one.

The Projects List(s)

The Projects list is not meant to hold plans or details about your projects themselves, nor should you try to keep it arranged by priority or size or urgency—it's just a comprehensive index of your open loops. You actually won't be working off of the Projects list during your moment-to-moment activities; for the most part, your calendar, action lists, and any unexpected tasks that come up will constitute your tactical and immediate focus. Remember, you can't *do* a project; you can only do the action steps it requires.

Being aware of the horizon represented by your projects, however, is critical for extending your comfort with your control and focus into longer reaches of time.

> A complete and current Projects list is the major operational tool for moving from tree-hugging to forest management.

The real value of the Projects list lies in the complete review it can provide (at least once a week), ensuring that you have action steps defined for all of your projects and that nothing is slipping through the cracks. A quick glance at this list from time to time will enhance your underlying sense of control. You'll also know that you have an inventory available to you (and to others) whenever it seems advisable to evaluate workload(s).

The Value of a Complete Projects List

The very broad and simple definition of a project that I have given (more than one action needed to achieve a desired result) provides an important net to capture the more subtle things that pull or push on your consciousness. If you work in an industry that is formally project focused (manufacturing, software, consulting, etc.), it may be challenging to realize that "look into getting a dog for our kids" and "find a good tailor" are projects! But whether you call them "projects" or something else, they still demand a certain kind of attention to relieve their pressure on your internal space.

Getting the inventory of all of those things complete, current, and clear for yourself, and acquiring the habit of maintaining it that way, could be one of the most valuable things you do to enable stress-free productivity for yourself from now on. Here are some of the reasons why:

- Critical for control and focus
- Alleviates subtle tensions
- Core of the Weekly Review
- Facilitates relationship management

Critical for Control and Focus   It is impossible to be truly relaxed and in your productive state when things you've told yourself you need to handle continue to pull at your mind—whether they be little or big. It seems that "I've got to get my driver's license renewed" can take up as much space in your head as "I need to formulate the agenda for next year's conference" when an external list of such things is not complete and reviewed regularly.

Alleviates Subtle Tensions   The smaller or more subtle things we tell ourselves we need to deal with create some of the more challenging stresses to handle, simply because they are not so much "in your face." Projects often don't show up in nice, neat packages. They start as what seems a simple situation, communication, or activity, but they slowly morph into something bigger than you expected. You thought you handled getting your daughter into preschool, but now there's a problem with the registration forms or a change in the logistical details. You thought the invoice you sent was complete and accurate, but now the client says he didn't agree to something you billed him for. Getting these kinds of situations identified and into your system with desired

Projects seldom show up in nice, neat packages. Small things often slip unexpectedly into bigger things.

outcomes for appropriate engagement creates a wealth of fresh energy with unexpected positive results.

Core of the Weekly Review   As I have indicated in other places, the Weekly Review is the critical success factor for marrying your larger commitments to your day-to-day activities. And a complete Projects list remains the linchpin for that orientation. Ensuring weekly that you're OK about what you're doing (or not doing) with a dog for your kids, along with what you're doing (or not doing) about next year's conference, is an essential practice. But that Projects list must already be there, in at least a somewhat recent form, before you have the capability to think about things from that perspective.

Facilitates Relationship Management   Whether you are in conversation with your boss, your staff, your partner, or your family, having a sense of control and overview of all of your commitments that may have relevance in your relationships with them is extremely valuable. Invariably there are challenges with allocating limited resources—your time, your money, your attention. And when others are involved with you in ways that pull on those resources, being able to negotiate (and frequently *re*negotiate) those explicit and implicit agreements is the only way to effectively relieve those inherent pressures. Once executives and spouses and staff people get the picture of the commitments of their work and life, it triggers extremely important and constructive conversations with those involved. But it doesn't happen without that complete list.

Where to Look for Projects Still to Uncover

There are three primary areas in which you are likely to have "hidden" projects:

• Current activities
• Higher-horizon interests and commitments
• Current problems, issues, and opportunities

Current Activities   Often there are projects that need to be captured from a simple inventory of your calendar, your action lists, and your workspaces.

What meetings are on your schedule—past or upcoming—because of some outcome you're committed to achieving that the meeting itself does not complete or resolve? You may notice that a conference call you've been scheduled for is about a client request for a new custom program he or she might want. Voila! A project—"Look into possible custom program for Client XYZ." You may have an evening orientation event calendared for parents at your son's school that reminds you that you have an issue to resolve about his schedule of classes. Personal or business trips coming up, conferences on your calendar, etc.—all should be assessed for projects that deserve acknowledging.

There are also very likely still unrecognized projects connected to the next actions on your lists. Many times people we work with have "Call Mario re: the fund-raising event" on their Calls list, but have not yet identified "Finalize the fund-raiser" as something that should be on their Projects list.

And—though it should be obvious but at times isn't—there are proposals or contracts to review in your briefcase, forms to fill out for the bank on your desk at home, or a broken watch in your purse that are actually project artifacts. Double-check that you have them all associated with the further and final outcomes instead of remaining workflow orphans.

Higher-Horizon Interests and Commitments   There is a good chance that you might still have subtle attention on some of your commitments and interests from a longer and higher view of your responsibilities, goals, visions, and core values.

A review of the accountabilities you're invested in professionally—the things you need to be doing well in your roles at work—and the areas of your life you need to keep up to certain standards will likely trigger some reminders of things that may have been taking some of your attention, for which defining a project about them will be valuable.

If you have professional goals, company objectives, and strategic plans, have you identified all the projects that they should engender for you, so that you can move on them appropriately? I have seldom had an executive pull out and review any long-range planning document without her realizing there is at least one project she needs to clarify for herself in regard to it. Are there things coming toward you further out in the future of your personal life that have started to pull on your attention to do something about them—kids or parents growing older, your retirement, life partner's aspirations, fun and creative things you'd love to start exploring? This kind of reflection often produces at least some "look into" kinds of projects that, once identified, will produce a greater sense of being on top of your bigger world.

Current Problems, Issues, and Opportunities   A very rich place from which to gather items for your inventory is the broad area of often-amorphous things that can disturb your focus if not recognized and dealt with by shaping them into real projects with action steps. These fall into three categories:

• Problems
• Process improvements
• Creative and capacity-building opportunities

When is a problem a project? Always. When you assess something as a problem instead of as something to simply be accepted as the way things are, you are assuming there is a potential resolution. Whether there is or not might still need to be determined. But at the very least you have some research to do to find out. "Look into improving Frederick's relationship with his school," "Resolve situation with landlord and building maintenance," and "Get closure on compensation dispute with business partner" are the kinds of very real projects that you might resist defining as such. When you actually do put words to it, put it on your list and create a next action for it; you will surprise yourself with a new level of elegance in the stress-free productivity game.

Invariably there are also projects lurking amid your administrative, maintenance, and workflow processes—in both the professional and personal arenas. What do you find yourself complaining about regarding your systems or simply how things are getting done (or not)? Is there anything frustrating about your procedures for filing, storage, communication, hiring, tracking, or record keeping? Does anything need improving in terms of your personal or business expense reporting, banking or investing processes, or how you keep in touch with friends and family? These are also the kinds of projects that usually become projects slyly—it's tricky to notice when they cross the line between mildly irritating and a real bother (or inspiration) that deserves to get done.

Finally, there might very well be things you've been telling yourself you'd like to learn or experience to expand your own development or creative expression. Would you like to learn Italian cooking or how to draw? Have you been telling yourself it would be great to take an online course in digital photography or social media marketing? It's very possible that many of these kinds of "might like to" projects would live just fine on your Someday/Maybe list. But as you gain greater familiarity with the effectiveness of GTD, you will want to take advantage of the methodology to more readily incorporate new, interesting, and useful experiences into your life by defining desired outcomes about them on the Projects list.

One List, or Subdivided?

Most people find that one list is the best way to go because it serves as a master inventory rather than as a daily prioritizing guideline. The organizing system merely provides placeholders for all your open loops and options so your mind can more easily make the necessary intuitive, moment-to-moment strategic decisions.

Frankly, it doesn't matter how many different lists of projects you have, so long as you look at the contents of *all* of them as often as you need to. For the most part you'll do that in one fell swoop during your Weekly Review.

Some Common Ways to Subsort Projects

There are some situations in which it makes good sense (and eases some anxieties!) to subsort a Projects list. Let's look at some usual options.

Personal/Professional   Many people feel more comfortable seeing their lists divided up between personal and professional projects. If you're among them, be advised that your Personal list will need to be reviewed as judiciously as your Professional one, and not just saved for weekends. Many actions on personal things will need to be handled on weekdays, exactly like everything else. And often some of the greatest pressures on professionals stem from the personal aspects of their lives that they are letting slip.

Delegated Projects   If you're a senior manager or executive, you probably have several projects that you are directly responsible for but have handed off to people who report to you. While you could, of course, put them on your Waiting For list, it might make better sense to create a "Projects—Delegated" list to track them. Your task will be simply to review the list regularly enough to ensure that everything on it is moving along appropriately.

Specific Types of Projects   Some people have as part of their work and lifestyle several different projects of the same type, which in some instances it may be valuable to group together as a sub-list of Projects. For example, a corporate trainer or a keynote speaker might maintain a separate category of "Projects—Presentations," with a chronological listing of all the upcoming events of that nature. These would be "projects" like the rest, in that they need to be reviewed for actions until they are completed; but it might be helpful to see them all organized on one list, in the order they are coming up on the calendar, apart from the other projects.

> The right amount of complexity is whatever creates optimal simplicity.

If you are a real estate agent, sell consulting services, or develop proposals for a relatively small number of prospective clients in any profession, you will likely find it useful to see all of your outstanding "sales relationships in progress" in one view. This could be a separate list in a planner or digital application, but to be optimally functional it would need to be complete and each item regularly reviewed for current actions.

Some people like to sort their projects by major areas of focus—parents tracking those about their children, an entrepreneur dividing projects by the various roles he's fulfilling (Finance, Sales, Operations), and the like.

Again, how you decide to group your projects is not nearly as critical as ensuring that your inventory is complete, current, and assessed sufficiently to get it off your mind. No matter how you organize it now, you will very likely change your structure as you get more experience using your system and as the nature of your focus shifts in work and life.

What About Subprojects?

Some of your projects will likely have major subprojects, each of which could in theory be seen as a whole project. If you're moving into a new residence, for instance, and are upgrading or changing much of what's there, you may have a list of actionable items like "Finalize the patio," "Upgrade the kitchen," "Set up home office space," and so on, all of which could in themselves be considered separate projects. Do you make all of this one entry on your Projects list—say, "Finish new home upgrades"—or do you write up each of the subprojects as an individual line item?

Actually, it won't matter, as long as you review all the components of the project as frequently as you need to in order to stay productive. No external tool or organizing format is going to be perfect for sorting both horizontally across and vertically down through all your projects; you'll still have to be aware of the whole in some cohesive way (such as via your Weekly Review). If you make the large project your one listing on your Projects list, you'll want to keep a list of the subprojects and/or the project plan itself as "project support material" to be reviewed when you come to that major item. I would recommend doing it this way if big pieces of the project are dependent on other pieces getting done first. In that scenario you might have subprojects with no next actions attached to them because they are in a sense waiting for other things to happen before they can move forward. For instance, you might not be able to start on "Upgrade the kitchen" until you have finished "Assess and upgrade home electrical system." Or, you can only afford one of your major home projects at a time, so keeping them lined up in order of your priorities would make sense. However, you might be able to proceed on "Finalize the patio" independent of the other subprojects. You would therefore want a next action to be continually current on any portion of this larger project that you *could* make progress on independently.

Don't be too concerned about which way is best. If you're not sure, I'd vote for putting your big projects on the Projects list and holding the sub-pieces in your project support material, making sure to include them in your Weekly Review. That often makes it easier to see the larger field of what's going on in your life from a higher perspective, at a glance. But if that arrangement doesn't feel quite right, try including the active and independent subprojects as separate entries on your master list.

There's no perfect system for tracking all your projects and subprojects the same way. You just need to know you *have* projects and, if they have associated components, where to find the appropriate reminders for them.*

> How you list projects and subprojects is up to you; just be sure you know where to find all the moving parts and review them as frequently as needed to keep them off your mind.

Project Support Materials

Project support materials are not project actions, and they're not project reminders. They're resources to support your actions and thinking about your projects.

Don't Use Support Material for Reminding Typically, people use stacks of paper, stuffed file folders, and/or a plethora of e-mails and digital documents as reminders that (1) they've got a project, and (2) they've got to do something about it. They're essentially making support materials serve as action reminders. The problem is that next actions and Waiting For items on these projects have usually not been determined and are psychologically still embedded in the stacks and the files and e-mails—giving them the aura of just more stuff that repels its (un)organizer instead of attracting him or her to action. It delivers an incessant subliminal chant: "Do something about me! Decide something about me! Follow up with something about me!" When you're on the run, in the heat of the activities of the day, files like that are the last things you'll want to pick up and peruse for actions. You'll actually go numb to the files and the piles because they don't prompt you to do anything and they simply create more mental noise and emotional anxiety.

> What continues to talk to you psychologically in your environment, demanding that you do something about it?

---

*As I write this, I'm in the throes of moving from California to Europe. For many months, I maintained one project on my Projects list: "Move to Amsterdam." Last week, as things became more immediate and necessary to deal with on multiple fronts, I unpacked that one project into fifteen—all of which I need to keep my eyes on weekly now, ranging from "Set up Dutch bank accounts" to "Finalize artwork storage in Santa Barbara."

If you're in this kind of situation you must first add the project itself to your Projects list, as a reminder that there's an outcome to be achieved. Then the action steps and Waiting For items must be put onto their appropriate action reminder lists. Finally, when it's time to actually *do* an action, like making a call to someone about the project, you can pull out all the materials you think you might need to have as support during the conversation.

To reiterate, you *don't* want to use support materials as your primary reminders of what to do—that should be relegated to your action lists. If, however, the materials contain project plans and overviews in addition to ad hoc archival and reference information, you may want to keep them a little more visibly accessible than you do the pure reference materials in your filing cabinet or on your computer. These are fine to store support stuff, too, as long as you have the discipline to pull out the file drawer or open the computer to the proper directory and files and take a look at the plans every time you do your Weekly Review. If not, you're better off storing those kinds of project support files (perhaps with printouts from computer files) in a standing file holder or a separate Pending stack tray on your desk or other visually available surface.

To return to the previous example of moving into a new residence, you could have a folder labeled "Upgrades—37 Pinkerton Place" containing all the plans and details and notes about the patio and kitchen and office area. In your Weekly Review, when you came to "Upgrade new residence" on your Projects list, you'd pull out the file for that project and thumb through all your notes to ensure that you weren't missing any possible next actions. Those actions would then get done, delegated, or deferred to your action lists, and the folder would be refiled until you needed it again for doing the actions or for your next Weekly Review.

Many people who interact with current and prospective clients have attempted to use client folders and/or client-relationship-management (CRM) software to "manage the account." The problem here is that some material is just facts or historical data that needs to be stored as background for when you might be able to use it, and some of what must be tracked are the actions required to move the relationships forward. The latter can be more effectively organized within your action-lists system. Client information is just that, and it can be folded into a general-reference file on the client or stored within a clients-focused library. But if I need to call a client, I don't want that reminder embedded anywhere but on a Calls list.*

Organizing Ad Hoc Project Thinking

In chapter 3, I suggested that you will often have ideas that you'll want to keep about projects but that are not necessarily next actions. Those ideas fall into the broad category of "project support materials," and may be anything from a notion about something you might want to do on your next vacation to a clarification of some major components in a project plan. These thoughts could come as you're driving down the freeway listening to a news story on the radio, or reading a relevant article. What do you do with that kind of material?

My recommendation here is that you consider where you're keeping tabs on the project or topic itself, how you might add information to it in that format, and where you might store any more extensive data associated with it. Most professionals will have several options for how to handle support materials, including attaching notes to a list item, organizing digital information in e-mail and/or databases, and maintaining paper-based files and notes in notebooks.

> There is no need ever to lose an idea about a project, theme, or topic.

Attached Notes Most organizing software allows you to attach a digital note to a list or calendar entry. If you're keeping a Projects list within the software, you can go to the project you had a thought about, open or attach a note to it, and type in your idea. This is an excellent way to capture "back of the envelope" project thinking. If your Projects list is paper based, you can attach a Post-it note next to

---

*Software technology will continue to advance the automation of workflow, with CRMs and other applications programmed to trigger action reminders, etc. In theory this would reduce the need for individual tracking of such items. In practice, each person still must engage with the work he or she is accountable for, generated by the software, and managing that within his or her holistic system. Additionally, the variables in our engagements and their activities are often so subtle and fast changing, even the most sophisticated technology will fall short of being totally trusted for such detailed direction in the foreseeable future.

the item on your master list or, if you're a low-tech type, on the item's separate sheet. In any case, you'll need to remember to look at the attachment when you review your project to make use of the data.

E-mail and Software Applications The digital world offers an infinite variety of ways to deal with project thoughts. E-mails that might contain good information related to your projects can be held in a dedicated e-mail reference folder, labeled accordingly. If you have a large volume of e-mails related to one project, consider creating two folders: "Johnson Partnership—Active" and "Johnson Partnership—Archive," or some such. You may also find it worthwhile, if you don't have one already, to set up a more rigorous kind of digital database for organizing your thinking on a project or topic. An enormous flowering of such tools has happened in this century—from simple and elegant cloud-based note-taking and notebook-organizing software that permits infinite customization for how it's used, to group-sharing file and project management systems, to personal project-organizing applications for everything from free-form mind mapping to organizing large writing and research endeavors.

The bad news about the good news of the huge assortment of options for digital project support is the ease with which we are seduced into spreading potentially meaningful information into such a multiplicity of locations and mechanisms that it can take us almost back to square one: we don't know where it all is, can't see it all integrated for appropriate overviewing from the right perspective at the right time, aren't sure exactly how to put what data where . . . so we wind up trying to keep it all coordinated back in our heads! I continually find interesting new ways to track relevant information for various things I'm doing, but I retain sanity only when I keep a clearly delineated and accessible Projects list and ensure that I'm scanning across any related parts of my system regularly for pertinent details.

> The inherent danger in the digital world is how much data can be spread into how many different places so easily, without coordinating links.

Paper-Based Files Having a separate file folder devoted to each project makes a lot of sense when you're accumulating paper-based materials; it may be low-tech, but it's an elegant solution nonetheless. Simplicity and ease of handling make for a good general-reference filing system—one that lets you feel comfortable about creating a folder for scraps of paper from a meeting. At times it's easier to overview and access project-related information for planning sessions and conversations using a physical folder than trying to use the digital pieces themselves in the moment. I will often print all potentially useful items pertaining to the project—spreadsheets, schedules, e-mails, Web pages, etc.—to have in hand as reference for those kinds of interactions.

Pages in Notebooks   A great advantage of paper-based loose-leaf notebooks is that you can dedicate a whole page or group of pages to an individual project. For years I maintained a midsize notebook with a Projects list in front and a Project Support section toward the back, where I always had some blank pages to capture any random thinking or plans and details about projects on my list. Though paper-based personal system components are increasingly giving way to their digital counterparts, the notebook model is a valuable one, supporting a more integrated and multilevel platform for well-oriented thinking.

Each of the methods previously described can be effective in organizing project thoughts. The key is that you must consistently look for any action steps inherent in your project notes, and review the notes themselves as often as you think it is necessary, given the nature of the project.

You'll also want to clear out many of your notes once they become inactive, unreal, or redundant, to keep the whole system from catching the "stale" virus. I've found a lot of value in capturing these types of thoughts, more for the way it consistently helps my thinking process than because I end up using every idea (most I don't!). But I try to make sure not to let my old thoughts stay around too long, pretending they're useful when they're not.

Organizing Nonactionable Data

Interestingly, one of the biggest problems with most people's personal management systems is that they blend a few actionable things with a large amount of data and material that has value but no action attached. Having good, consistent structures with which to manage the nonactionable items in our work and lives is as important as managing our action and project reminders. When the nonactionable items aren't properly managed, they clog up the whole process.

Nonactionable items fall into three large categories: reference materials, reminders of things that need no action now but might at a later date, and things that you don't need at all (trash).

Reference Materials

Much of what comes across your desk and into your life in general is reference material. There's no action required, but it's information that you want to keep, for a variety of reasons. Your major decisions will be how much to keep, how much room to dedicate to it, what form it should be stored in, and where. Much of that will be a personal or organizational judgment call based upon legal or logistical concerns or personal preferences. The only time you should have attention on your reference material is when you need to change your system in some way because you have too much or too little information, given your needs or preferences.

The problem most people have psychologically with all their stuff is that it's still *stuff*—that is, they haven't decided what's actionable and what's not. Once you've made a clean distinction about which is which, what's left as reference should have no pull or incompletion associated with it—it's just your library. Your only decision then is how big a library you want. When you've fully implemented this action-management methodology, you can be as big a pack rat as your space (physical and digital) will allow. As I've increased the size of the hard disk on my computer and added an almost infinite backup capability on attached drives and in the cloud, I've kept that much more e-mail in my archives and that many more digital photographs. The more the merrier, as far as I'm concerned, since increasing the volume of pure reference material adds no psychological weight.

The Variety of Reference Systems

Reference material now shows up in many forms (topics and media), with numerous ways to organize it. What follows is a brief discussion of some of the most common.

- General-reference filing—paper, e-mail, and simple digital storage
- Large-category filing
- Contact managers
- Libraries and archives

> Your reference and filing system should be a simple library of data, easily retrievable—not your reminder for actions, projects, priorities, or prospects.

General-Reference Filing   As I've emphasized in previous chapters, a good filing system is critical for processing and organizing your stuff. It's also a must for dealing with the paper-based material and ad hoc digital information that are valuable to you for one reason or another, and you'll need a way to store both. Ideally you already set up a general-reference filing system as you were processing "in." You need to feel comfortable storing even a single piece of paper that you might want to refer to later, or an article you read online, and your general-reference system must be informal and accessible enough that it's a snap to file something away, right at hand where you do your work and personal administration and review. If you're not set up that way yet, look back at chapter 4 for help on this topic.

Most people wind up needing from one to four physical file drawers, many dozens of e-mail reference folders, and other digital storage locations and categories that can range from a few to hundreds.* The Web itself is nothing more than a huge digital filing cabinet, which both relieves the need to create your own digital reference library and produces a huge amount of the type of information that you will likely want to collect and organize within your own system. The ever-increasing plethora of information and ways to access and organize it only forces the necessity to distinguish nonactionable from actionable inputs, and to create and maintain an easily usable system of reference data storage.

Large-Category Filing   Any topic that requires more than fifty folders and/or major documents should probably be given its own section, drawer, or digital database, with its own alpha-sorted or other easily searchable system. For instance, if you're managing a

---

*As a bit of a foodie, I have kept track of any restaurant around the world I might want to patronize (from experience or referrals). It's in a software application that allows me to look under, for example, "Locales—London—Restaurants" and see my list. Just that one topic, restaurants I might want to visit, populates hundreds of folders and subfolders on my computer.

corporate merger and need to keep hold of a lot of the paperwork, you may want to dedicate two or three whole file cabinets to hold all the documentation required in the due-diligence process. If gardening or sailing or cooking is your passion, you may need at least a whole file drawer for each of those designated hobbies.

Bear in mind that if your area of focus has support material that could blend into other areas of focus, you may run into the dilemma of whether to store the information in general reference or in the specialized reference files. When you read a great article about wood fencing and want to keep it, does that go in your Garden cabinet or in the general system with other information about home-related projects? As a rule, it's best to stick with one general-reference system except for a very limited number of discrete topics.

Contact Managers   Much of the information that you need to keep is directly related to people in your network. You need to track contact information of all sorts—mobile, home, and office phone numbers, e-mail addresses, and so on. In addition, if you find it useful, you may want to maintain information about their birthdays, names of family members, hobbies, interests, etc. In a more rigorous professional vein, you may need or want to track hire dates, performance-review dates, goals and objectives, and other potentially relevant data for staff development and legal purposes.

The "contacts" section of most of the digital and paper organizers (along with the calendar) has probably been the most commonly used component. Everyone needs to keep track of phone numbers and e-mail addresses. It's instructive to note that this is purely and simply reference material. No action is required—this is just information that you might need to access in the future. As digital as the world seems to have become, many people still have stacks of collected business cards that are subtly yelling at them, "Decide something about me! Do something with me!"

But once you have filtered actionable items out of those inputs, there's no big mystery about how to organize contact information, aside from the logistics for your individual needs. Again, the only problem comes up when people try to make their contact manager serve as a tool for reminding them about things they need to do. That doesn't work (unless it's part of a well-functioning CRM system that includes both customer information and action triggers appropriately assigned and incorporated). As long as all the actions relative to people you know have been identified and tracked in your action reminder lists, there's no role for a contact manager to fill other than being a data store.

The only issue (or opportunity) then becomes how much information you need to keep and where and in what equipment you need to keep it in order to have it accessible when you want it. Nothing's perfect in that regard, but as the mobile digital Internet-connected tools increase in power, along with their connection to various data stores, both the ease of access and the confusion of options will increase in this regard.

Libraries and Archives: Personalized Levels   Information that might be useful lives at many levels. You could probably find out pretty much anything if you were willing to dig deep enough. The question of how much to keep, how close, and in what form will be a changing reality, given the variables of your needs, your particular comfort levels with data, and the technology that turbocharges your relationship to global information. Relative to your personal organization and productivity, this is not a core issue, so long as all of your projects and actions are in a control system that you work with regularly. Reference material in all its forms then becomes nothing more or less than material to capture and create access to according to your particular proclivities, requirements, and capabilities.

> If material is purely for reference, the only issue is whether it's worth the time and space to keep it.

Some degree of consistency will always make things easier. What kinds of things do you need with you all the time? Those must go into your ubiquitously available mobile device or notebook. What do you need for meetings or off-site events? That should be put into your briefcase, pack, satchel, or purse. What might you need when you're working in your office? That should be put into your personal filing system or your networked computer. What about rare situations relative to your job? Material needed for those could be archived in departmental files, off-site storage, or deep in the digital cloud. What could you find on the Web anytime you might need it? You don't need to do anything with that information, unless you require it when you're away from a good Internet connection, in which case you should print the data out when you're online and store it in a file you can take with you.

Do you see how that personal organization of reference material is simply a logistical and purpose-based one? Distinguishing actionable from nonactionable things is the first key success factor in this arena. Second is determining what your potential use of the information is, and therefore where and how it should be stored. Once these are addressed, you have total freedom to manage and organize as much or as little reference material as you want. There is no "perfect" reference system. Its structures and content demand a highly individual decision that ought to be based on the ratio of the value received to the time and effort required for capturing and maintaining it. You are better off starting with real information you want to keep, deciding the best place to put it so it's retrievable, and crafting that from the ground up than trying to choose or design a system theoretically. You will definitely hone your reference libraries into a larger, more sensible framework as time goes on, but that will best be built from upgrading how you're managing your day-to-day realities. Tolerate some ambiguity here, in terms of figuring out the best way to do it all. The key will be some regular overviewing and reassessment of your system, and dynamically course-correcting as needed.

Someday/Maybes

The second thing to deal with in organizing nonactionable items is how to track things that you want to reassess in the future. These could range from a special trip you might want to take one day, to books you might want to read, to projects you might want to tackle in the next fiscal year, to skills and talents you might want to develop. For a full implementation of this model you'll need some sort of "back burner" or "on hold" component.

Someday/Maybes are not throwaway items. They may be some of the most interesting and creative things you'll ever get involved with.

There are several ways to stage things for later review, all of which will work to get them off your current radar and your mind. You can put the items on various versions of Someday/Maybe lists or trigger them on your calendar or in a digital or paper-based tickler system.

Someday/Maybe List

It's highly likely that if you did a complete mind sweep when you were collecting things from your mental space, you came up with some things you're not sure you want to commit to. "Learn Spanish," "Get Marcie a horse," "Climb Mt. Washington," "Write a mystery novel," and "Get a vacation cottage" are typical projects that fall into this category.

If you haven't already done it, I recommend that you create a Someday/Maybe list in whatever organizing system you've chosen. Then give yourself permission to populate that list with all the items of that type that have occurred to you so far. You'll probably discover that simply having the list and starting to fill it out will cause you to come up with all kinds of creative ideas.

You may also be surprised to find that some of the things you write on the list will actually come to pass, almost without your making any conscious effort to make them happen. If you acknowledge the power of the imagination to foster changes in perception and performance, it's easy to see how having a Someday/Maybe list out in front of your conscious mind could potentially add many wonderful adventures to your life and work. We're likely to seize opportunities when they arise if we've already identified and captured them as a possibility. That has certainly been my own experience: learning to play the flute and how to sail in the open ocean started in this category for me. In addition to your in-tray, there are two rich sources to tap for your Someday/Maybe list: your creative imagination and your list of current projects.

> Activating and maintaining your Someday/Maybe category unleashes the flow of your creative thinking—you have permission to imagine cool things to do without having to commit to doing anything about them yet.

Make an Inventory of Your Creative Imaginings What are the things you really might want to do someday if you have the time, money, and inclination? Write them on your Someday/Maybe list. Typical categories include:

- Things to get or build for your home
- Hobbies to take up
- Skills to learn
- Creative expressions to explore
- Clothes and accessories to buy
- Toys (hi-tech and otherwise!) to acquire
- Trips to take
- Organizations to join
- Service projects to contribute to
- Things to see and do

Reassess Your Current Projects Now's a good time to review your Projects list from a more elevated perspective (that is, the standpoint of your job, goals, and personal commitments) and consider whether you might transfer some of your current commitments to Someday/Maybe. If on reflection you realize that an optional project doesn't have a chance of getting your attention for the next few months or more, move it to this list.

People have at times found it useful even to subcategorize their Someday/Maybe projects. There might be a significant difference for you to think about projects you really want to do around your home as soon as you have the resources versus your "bucket list" kind of fantasies, such as climbing a mountain in Nepal or creating a foundation for disadvantaged kids. In a company this might be a distinction between "parking lot" ideas ("Let's save that to discuss at our next quarterly meeting") and keeping track of the projects you might energize when and if significant capital shows up. The key here is to pay attention, as you experiment with these options, to whether your lists and subcategories are unnerving or energizing you.

Special Categories of Someday/Maybe

More than likely you have some special interests that involve lots of possible things to do. It can be fun to collect these on lists. For instance:

- Food—recipes, menus, restaurants, wines
- Children—things to do with them

- Books to read
- Music to download
- Movies to see
- Gift ideas
- Web sites to explore
- Weekend trips to take
- Ideas—Misc. (meaning you don't know where else to put them!)

These kinds of lists can be a cross between reference and Someday/Maybe—reference because you can just collect and add to lists of good wines or restaurants or books, to consult as you like; Someday/Maybe because you might want to review the listed items on a regular basis to remind yourself to try one or more of them at some point.

In any case, this is another great reason to have an organizing system that makes it easy to capture things that may add value and variety and interest to your life—without clogging your mind and work space with undecided, unfinished business.

The Danger of "Hold and Review" Files and Piles

Many people have created some sort of "Hold and Review" pile or file (or whole drawer or e-mail folder) that vaguely fits within the category of Someday/Maybe. They tell themselves, "When I have time, I may like to get to this," and a "Hold and Review" file seems a convenient place to put it. I personally don't recommend this particular kind of subsystem, because in virtually every case I have come across, the person held but didn't review, and there was numbness and resistance about the stack and contents. The value of someday/maybe disappears if you don't put your conscious awareness back onto it with some consistency.

> *What lies in our power to do, lies in our power not to do.*
>
> —*Aristotle*

Also, there's a big difference between something that's managed well, as a Someday/Maybe list, and something that's just a catchall bucket for stuff. Usually much of that stuff needs to be tossed, some of it needs to go into Read/Review, some needs to be filed as reference, some belongs on the calendar or in a tickler file (see page 182) for review in a month or perhaps at the beginning of the next quarter, and some items actually have next actions on them. Many times, after appropriately processing someone's "Hold and Review" drawer or file, I've discovered there was nothing left in it!

Using the Calendar for Future Options

Your calendar can be a very handy place to park reminders of things you *might* want to consider doing in the future. Most of the people I've coached were not nearly as comfortable with their calendars as they could have been; otherwise they probably would have found many more things to put in there.

One of the three uses of a calendar is for *day-specific information*. This category can include a number of things, but one of the most creative ways to utilize the calendar function is to enter things that you want to take off your mind and reassess at some later date. Here are a few of the myriad things you should consider inserting:

- Triggers for activating projects
- Events you might want to participate in
- Decision catalysts

Triggers for Activating Projects   If you have a project that you don't really need to think about now but that deserves a flag at some point in the future, you can pick an appropriate date and put a reminder about the project in your calendar for that day. It should go in some day-specific (versus time-specific) calendar slot for the things you want to be reminded of on that day; then when the day arrives, you see the reminder and insert the item as an active project on your Projects list. Typical candidates for this treatment are:

- Special events with a certain lead time for handling (product launches, fund-raisers, etc.)
- Regular events that you need to prepare for, such as budget reviews, annual conferences, planning events, or meetings (e.g., when should you add next year's "Annual sales conference" or "Get kids set up for next school year" to your Projects list?)
- Key dates for significant people that you might want to do something about (birthdays, anniversaries, holiday gift giving, etc.)

Events You Might Want to Participate In   You probably get notices constantly about seminars, conferences, speeches, and social and cultural events that you may want to decide about attending as the time gets closer. So figure out when that closer time is and put a trigger in your calendar on the appropriate date—for example:

> "Chamber of Commerce breakfast tomorrow?"
> "Lions football tickets go on sale today"
> "BBC special on climate change at 8:00 p.m."
> "Garden Club tea next Saturday"

If you can think of any jogs like these that you'd like to put into your system, do it now.

Decision Catalysts   Once in a while there may be a significant decision that you need to make but can't (or don't want to) right away. That's fine, in terms of your own self-management process, as long as you've concluded that the additional information you need has to come from an *internal* rather than an *external* source (e.g., you need to sleep on it), or there is a good reason to delay your decision until a last responsible moment (allowing all factors to be as current as possible before you choose how to move on it). But in order to move to a level of OK-ness about *not* deciding, you'd better put out a safety net that you can trust to get you to focus on the issue appropriately in the future. A calendar reminder can serve that purpose.*

> It's OK to decide not to decide—as long as you have a decide-not-to-decide system.

Some typical decision areas in this category include:

• Hire/fire
• Merge/acquire/sell/divest
• Change job/career
• Potential strategy redirection

---

*If you are using a group-accessible calendar, you obviously must maintain discretion about those kinds of triggers. Digital calendars usually have "private" categorization functions you can use for entries you don't necessarily want everyone to see.

This is a big topic to devote so little space to, I know, but go ahead and ask yourself, "Is there any major decision for which I should create a future trigger, so I can feel comfortable just 'hanging out' with it for now?" If there is, put some reminder in your calendar to revisit the issue.

The "Tickler" File

One elegant way to manage nonactionable items that may need an action in the future is the tickler file.* A three-dimensional version of a calendar, the original version of this allows you to hold *physical* reminders of things that you want to see or remember—not now, but in the future. It can be an extremely functional tool, allowing you to in effect set up your own postal service and "mail" things to yourself for receipt on a designated future date. I have used a tickler file for years. Even though technology has made reminders of this sort more easily digitized in software and mobile access devices, it's possible that numerous things for you are more easily managed in this low-tech manner. The promise of digital management of such things is marching forward incessantly, but there remain many things in my personal system that are more efficiently managed by physical particles as reminders.

Essentially the tickler file is a simple file-folder system that allows you to distribute paper and other physical reminders in such a way that whatever you want to see on a particular date in the future "automatically" shows up that day in your in-tray.

If you have a secretary or assistant, you can entrust at least a part of this task to him or her, assuming that he or she has some working version of this or a similar system. Typical examples would be:

- "Hand me this agenda the morning of the day I have the meeting."
- "Give this back to me on Monday to rethink, since it applies to our board meeting on Wednesday."
- "Remind me about the Hong Kong trip two weeks ahead, and we'll plan the logistics."

---

*Also referred to as a "suspense," "bring forward," "perpetual," or "follow-up" file.

Then every day of the week, that day's folder is pulled and reviewed.

Even if you are in a high-level professional role, while you can (and probably should) utilize staff to handle as much of this as is appropriate, I recommend that, if you can integrate it into your lifestyle, you maintain your own tickler file functionality. There are many useful things you can do, at least some of which you may want to avail yourself of outside the pale of your assistant's responsibilities. I use my tickler file to manage travel documents I need at hand on a certain day, reminders of birthdays and special events upcoming (that would take up too much visual room on my digital calendar), printouts of interesting things to explore when I might have more time in a couple of months, etc.

Bottom line: the tickler file demands only a one-second-per-day new behavior to make it work, and it has a payoff value exponentially greater than the personal investment. It represents a unique executive function: deciding not to decide until a certain point.

Setting Up a Tickler File   If you are doing this in a physical system, you need forty-three folders—thirty-one labeled "1" through "31," and twelve more labeled with the names of the months of the year. The daily files are kept in front, beginning with the file for tomorrow's date (if today is October 5, then the first file would be "6"). The succeeding daily files represent the days of the rest of the month ("6" through "31"). Behind the "31" file is the monthly file for the next month ("November"), and behind that are the daily files "1" through "5." Following that are the rest of the monthly files ("December" through "October"). The next daily file is emptied into your in-tray every day, and then the folder is refiled at the back of the dailies (at which point, instead of October 6, it represents *November* 6). In the same way, when the next monthly file reaches the front (on October 31 after you empty the daily file, the "November" file will be the next one, with the daily files "1" through "31" behind it), it's emptied into the in-tray and refiled at the back of the monthlies to represent November a year from now. This is a perpetual file, meaning that at any given time it contains files for the next thirty-one days and the next twelve months.

The big advantage of using file folders for your tickler system is that they allow you to store actual documents (the form that needs to be filled out on a certain day, the meeting agenda that needs to

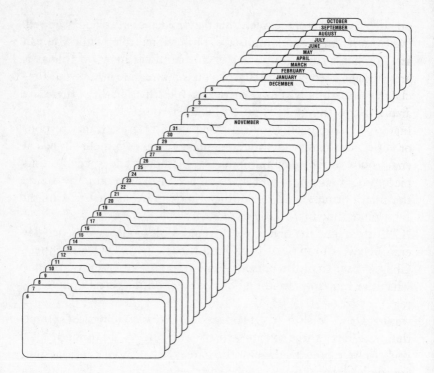

FILE-FOLDER-STYLE SETUP (OCTOBER 5)

be reviewed then, the invoice that you're holding payment on until that day, etc.).

In order for the system to work, you must check and update it every day. If you forget to empty the daily file, you won't trust the system to handle important data, and you'll have to manage those things some other way. If you leave town (or don't access the file on the weekend), you must be sure to check the folders for the days you'll be away, *before* you go.

Checklists: Creative and Constructive Reminders

The last topic in personal system organization that deserves some attention is the care and feeding of checklists, those "recipes of potential ingredients" for projects, work processes and procedures, events, and areas of value, interest, and responsibility. In essence, any of the lists or categories of reminders we've already discussed are checklists, in that they serve the function of providing things to check or review to ensure that you're not missing something in that area. The more common idea of checklists, however, refers to a listing of the contents of a topic, procedure, or some arena of interest or activity, to be utilized either at a specific time or whenever you engage in a particular kind of activity. These can range from big-picture outlines of areas of focus in your job or your life down to the detailed instructions of how to load pictures onto a Web site.

Many years ago Alfred North Whitehead cogently observed, "Civilization advances by extending the number of important operations which we can perform without thinking about them." Checklists provide the micro version of that macro observation: whenever you have to think about anything, either because of some regularity of a refreshed view ("At the end of every calendar year, I want/need to . . .") or a specific situation that requires more detail than you can easily recall ("Before I deliver a seminar, I need to . . ."), you should entrust those jobs to your "external mind"—your management system that holds the details you need to engage with at appropriate times.*

There are an infinite number of possible checklists that allow you to have more relaxed control in various situations across your life and work. If you ever refer to a recipe in a cookbook in order to prepare a specific dish, you're using a checklist to boost your focus and productivity. If your board has tasked you with three key initiatives or outcomes for the year, reviewing those prior to your board meeting would be utilizing a checklist.

Because I am describing the process of clarifying and organizing what may be on your mind, to begin to implement this system I'll focus on a common set of topics that emerge for people, for which checklists are often the best solution.

---

*A powerful exposition of this function and its value (and the costs of not paying attention to it!) was laid out in Atul Gawande's book *The Checklist Manifesto: How to Get Things Right* (Metropolitan Books, 2009).

Things You Want to Pay Attention To

Often, when we are working with people to clear up what is on their minds, what shows up are things like this:

- Exercise more regularly
- Spend more quality time with my kids
- Do more proactive planning for my division
- Maintain good morale on my team
- Ensure we're in alignment with corporate strategy
- Keep the client billing process up-to-date
- Focus more on my spiritual practices
- Pay more attention to the individual goals of my staff members
- Keep myself motivated in my job
- Keep current conversations and updates going with key people in my company

What should you do with these "fuzzier" kinds of internal commitments and areas of attention?

First, Identify Inherent Projects and Action

For much of this kind of stuff, there is still a project and/or an action that needs to be defined. "Exercise more regularly" *really* translates for many people into "Set up regular exercise program" (project) and "Call Sally for suggestion about gyms and personal trainers" (real action step). In such cases, inherent projects and actions still need to be clarified and organized into a personal system. Or "Maintain good morale on my team" should become a project ("Explore team-building processes for my department") with a specific action step ("E-mail our HR director to get her input on this opportunity").

But there *are* some things that don't quite fit into that category, and often, appropriate checklists are needed to address them.

Blueprinting Key Areas of Work and Accountability

Objectives like "Maintain good physical conditioning" or "Keep my team motivated" may still need to be built into some sort of overview checklist that will be reviewed regularly. You have multiple layers of outcomes and standards playing on your psyche and your choices at any point in time, and knowing what those are, at all the different levels, is always a good idea (and yet not so easy to habitually maintain and adhere to).

I suggested earlier that there are at least six levels of your "work" that could be defined and that each level deserves its own acknowledgment and evaluation. A complete inventory of everything you hold important and are committed to on each of these levels would represent an awesome checklist. It might include:

- Career goals
- Service
- Family
- Relationships
- Community
- Health and energy
- Financial resources
- Creative expression

And then moving down a level, within your job, you might want some reminders of your key areas of responsibility, your staff, your values, and so on. A list of these might contain points like:

- Team morale
- Processes
- Timelines
- Staff issues
- Workload
- Communications
- Technology

All of these items could in turn be included on the lists in your personal system, as reminders to you, as needed, to keep the ship on course, on an even keel. Many times the value is simply to affirm that the specific area is OK as is; nothing needs to be added or changed. But *knowing* that adds to your relaxed focus.

The More Novel the Situation, the More Control Required

The degree to which any of us needs to maintain checklists and external controls is directly related to our unfamiliarity with the area of responsibility. If you've been doing what you're doing for a long time, and there's no pressure on you to change in that area, you probably need minimal external personal organization to stay on cruise control. You know when things must happen and how to make them happen, and your system is fine, status quo. You could manage those in your sleep. Often, though, that's not the case.

Did you ever have to go through some prescribed procedure to manage a discrete kind of financial transaction, log in and refresh a software application, or even go through several necessary steps to check in to a friend's vacation cabin, and you had the experience of asking yourself, "Wait a minute, what do I need to do, now?" In any of those situations you may want or need to repeat, you need a checklist. I am dangerously semiliterate in terms of computers and software, and whenever I get instruction from our IT experts about how to fix some recurring glitch, it is easy to convince myself I will remember what they told me. I have learned (too many times the hard way) to create checklists for them.

Many times you'll want some sort of checklist to help you maintain a focus until you're more familiar with what you're doing. If your CEO suddenly disappeared, for example, and you instantly had to fill her shoes, you'd need some overview and outlines in front of you for a while to ensure that you had all the mission-critical aspects of the job handled. And if you've just been hired into a new position, with new responsibilities that are relatively unfamiliar to you, you'll want a framework of control and structure, if only for the first few months. As we have instituted a novel organizational structure and operating system in our company, we have been using many critical checklists to support our meeting practices for its implementation, until they become automatic.

Checklists can be highly useful to let you know what you *don't* need to be concerned about.

There have been times when I needed to make a list of areas that I had to handle temporarily, until things were under control. For instance, when my wife and I decided to create a brand-new structure for a business we'd been involved with for many years, I took on areas of responsibility I'd never had to deal with before—namely, accounting, computers, marketing, legal, and administration. For several months I needed to keep a checklist of those responsibilities in front of me to ensure that I filled in the blanks everywhere and managed the transition as well as I could. After the business got onto "cruise control" to some degree, I no longer needed that list.

Checklists at All Levels

Be open to creating any kind of checklist as the urge strikes you. The possibilities are endless—from "Core Life Values" to "Things to Take Camping" to "Potential Holiday Gifts." Making lists, ad hoc, as they occur to you, is one of the most powerful yet subtlest and simplest procedures that you can install in your life.

To spark your creative thinking, here's a list of some of the topics of checklists I've seen and used over the years:

- Job Areas of Responsibility (key responsibility areas)
- Exercise Regimens (muscle resistance training programs)
- Travel Checklist (everything to take on or do before a trip)
- Weekly Review (everything to review and/or update on a weekly basis)
- Training Program Components (all the things to handle when putting on an event, front to back)
- Key Clients
- People to Stay in Touch With (all the people you might want to connect with in your network)
- Year-end Activities (all the actions for closing up for the time period)
- Personal Development (things to evaluate regularly to ensure personal balance and progress)
- Jokes

Capability and willingness to instantly make a checklist, accessible and used when needed, is a core component of high-performance self-management.

Get comfortable with checklists, both ad hoc and more permanent. Be ready to create and eliminate them as required. Make sure you have an easily accessed place to put a new list that's also attractive and even fun to engage with—in a loose-leaf notebook or in a software application that is readily available. Appropriately used, checklists can be a tremendous asset in enhancing personal productivity and relieving mental pressure.

If in fact you have now *captured* everything that represents an open loop in your life and work, *clarified* and processed each one of those items in terms of what it means to you and what actions are required, and *organized* the results into an intact system that holds a current and complete overview—large and small—of all your present and "someday" projects, then you're ready for the next step of implementation in the art of stress-free productivity: the reflection process.

8

Reflecting: Keeping It All Fresh and Functional

THE PURPOSE OF this whole method of workflow management is not to let your brain become lax, but rather to enable it to be free to experience more elegant, productive, and creative activity. In order to earn that freedom, however, your brain must engage on some consistent basis with all your commitments and activities. You must be assured that you're doing what you need to be doing, and that it's OK to be *not* doing what you're not doing. That facilitates the condition of *being present*, which is always the optimal state from which to operate. Reviewing your system on a regular basis, reflecting on the contents, and keeping it current and functional are prerequisites for that kind of clarity and stability.

If you have a list of calls you must make, for example, the minute that list is not totally current with *all* the calls you need to make, your brain will not trust the system, and it won't get relief from its lower-level mental tasks. It will have to take back the job of remembering, processing, and reminding, which, as you should know by now, it doesn't do very effectively.

All of this means your system cannot be static. In order to support appropriate action choices, it must be kept up-to-date. And it should trigger consistent and appropriate evaluation of your life and work at several horizons.

There are two major issues that need to be handled at this point:

- What do you look at in all this, and when?
- What do you need to do, and how often, to ensure that all of it works as a consistent system, freeing you to think and manage at a higher level?

A real review process will lead to enhanced and proactive new thinking in key areas of your life and work. Such thinking emerges from both focused concentration and serendipitous brainstorming, which will be triggered and galvanized by a consistent personal review of your inventory of actions and projects.

What to Look At, When

Your personal system and behaviors need to be established in such a way that you can see all the action options you need to see, *when* you need to see them. This is really just common sense, but few people actually have their processes and their organization honed to the point where they are as functional as they could be.

When you have access to a phone and any discretionary time, you ought to at least glance at the list of all the phone calls you need to make, and then either direct yourself to the best one to handle or give yourself permission to feel OK about not bothering with any of them. When you're about to go in for a discussion with your boss or your partner, take a moment to review the outstanding agendas you have with him or her, so you'll know that you're using your time most effectively. When you need to pick up something at the dry cleaner, first quickly review all the other errands that you might be able to do en route.

> A few seconds a day is usually all you need for review, as long as you're looking at a sufficient amount of the right things at the right time.

People often ask me, "How much time do you spend looking at your system?" My answer is simply, "As much time as I need to feel comfortable about what I'm doing." In actuality it's an accumulation of two seconds here, three seconds there. What most people don't realize is that my lists are in one sense my office. Just as you might have Post-its and stacks of documents that represent work to do at your workstation, so do I on my Next Actions lists and calendar. Assuming that you've completely collected, processed, and organized your stuff, you'll most likely take only a few brief moments here and there to access your system for day-to-day reminders.

Look at Your Calendar First . . .

Your most frequent review will probably be of your daily calendar, and your daily tickler folder if you're maintaining one, to see the "hard landscape" and assess what has to get done. You need to know the time and space parameters first. Knowing that you have nonstop meetings from eight a.m. to six p.m., for example, with barely a half-hour break for lunch, will help you make necessary decisions about any other activities.

. . . Then Your Action Lists

After you review all your day- and time-specific commitments and handle whatever you need to about them, your next most frequent area for review will be the lists of all the actions you could possibly do in your current context. If you're in your office, for instance, you'll look at your lists of calls, computer actions, and in-office things to do. This doesn't necessarily mean you will be *doing* anything on those lists; you'll just evaluate them against the flow of other work coming at you to ensure that you make the best choices about what to deal with. You need to feel confident that you're not missing anything critical.

> *The maintenance of life and the pursuit of happiness are not two separate issues.*
> —*Ayn Rand*

Frankly, if your calendar is trustworthy and your action lists are current, they may be the only things in the system you'll need to refer to more than every couple of days. There have been many days when I didn't need to look at *any* of my lists, in fact, because it was clear from the front end—my calendar—what I *wouldn't* be able to do.

The Right Review in the Right Context

You may need to access any one of your lists at any time. When you and your life partner are decompressing at the end of the day, and you want to be sure you'll take care of the "business" the two of you manage together about home, family, and/or personal life, you'll want to look at your accumulated agendas for him or her. On the other hand, if your boss pops in for a face-to-face conversation about current realities and priorities, it will be highly functional for you to have your Projects list up-to-date and your Agenda list for him or her right at hand. When you suddenly get a text invitation for an unplanned but highly strategic lunch meeting with a potential client who just showed up, how fast can you "clear the deck," print relevant data, and renegotiate other commitments to be fully present for that engagement, which, if it goes well, may extend into the afternoon?

Updating Your System

The real trick to ensuring the trustworthiness of the whole organization system lies in regularly refreshing your thinking and your system from a more elevated perspective. That's impossible to do, however, if your lists fall too far behind your reality. You won't be able to fool yourself about this: if your system is out of date, your brain will be forced to fully engage again at the lower level of remembering.

To make knowledge productive, we will have to learn to see both forest and tree. We will have to learn to connect.

—Peter F. Drucker

This is perhaps the biggest challenge of all. Once you've tasted what it's like to have a clear head and feel in control of everything that's going on, can you do what you need to do to maintain that as an operational standard? The many years I've spent researching and implementing this methodology with countless people have proved to me that the magic key to the sustainability of the process is the Weekly Review.

The Power of the Weekly Review

If you're like me and most other people, no matter how good your intentions may be, you're going to have the world come at you faster than you can keep up. Many of us seem to have it in our natures to consistently entangle ourselves in more than we have the ability to handle. We book ourselves in back-to-back meetings all day, go to after-hours events that generate ideas and commitments we need

to deal with, and get embroiled in engagements and projects that have the
potential to spin our creative intelligence into cosmic orbits.

> You will invariably take in more
> opportunities than your system can
> process on a daily basis.

That whirlwind of activity is precisely what makes the Weekly
Review so valuable. It builds in some capturing, reevaluation, and
reprocessing time to keep you in balance. There is simply no way to
do this necessary regrouping while you're trying to get everyday
work done.

The Weekly Review will also sharpen your intuitive focus on
your important projects as you deal with the flood of new input and
potential distractions coming at you the rest of the week. You're
going to have to learn to say no—faster, and to more things—in
order to stay afloat and comfortable. Having some dedicated time
in which to at least get up to the project level of thinking goes a
long way toward making that easier.

What Is the Weekly Review?

Very simply, the Weekly Review is whatever you need to do to get
your head empty again and get oriented for the next couple of
weeks. It's going through the steps of workflow management—
capturing, clarifying, organizing, and reviewing all your outstanding commitments, intentions, and inclinations—until you can
honestly say, "I absolutely know right now everything I'm not doing but could be doing if I decided to."

From a practical standpoint, here is the three-part drill that can
get you there: get *clear*, get *current*, and get *creative*. Getting clear
will ensure that all your collected stuff is processed. Getting current will ensure that all your orienting "maps" or lists are reviewed
and up-to-date. The creative part happens to some degree automatically, as you get clear and current—you will naturally be generating ideas and perspectives that will be adding value to your
thinking about work and life.

Get Clear

This is the initial stage of gathering up all the loose ends that have
been generated in the course of your busy week. Notes taken in

meetings, receipts and business cards you've collected, notices from your kids' schools, and all the miscellaneous inputs that, in spite of yourself, have accumulated in all the weird little pockets and places in your purse, briefcase, smartphone texts, jacket, and on your dressing-room counter, in addition to what's shown up in your standard input channels like your e-mail in-tray and social media.

Collect Loose Papers and Materials   Pull out all miscellaneous pieces of paper, business cards, receipts, and so on that have crept into the crevices of your desk, clothing, and accessories. Put it all in your in-tray for processing.

Get "In" to Empty   Review any meeting notes and miscellaneous scribbles on notepaper or in your mobile devices. Decide and list any action items, projects, waiting-fors, calendar events, and someday/maybes, as appropriate. File any reference notes and materials. Get the "in" areas of e-mails, texts, and voice mails to zero. Be ruthless with yourself, processing all notes and thoughts relative to interactions, projects, new initiatives, and input that have come your way since your last download, and purging those not needed.

Empty Your Head   Put into writing or text (in appropriate categories) any new projects, action items, waiting-fors, someday/maybes, and so forth that you haven't yet captured and clarified.

Get Current

You need to "pull up the rear guard" now and eliminate outdated reminders in your system and get your active lists up-to-date and complete. Here are the steps:

Review "Next Actions" Lists   Mark off completed actions. Review for reminders of further action steps to record. Many times I've been moving so fast I haven't had a chance to mark off many completed items on my list, much less figure out what to do next. This is the time to do that.

Review Previous Calendar Data   Review the past two to three weeks of calendar entries in detail for remaining or emergent action items, reference information, and so on, and transfer that data into the active system. Grab every "Oh! That reminds me . . . !" with its associated actions. You will likely notice meetings and events that you attended, which trigger thoughts of what to do next about the content. Be able to archive your past calendar with nothing left uncaptured.

Review Upcoming Calendar Look at further calendar entries (long- and short-term). Capture actions about projects and preparations required for upcoming events. Your calendar is one of the best checklists to review regularly, to prevent last-minute stress and trigger creative front-end thinking.* Upcoming travel, conferences, meetings, holidays, etc. should be assessed for projects to add to your "Projects" and "Next Actions" lists for any of those situations that are already on your radar but not yet on cruise control.

Review "Waiting For" List Any needed follow-up? Need to send an e-mail to get a status on it? Need to add an item to someone's Agenda list to update when you'll talk with him or her? Record any next actions. Check off any already received.

Review "Projects" (and "Larger Outcome") Lists Evaluate the status of projects, goals, and outcomes, one by one, ensuring that at least one current kick-start action for each is in your system. Browse through any active and relevant project plans, support materials, and any other work-in-progress material to trigger new actions, completions, waiting-fors, etc.

Review Any Relevant Checklists Is there anything else that you haven't done, that you need or want to do, given your various engagements, interests, and responsibilities?

Get Creative

This methodology is not simply about cleaning up and getting closure. Those are critical factors, to be sure, to utilize for clarity and

---

*This is especially true if other people have authority to add entries to your calendar. It's very easy to be uncomfortably surprised with meetings you suddenly notice that were scheduled by someone else!

focus. Ultimately, though, the prime driver for my own exploration in this field has been creating the space to catalyze and access new, creative, and valuable thinking and direction. To a great extent, that's actually not something you need to exert a lot of energy to achieve, if you have gotten this far in implementing this methodology. We are naturally creative beings, invested in our existence to live, grow, express, and expand. The challenge is not to *be* creative— it's to eliminate the barriers to the natural flow of our creative energies. Practically speaking, it's about getting your act together, letting spontaneous ideas emerge, capturing them, and utilizing their value. If you, in the process of reading and applying any of these techniques, have had any kind of "Aha! That reminds me . . ." or "Hmmm, I think I might want to . . . ," because you externalized your thinking and reflected on it, then you're already demonstrating the naturalness of this process.

> *"Point of view" is that quintessentially human solution to information overload, an intuitive process of reducing things to an essential relevant and manageable minimum. . . . In a world of hyperabundant content, point of view will become the scarcest of resources.*
>
> *—Paul Saffo*

As I said, there may not be anything you need to focus on at this point, since probably most of your creative thinking will have already shown up and been integrated in this process. However, there are a couple of additional triggers that you might find valuable to finish off this process.

Review "Someday/Maybe" List Check for any projects that may have become more interesting or valuable to activate, and transfer them to Projects. Delete any that have simply stayed around much longer than they should, as the world and your interest have changed enough to take them off even this informal radar. Add any emerging possibilities that you've just started thinking about.

Be Creative and Courageous Are there any new, wonderful, hare-brained, creative, thought-provoking, risk-taking ideas you can capture and add into your system, or "external brain"?

This review process is common sense, but few of us do it as well or consistently as we could, which means as regularly as we should to keep a clear mind and a sense of relaxed control. Granted, its scope is daunting, especially if you haven't yet structured and populated your personal system to have reasonably current and complete data. And even if you have a decent center of control, given the pressures and demands of your day-to-day world, seldom is it obvious or easy to make this kind of reflection and recalibration event happen.

The Right Time and Place for the Review

The Weekly Review is so critical that it behooves you to establish good habits, environments, and tools to support it. Once your comfort zone has been established for the kind of relaxed control that *Getting Things Done* is all about, you won't have to worry too much about making yourself do your review—you'll *have* to, in order to get back to your personal standards again.

Until then, do whatever you need to, once a week, to trick yourself into backing away from the daily grind for a couple of hours—not to zone out, but to rise up at least to the horizon of all your projects and their statuses, and to catch up with everything else that relates to what's pulling on your attention.

If you have the luxury of an office or work space that can be somewhat isolated from the people and interactions of the day, and if you have anything resembling a typical five-day workweek, I recommend that you block out two hours early in the afternoon of your last workday for the review. Three factors make this an ideal time:

- The events of the week are likely to be still fresh enough for you to be able to do a complete postmortem ("Oh, yeah, I need to make sure I get back to her about . . .").
- When you (invariably) uncover actions that require reaching people at work, you'll still have time to do that before they leave for the weekend.
- It's great to clear your mental decks so you can go into the weekend ready for refreshment and recreation, with nothing else pulling on you unnecessarily.

You may be the kind of person, however, who doesn't have normal weekends. I, for example, often have as much to do on those days as I do midweek. But I do have the luxury(?) of enduring

Every now and then go away and have a little relaxation. To remain constantly at work will diminish your judgment. Go some distance away, because work will be in perspective and a lack of harmony is more readily seen.

—*Leonardo da Vinci*

frequent long plane trips, which provide an ideal opportunity for me to catch up. Many people have tailored their own Weekly Review habits to fit with their lifestyles, ranging from a standard time at their favorite coffeehouse every Saturday morning to the time on Sunday they sat in the rear of their church during their daughter's choir practice.

Whatever your lifestyle, you need a weekly regrouping ritual. You likely have something like this (or close to it) already. If so, leverage the habit by adding into it a higher-altitude review process.

The people who find it hardest to make time for this review are those who have constantly on-demand work and home environments, with zero built-in time or space for regrouping. The most stressed professionals I have met are the ones who have to be mission-critically reactive at work (e.g., high-level equities traders and chiefs of staff) and then go home to a couple of under-ten-year-old children and a spouse who also had a hard day at work. Some of them fortunately have a one-hour train commute.

If you recognize yourself in that picture, your greatest challenge will be to build in a consistent process of regrouping, with your world not directly in your face. You'll need to either accept the requirement of an after-hours time at your desk on a Friday night or establish a relaxed but at-work kind of location and time at home.

Executive Operational Review Time   I've coached many executives to block out two hours on their calendars at the end of their workweek. For them the biggest problem is how to balance quality thinking and catch-up time with the urgent demands of mission-critical interactions. This is a tough call. The most senior and savvy of them, however, know the value of sacrificing the seemingly urgent for the truly important, and they create their islands of time for some version of this

Your best thoughts about work won't happen while you're at work.

process. One of our clients, head of executive development for one of the largest companies in the world, suggested that building in quality time for review and regrouping in order to trust one's intuitive decision making is both critical and sorely lacking in the higher echelons of his organization.

Even the executives who have integrated a consistent reflective space for their work, though, often seem to give short shrift to the more mundane review and catch-up process at the Horizon 1 (Projects) level. Between wall-to-wall meetings and ambling around your koi pond with a glass of wine at sunset, there's got to be a slightly elevated level of review required for operational control and focus. If you think you have all your open loops fully identified, clarified, assessed, and actionalized, you're probably kidding yourself.

> *Thinking is the very essence of, and the most difficult thing to do in, business and in life. Empire builders spend hour-after-hour on mental work . . . while others party. If you're not consciously aware of putting forth the effort to exert self-guided integrated thinking . . . then you're giving in to laziness and no longer control your life.*
>
> —David Kekich

The "Bigger Picture" Reviews

Yes, at some point you must clarify the larger outcomes, the long-term goals, the visions and principles that ultimately drive, test, and prioritize your decisions.

What are your key goals and objectives in your work? What should you have in place a year or three years from now? How is your career going? Is this the lifestyle that is most fulfilling to you? Are you doing what you really want or need to do, from a deeper and longer-term perspective?

The explicit focus of this book is not teasing out those Horizon 3-to-5 levels. Urging you to operate from a higher perspective is, however, its *implicit* purpose—to assist you in making your total life expression more fulfilling and better aligned with the bigger game you're all about. As you increase the speed and agility with which you clear the Ground and Horizon 1 levels of your life and work, be sure to revisit the other levels you're engaged in, as needed, to maintain a truly clear head.

> Trying to create goals before you have confidence that you can keep your everyday world under control will often undermine your motivation and energy rather than enhance them.

How often you ought to challenge yourself with that type of wide-ranging review is something only you can know. The principle I must affirm at this juncture is this:

You need to assess your life and work at the appropriate horizons, making the appropriate decisions, at the appropriate intervals, in order to really come clean. That's a lifelong invitation and obligation to yourself, to fulfill whatever your unfinished destiny or intentionality happens to be.

Over the years I have discovered, through my own experience as well as being intimately involved with scores of people in their day-to-day worlds, that getting ultimately grounded and in control of the mundane aspects of life produces a rich field of natural inspiration about our higher-level stuff. It is because of our deeper drives and inclinations that we have embroiled ourselves in the complexities and commitments that often create confusion and the sense of being overwhelmed. You felt a profound need to have children; now you've got them, and each one is a major business to manage for at least two decades. You've felt impelled to be creative and produce recognized (and monetized) value in the world; so you've built a business or committed to a lofty professional career, and you're now buried in many more things than you feel you can handle.

In order to understand the world, one has to turn away from it on occasion.

—*Albert Camus*

More goals may not be necessary for you now—you need comfort with the ones you've already put in motion, and the confidence that you can execute elegantly on any new ones.

We can always use a refreshed view of our visions, values, and objectives, indeed. But in my experience you'll resist that conversation with yourself if you don't think you're handling the world you've already created for yourself very well! How long does it take to change a goal or picture of what you want? Not much time, if any. How long will it take you to feel confident that you can deliver to yourself the outcomes you commit to? My experience is that it will be at least two years of implementing and habituating this methodology to get to that level of self-confidence. That's not bad news—it's just news. The good news is that getting more control at the more mundane and operational levels of your life and work is immediately available as you start to apply these best practices, and it will likely open up real aspects of your bigger game that you wouldn't be able to recognize or leverage without it.

An additional aspect of this future-thinking dynamic is the value of staying immensely flexible and informal about goal setting. A significant change in this area has been pioneered in the software world, as "agile programming" has become the norm for successful start-ups. Have a vision, do your best to imagine what it might look like, get cranking on producing something as a viably marketable first iteration, and then "dynamically steer," maturing both

> The world itself is never overwhelmed or confused—only we are, due to how we are engaged with it.

your vision as well as how to implement it, based on real feedback from your real world. The message is: positive future thinking is critical and fabulous, but it's most effectively manifested when it is tied to a confidence of execution in the material world, with responsiveness and course correction built in.

Which brings us to the ultimate point and challenge of all this personal capturing, clarifying, organizing, and reflecting methodology: It's 9:22 a.m. Wednesday morning—what do you do?

Engaging: Making the Best Action Choices

WHEN IT COMES to your real-time, plow-through, get-it-done workday, how do you decide what to do at any given point?

As I've said, my simple answer is, trust your heart. Or your spirit. Or, if you're allergic to those kinds of words, try these: your gut, the seat of your pants, your liver, your intuition—whatever works for you as a reference point that has you step back and access whatever you consider the source of your inner wisdom. If you've ever made thoughtful versus knee-jerk and reactive choices, you'll know what I mean.

Ultimately and always you must trust your intuition. There are many things you can do, however, that can enhance that trust.

That doesn't mean you throw your life to the winds—unless, of course, it does. I actually went down that route myself with a vengeance at one point in my life, and I can attest that the lessons were valuable, if not necessarily necessary.*

As outlined in chapter 2 (pages 52–57), I have found three priority frameworks to be enormously helpful in the context of deciding actions:

---

*There are myriad ways to give it all up. You can ignore the physical world and its realities and trust in the universe. I did that at one point, in my own particular way, and it was a powerful experience. And one I wouldn't wish on anyone. I tried to check out of my practical connections, though I didn't choose to end my life (but it was a close call!). I had much to learn about cooperating with the world I'd chosen to play in. But surrendering to your inner awareness, and its intelligence and advice for the worlds you live in, is the higher ground. Trusting yourself and the source of your intelligence is the most elegant version of experiencing freedom and manifesting personal productivity.

- The four-criteria model for choosing actions in the moment
- The threefold model for evaluating daily work
- The six-level model for reviewing your own work

These happen to be shown in reverse hierarchical order—that is, the reverse of the typical strategic top-down perspective. In keeping with the nature of the *Getting Things Done* methodology, I have found it useful to once again work from the bottom up, meaning I'll start with the most mundane levels.

The Four-Criteria Model for Choosing Actions in the Moment

Remember that you make your action choices based on the following four criteria, in order:

- Context
- Time available
- Energy available
- Priority

Let's examine each of these in light of how you can best structure your systems and behaviors to take advantage of its dynamics.

Context

At any point in time, the first thing to consider is, what could you possibly do, where you are, with the tools you have? Do you have a phone? Do you have access to the person you need to talk with face-to-face about three agenda items? Are you at the store where you need to buy something? If you can't do the action because you're not in the appropriate location or don't have the appropriate tools, don't worry about it.

As I've said, it's often helpful to organize your action reminders by context—Calls, At Home, At Computer, Errands, Agenda for Joe, Agenda for Staff Meeting, and so on. Since context is the first criterion that comes into play in your best choice of actions, context-sorted lists prevent unnecessary reassessments about what to do. If you have a bunch of things to do on one to-do list, but you actually can't do many of them in the same context, you force yourself to continually keep reconsidering *all* of them.

If you have traveled to meet a client at her office and on arrival discover that the meeting will be delayed for fifteen minutes, you will want to refer to your Calls list for something you could do to use your time productively. Your action lists should fold in or out, based on what you could possibly do at any time.

> *You have freedom when you are easy in your harness.*
>
> —*Robert Frost*

A second real benefit accrues from organizing action reminders by appropriate context: in itself that forces you to make the all-important determination about the next physical action on your stuff. All of my action lists are set up this way, so I have to decide on the very next physical action before I can know which list to put an item on. (Is this something that requires the computer? A phone? Being in a store? Talking in real time with my wife?) People who give themselves a Miscellaneous action list (i.e. one not specific in context) often let themselves slide in the next-action decision, too.

I frequently encourage people I'm working with to structure their list categories early on as they're processing their in-trays, because that automatically grounds their projects in the real things that need to get done to get them moving.

Creative Context Sorting

As you begin to implement this methodology consistently, you will invariably find inventive ways to tailor your own contextual categories to fit your situation. Though sorting by the tool or physical location required is most common, there are often other uniquely useful ways to filter your reminders.

Before I go on a long trip, I will create "Before Trip" as a temporary category into which I will move everything from any of my action lists that *must* be handled before I leave. That becomes the only list I need to review, until they're all done. At times I have had many next actions that required me to be in "creative writing" mode; though those actions were At Computer, they required a different time and frame of mind than the rest of the things I needed to do at my laptop. It was much more relaxing and productive to manage my focus by sorting those onto a different, Creative Writing action list. I currently divide my computer-required actions into those that don't require an Internet connection, those that do, and those that are just surfing (potentially fun or interesting things on the Web to explore).

Over the years I have seen people effectively use categories such as "Brain Gone" (for simple actions requiring no mental horsepower) and "Less Than 5-Minute" (for getting quick "wins"). At times people feel more comfortable sorting their reminders by the areas of focus in their life and work—"Financial," "Family," "Administrative," etc. Recently someone shared with me the value she found in categorizing actions based upon the immediate emotional reward for doing them—service to others, life stability, abundance building, etc. There is no "right" way to structure your Next Actions lists—only what works best for you, and that part of your system will likely change as your life does.*

If you are a novice to this process, these details and distinctions may seem unnecessary or overwhelming. Just keep in mind that when you actually identify all the next actions you are committed to taking to fulfill your commitments in life and work, you will likely have many more than a hundred. To truly implement an effective "external brain" and garner its amazing results, managing this ground-floor level of your work with this degree of sophistication will pay off immeasurably.

---

*In an ideal world, you could see all your next-action reminders any way you wanted to see them: time, brain-power, location, or tool required; emotional payoff; area of life served; goals and projects supported. The issue is: How much structure is too much, for the potential value of it? If you have to think and work too much to input content into your system, you won't do it. The digital applications for list and category management increasingly give us more opportunities to slice and dice our information in multiple new ways, but care must always be taken to evaluate if the energy required to utilize the system in the "heat of battle" is worth it. (You could have created this context-specific sorting functionality since the first software spreadsheet programs were introduced, by structuring columns and building sorting macros. But do I need to go through all that just to insert "Call my brother" as a reminder?!)

Time Available

The second factor in choosing an action is how much time you have before you have to do something else. If your meeting is starting in ten minutes, you'll most likely select a different action to do right now than you would if the next couple of hours were clear.

Obviously, it's good to know how much time you have at hand (hence the value of accessible calendar and timepiece). A total-life action-reminder inventory will give you maximum information about what you need to do, and make it much easier to match your actions to the windows you have. In other words, if you have ten minutes before that next meeting, find a ten-minute thing to do. If your lists have only the big or important things on them, no item listed may be possible to handle in a ten-minute period—especially if they are missing next-action reminders. If you're going to have to do those shorter action things anyway, the most productive way to get them done is to utilize the little "weird time" windows that occur throughout the day.

Additionally there are many times when you have been head down in some mentally intensive endeavor for a couple of hours, and you'd like to shift your focus and get some easy wins. Then it's great to "snack" on your action lists for some simple things to complete easily and quickly. Change a restaurant reservation, call a friend and wish him or her happy birthday, order birdseed, or just walk next door to the market or pharmacy for something on your Errands list.

Energy Available

Although you can increase your energy level at times by changing your context and redirecting your focus, you can do only so much. The tail end of a day taken up by a marathon budget-planning session is probably not the best time to call a prospective client, start drafting a performance-review policy, or broach a new and sensitive topic with your life partner. It might be better to call an

We all have times when we think more effectively, and times when we should not be thinking at all.

—Daniel Cohen

airline to change a reservation, process some expense receipts, step out on your patio and watch the sunset, skim a trade journal, or just clean up a desk drawer.

Just as having all your next-action options available allows you to take advantage of various time slots, knowing about everything you're going to need to process and do at some point will allow you to match productive activity with your vitality level.

I recommend that you always keep an inventory of things that need to be done that require very little mental or creative horsepower. When you're in one of those low-energy states, do those things. Casual reading (magazines, articles, catalogs, Web surfing), contact data that needs to be inputted, file purging, backing up your computer, even just watering your plants and filling your stapler—these are some of the myriad things that you need or want to deal with sometime anyway.

This is one of the best reasons for having very clean edges to your personal management system: it makes it easy to continue doing productive activity when you're not in top form. If you're in a low-energy mode and your reading material is disorganized, your receipts are all over the place, your filing system is chaotic, and your in-tray is dysfunctional, it just seems like too much work to find and organize the tasks at hand, so you simply avoid doing anything at all and then you feel even worse. One of the best ways to increase your energy is to close some of your loops. So always be sure to have some easy loops to close, right at hand.*

> There is no reason not to be highly productive, even when you're not in top form.

These first three criteria for choosing action (context, time, and energy) bespeak the need for a complete next-action reminder system. Much of the time you won't be in a mode to do that kind of coordinated and organized thinking; it needs to have *already been done*. If it is, you can operate much more "in your zone" and choose from delineated actions that fit the situation.

---

*Granted, it's a fine line between something that doesn't require a lot of energy because it's the most productive thing to do in the moment and doing it to avoid doing the tougher stuff you know you *ought* to be doing!

Priority

Given the context you're in and the time and energy you have, the obvious next criterion for action choice is relative priority: "Out of all my remaining options, what is the most important thing for me to do?"

> It is impossible to feel good about your choices unless you are clear about what your work really is.

"How do I decide my priorities?" is a question I frequently hear from people. It springs from their experience of having more on their plate to do than they can comfortably handle. They know that some hard choices have to be made, and that some things may not get done at all.

At the end of the day, in order to feel good about what you didn't get done, you must have made some conscious decisions about your accountabilities, goals, and values. That process invariably includes an often-complex interplay with the goals, values, and directions of the organization(s) and significant people in your life, and with the importance of those relationships to you. This criterion is addressed by utilizing the six-horizon commitment model I've described and will elaborate on shortly.

The Threefold Model for Evaluating Daily Work

Setting priorities assumes that some things will be more important than others, but important relative to what? In this context, the answer is, to your work—that is, the job(s) you have accepted from yourself and/or from others. This is where the next two frameworks need to be brought to bear in your thinking. They're about defining your work. Keep in mind that though much of this methodology will be within the arena of your professional focus, I'm using "work" in the universal sense, to mean anything you have a commitment to make happen, personally as well as professionally.

These days, daily work activity itself presents a relatively new type of challenge to most professionals, something that it's helpful to understand as we endeavor to build the most productive systems. As I explained earlier, during the course of the workday, at any point in time, you'll be engaged in one of three types of activities:

- Doing predefined work
- Doing work as it shows up
- Defining your work

You may be doing things on your action lists, doing things as they come up, or processing incoming inputs to determine what work needs to be done with them, then or later, from your lists.

This is common sense. But many people let themselves get sucked into the second activity—dealing with unplanned and unexpected things that show up—much too easily, and let the other two slide, to their detriment.

> It is often easier to get wrapped up in the urgent demands of the moment than to deal with your in-tray, e-mail, and the rest of your open loops.

Let's say it's 10:26 a.m. Monday, and you're in your office. You've just ended a half-hour unexpected phone call with a prospective client. You have three pages of scribbled notes from the conversation. There's a meeting scheduled with your staff at eleven, about half an hour from now. You were out late last night with your spouse's parents and are still a little frayed around the edges (you told your father-in-law you'd get back to him about . . . what?). Your assistant just put two arriving international express packages on your desk, and additionally says he needs to talk with you about three urgent meeting requests he doesn't know how you want handled. You have a major strategic-planning session coming up in two days, for which you have yet to formulate your ideas. The oil indicator light in your car came on as you drove to work this morning. And your boss hinted as you passed her earlier in the hall that she'd like your thoughts on the e-mail she sent you last night, before this afternoon's three o'clock meeting.

Are your systems set up to maximally support dealing with this reality, at 10:26 on Monday morning? If you're still keeping things in your head, and if you're still trying to capture only the "critical" stuff in your lists, I suggest that the answer is no.

I've noticed that people are actually more comfortable dealing with surprises and crises than they are taking control of processing, organizing, reviewing, and assessing that part of their work that is *not* as self-evident. It's easy to get seduced into "busy" and "urgent" mode, especially when you have a lot of unprocessed and relatively out-of-control work on your desk, in your e-mail, and on your mind.

In fact, much of our life and work *does* just show up in the moment, and it often becomes the priority when it does. It's indeed true for most professionals (and parents of young children!) that the nature of their job requires them to be instantly available to handle new work as it appears in many forms. For instance, you need to pay attention to your boss when he shows up and wants a few minutes of your time. You get a request from a senior executive that suddenly takes precedence over anything else you thought you needed to do today. You find out about a serious problem fulfilling a major customer's order, and you have to take care of it right away. Or your baby develops a serious cough.

Success is learning to deal with Plan B.

—Unknown

These are all understandable judgment calls. But the angst begins to mount when the other actions on your lists are not reviewed and renegotiated by you or between you and everyone else. The constant sacrifices of not doing the work you have defined on your lists can be tolerated only if you *know* what you're not doing. That requires regular processing of your in-tray (defining your work) and consistent review of complete lists of all your predetermined work.

If choosing to do work that just showed up instead of doing work you predefined is a conscious choice based on your best call, that's playing the game the most effective way you can. Most people, however, have major improvements to make in how they clarify, manage, and renegotiate their total inventory of projects and actions. If you let yourself get caught up in the urgency of the moment, without feeling comfortable about what you're *not* dealing with, the result is frustration and anxiety. Too often the stress and reduced effectiveness are blamed on the surprises. If you know what you're doing and what you're *not* doing, surprises are just another opportunity to be flexible and creative, and to excel.

There are no interruptions—there are only mismanaged inputs.

Another reason people consider unexpected demands or requests negative is because they don't trust their own system and behaviors to be able to put a "bookmark" on any resulting action that needs to be taken, or on the work they're doing at the moment. They know they need do something about the new work that just showed up, but they don't trust that a simple note in their own in-tray will ensure it is handled with proper timing. So they stop their previous work and immediately go do what was just requested or required of them, complaining about the interruption that just disturbed their life. There are no interruptions, really—there are simply mismanaged occurrences.

In addition, when the in-tray and the action lists get ignored for too long, random things lying in them tend to surface as emergencies later on, adding more unexpected work-as-it-shows-up to fuel the fire.

Many people use the inevitability of an almost infinite stream of immediately evident things to do as a way to avoid the responsibilities of defining their work and managing their total inventory. It's easy to get lured into not-quite-so-critical stuff that is right at hand, especially if your in-tray and your personal organization are out of control. Too often "managing by wandering around" is an excuse for getting away from amorphous piles of stuff.

This is where the need for the *Getting Things Done* methodology really shows up. Most people did not grow up in a world where defining the edges of work and managing huge numbers of open loops were required. But when you've developed the skill and habits of processing input rapidly into a rigorously defined system, it becomes much easier to trust your judgment calls about the dance of what to do, what to stop doing, and what to do instead.

The Moment-To-Moment Balancing Act

At a master level, you can shift like lightning from one foot to the other and back again. While you're processing your in-tray, for example, you assistant enters to tell you about a situation that needs immediate attention. No sweat—your in-tray and e-mail are still there, with everything still to be processed in a coordinated view, ready to be picked up again when you can get back to it. While you're on hold on the phone, you can be reviewing your action lists and getting a sense of what you're going to do when the call is done. When your infant is crawling around in the living room and you're highly attuned to anything unusual you might have to respond to, you can be handling simple Web-surfing research on your At Computer list. While you wait for a meeting to start, you

To ignore the unexpected (even if it were possible) would be to live without opportunity, spontaneity, and the rich moments of which "life" is made.

—Stephen Covey

can work down the Read/Review stack you've brought with you. And when the conversation you weren't expecting with your boss shrinks the time you have before your next meeting to twelve minutes, you can easily find a way to use that window to good advantage.

You can only do one of these work activities at a time. If you stop to talk to someone in his or her office, you're not working off your lists or processing incoming stuff. The challenge is to feel confident about what you have decided to do.

So how do you decide? This again will involve your intuitive judgments—how important is the unexpected work, against all the rest? How long can you let your in-tray go unprocessed and all your stuff unreviewed and trust that you're making good decisions about what to do?

People often complain about the interruptions that prevent them from doing their work. But interruptions are unavoidable in life. When you become elegant at dispatching what's coming in and are organized enough to take advantage of "weird time" windows that show up, you can switch between one task and the other rapidly.

Do unexpected work as it shows up, not because it is the path of least resistance, but because it is the thing you need to do vis-à-vis all the rest.

You can be processing e-mails while you're on hold on a conference call. Research has now proven that you can't actually multitask, i.e. put conscious focused attention on more than one thing at a time; and if you are trying to, it denigrates your performance considerably. If your head is your only system for placeholding, you will experience an attempted multitasking internally, which is psychologically impossible and the source of much stress for many people. If you have established practices for parking still-incomplete items midstream, however, your focus can shift cleanly from one to the next and back again, with the precision of a martial artist who appears to fight four people at once, but who in reality is simply rapidly shifting attention.

Nonetheless, even if you are a "black belt" in capturing and bookmarking what's going on, you must still learn to make quick and appropriate choices among those many tasks to keep a healthy balance of your workflow. Your choices will still have to be calibrated against your own clarity about the nature and goals of your work.

Your ability to deal with surprise is your competitive edge, and a key to sanity and sustainability in your lifestyle. But at a certain point, if you're not catching up and getting things under control, staying busy with only the work at hand will undermine your effectiveness. And ultimately, in order to know whether you should stop what you're doing and do something else, you'll need to have a good sense of all your roles and how they fit together in a larger context. The only way you can have that is to evaluate your life and work appropriately at multiple horizons.

The Six-Level Model for Reviewing Your Own Work

The six levels of work as we saw in chapter 2 (pages 54–56) may be thought of in terms of altitude, as in the floors of a building:

• Horizon 5: Life
• Horizon 4: Long-term visions
• Horizon 3: One- to two-year goals
• Horizon 2: Areas of focus and accountability
• Horizon 1: Current projects
• Ground: Current actions

It makes sense that each of these levels should enhance and align with the ones above it. In other words, your priorities will sit in a hierarchy from the top down. Ultimately, if the phone call you're supposed to make clashes with your life purpose or values, to be in sync with yourself you won't make it. If your job structure doesn't match up with where you need to be a year from now, you should rethink how you've framed your areas of focus and roles, if you want to get where you're going most efficiently.

Let's look at that first example from the bottom up. The phone call you need to make (action) is about the deal you're working on (project), which would increase sales (accountability). This particular deal would give you the opportunity to move up in the sales force

Your work is to discover your
work and then with all your
heart to give yourself to it.

　　　　　—*Buddha*

(job goal) because of the new market your company wants to penetrate (organization vision). And that would get you closer to the way you want to be living, both financially and professionally (life).

Or, from the other direction, you've decided that you want to be your own boss and unlock some of your unique assets and talents in a particular area that resonates with you (life). So you create a business for yourself (vision), with some short-term key operational objectives (job goal). That gives you some critical roles you need to fulfill to get it rolling (accountability), with some immediate outcomes to achieve (projects). On each of those projects you'll have things you need to do, as soon as you can do them (next actions).

The healthiest approach for relaxed control and inspired productivity is to manage all the levels in a balanced fashion. At any of those levels, it's critical to identify all the open loops, all the incompletions, and all the commitments that you have right now, as best you can. They all came, consciously or not, from the urges, pulls, and pushes from these multiple levels within you. Without an acceptance and an objective assessment of what's true in the present, and feeling confident you can manage what you've created, it's always difficult to cast off for new shores. What's in your e-mail? What are the projects you need to start or complete with your kids? What do you need to handle in your current roles at the office? What's pushing you to change or attracting you to create in the next months or years? These are all open loops in your head, though often it takes deeper and more introspective processes to identify the bigger goals and subtler inclinations.

There is magic in being in the present in your life. I'm always amazed at the power of clear observation simply about what's going on, what's true. Finding out the exact details of your personal finances, clarifying the historical data about the company you're buying, or getting the facts about who really said what to whom in an interpersonal conflict can be constructive, if not absolutely necessary and downright healing.

The best place to succeed is where
you are with what you have.

　　　　　—*Charles Schwab*

Getting things done, and feeling good about it, means being willing to recognize, acknowledge, and appropriately engage with all the things within the ecosystem of your consciousness. Mastering the art of stress-free productivity requires it.

Working from the Bottom Up

In order to create productive alignment in your life, you could quite reasonably start with a clarification from the top down. Decide why you're on the planet. Figure out what kind of life and work and lifestyle would best allow you to fulfill that contract. What kind of job and personal relationships would support that direction? What key things would you need to put in place and make happen right now, and what could you do physically as soon as possible to kick-start each of those?

> You're never lacking in opportunities to clarify your priorities at any level. Pay attention to which horizon is calling you.

In truth, you can approach your priorities from any level, at any time. I always have something that I could do constructively to enhance my awareness and focus on each level. I'm never lacking in more visions to elaborate, goals to reassess, projects to identify or create, or actions to decide on. The trick is to learn to pay attention to the ones you need to, at the appropriate time, to keep you clear and present with whatever you're doing.

Because everything will ultimately be driven by the priorities of the level above it, any formulation of your priorities would obviously most efficiently begin at the top. For example, if you spend time prioritizing your work and then later discover that it's not the work you think you ought to be doing, you may have wasted time and energy that could have been better spent defining the next job you really want. The problem is that without a sense of control at the implementation level (current projects and actions), and without trust in your own ability to manage those levels appropriately, trying to manage yourself from the top down often creates frustration.

> Trying to manage from the top down when the bottom is out of control may be the *least* effective approach.

From a practical perspective, I suggest going from the bottom up instead. I've coached people from both directions, and in terms of lasting value, I can honestly say that getting someone in control of the details of his or her current physical world, and then elevating the focus from there, has never missed.

The primary reason to work from this bottom-up direction is that it clears your inner decks to begin with, allowing your creative attention to focus on the more meaningful and elusive visions that you may need to challenge yourself to identify. Also, this particular method has a high degree of flexibility and freedom, and it includes a thinking and organizing practice that is universal and effective no matter what it's focused on. That makes it worth learning, no matter what the actual content you're dealing with at the moment may be. Change your mind and this process will help you adjust with maximum speed. It takes no time to reset a vision or goal, but learning to objectify and execute on it in a streamlined, coordinated, and stress-free way is an art that must be learned and practiced. Knowing you have that ability will give you permission to play a bigger game. It's truly empowering.

> Handle what has your attention and you'll then discover what *really* has your attention.

I have learned over the years that the most important thing to deal with is whatever is most on your mind. The fact that you think it shouldn't be on your mind is irrelevant. It's there, and it's there for a reason. "Buy cat food" may certainly not rank high on some theoretical prioritizing inventory, but if that's what's pulling on you the most, in the moment, then handling it in some way would be Job One. Once you handle what has your attention, it frees you up to notice what *really* has your attention. Which, when you handle that, will allow you to see what *really* has your attention, and so on. Almost without exception the executives I have worked with are most plagued by the management of the nitty-gritty of their workaday world—e-mails, meetings, travel, projects going off the rails, etc. When they begin to get all that under control, their attention invariably turns to areas of focus and interest from a higher perspective—family, career, and quality-of-life stuff. So don't worry about what horizon or what content of your life is the highest priority to deal with—deal with what's present. When you do, you will more effectively uncover and address what's really true and meaningful for you.*

While Horizon 5 (purpose and principles) is obviously the most important context within which to set priorities, experience has shown me that when we understand and implement *all* the levels of work in which we are engaged, especially the Ground and Horizon 1 levels, we gain greater freedom and resources to do the bigger work that we're all about. If your boat is sinking, you really don't care in which direction it's pointed! Although a bottom-up approach is not a conceptual priority, from a practical perspective it's a critical factor in achieving a balanced, productive, and comfortable life.

Ground The first thing to do is make sure your action lists are complete, which in itself can be quite a task. Those who focus on gathering and objectifying all of those items discover that there are many (often of some importance) they've forgotten, misplaced, or just not recognized.

Aside from your calendar, if you don't have at least fifty next actions and waiting-fors, including all the agendas for people and meetings, I would be skeptical about whether you really had *all* of them. If you've followed through rigorously with the steps and suggestions in part 2, though, you may have them already. If not, and you do want to get this level up-to-date, set aside some time to work through chapters 4 through 6 in real implementation mode.

When you've finished getting this level of control current, you'll automatically have a more grounded sense of immediate priorities, which is almost impossible to achieve otherwise.

Horizon 1 Finalize your Projects list. Does it truly capture all the commitments you have that will require more than one action to get done? That will define the boundaries of the kind of week-to-week operational world you're in and allow you to relax your thinking for longer intervals.

If you make a complete list of all of the things you want to have

---

*This is very likely one reason someone may resist the acceptance and implementation of the *Getting Things Done* methodology. Some of those higher-horizon issues, which consequently may surface, would be too unpleasant to confront. Being busy and overwhelmed can be, paradoxically, at least a temporarily effective way to stay comfortable.

Taking the inventory of your current work at all levels will automatically produce greater focus, alignment, and sense of priorities.

happen in your life and work at this level, you'll discover that there are actions you need to do that you didn't realize. Just creating this objective inventory will give you a firmer basis on which to make decisions about what to do when you have discretionary time. Invariably when people get their Projects list up-to-date, they discover there are several things that could be done readily to move things they care about forward.

Very few people have this clear data defined and available to themselves in some objective form. Before any discussion about what should be done this afternoon can take place, this information must be at hand.

Again, if you've been putting into practice the methodology of *Getting Things Done*, your Projects list will be where it needs to be. For most of the people we coach, it takes ten to fifteen hours of capturing, clarifying, and organizing to get to the point of trusting the thoroughness of their inventory.

And to achieve the most pristine level of "mind like water" (nothing on your mind except what's present in the moment), Horizon 1 is the level that seems to incorporate some of the most interesting challenges. For all of us, there are situations and circumstances that emerge that bother, interest, or distract us, but with which it is not immediately obvious or evident how to engage. Your son has a problem with his math teacher; you are frustrated with how long it takes to implement a procedure in your company; you have a concern about the person running your fund-raising committee; you keep thinking you ought to be rekindling your interest in painting; etc. Quieting that subtle noise requires identifying objective outcomes for each of those (a project), with accompanying next actions placed into your trusted system. Playing consistently at this level of the stress-free productivity game is a hallmark of its mastery.

Horizon 2   This is the level of "current job responsibilities" and "areas of my life to maintain at an appropriate standard." What are the hats you wear, the roles you play? Professionally, this would relate to your current position and work. Personally, it would include the areas of responsibility you've taken on in your family, in your community, and of course with yourself as a functioning person.

You may have some of these roles already defined and written out. If you've recently taken a new position and there's an agreement or contract about your areas of accountability, that would certainly be a good start. If you've done any kind of personal goal-setting and values-clarifying exercises in the past and still have any materials you created then, add those to the mix.

> If you're not totally sure what your job is, it will always feel overwhelming.

Next I recommend that you make and keep a list called "Areas of Focus." You might like to separate this into "Professional" and "Personal" sublists, in which case you'll want to use them both equally for a consistent review. This is one of the most useful checklists you can create for your own self-management. It won't require the kind of once-a-week recalibration that the Projects list will; more likely it will have meaning on a longer recursion cycle. Depending on the speed of change in some of the more important areas of your life and work, this should be used as a trigger for potential new projects every one to three months.

You probably have somewhere between four and seven key areas of responsibility in your work, and a similar number personally. Your job may include things like staff development, systems design, long-range planning, administrative support, customer service, and marketing; or accountabilities for facilities, fulfillment, quality control, asset management, and so on. If you're your own business, your attention will be on many more areas than if you have a very specialized function in a large organization. The rest of your life might entail areas of focus such as parenting, partnering, spiritual community, health, volunteering, home management, personal finances, self-development, creative expression, and so forth. And each one of those specific areas could be broken down into useful subcategories. "Parenting" could generate separate checklists for each of your children. "Marketing" can include "Program Design," "Research," "Social Media," etc.

The operational purpose of the Areas of Focus list is to ensure that you have all your projects and next actions defined, so you can manage your responsibilities appropriately. If you were to create an accounting of those and evaluate them objectively, in terms of what you're doing and should be doing, you'll undoubtedly uncover projects you need to add to your Projects list. You may, in reviewing the list, decide that some areas are just fine and are being taken care of. Then again, you may realize that something has been bugging or intriguing you in one area and that a project should be created to deal with it. "Areas of Focus" is really just a more abstract and refined version of the Triggers list we covered earlier.

Every person I have worked with in the past thirty years has uncovered at least two or three important gaps at this level of discussion. For instance, a common role a manager or executive has is "staff." Upon reflection, most realize they need to add a project or two in that area, such as "Upgrade support office procedures," "Research hiring a chief of staff," or "Upgrade performance review processes." Or when objectifying the accountabilities for aspects of one's personal life, often projects like "Research yoga classes" and "Set up summer activities for the kids" show up.

A discussion of priorities would have to incorporate all of these levels of current agreements between you and others. If you get this professional "job description" checklist in play and keep it current, you'll probably be more relaxed and in control than most people in our culture. Few people are doing only what they were hired to do, and keeping clear about new and changing expectations needs to be a constantly updated conversation. Equally few people maintain a consistent and objective overview of all the relevant areas of their balanced life—family, fun, or finances—with a mind to execute on the gaps. Driving your thinking and systems from these levels will go a long way toward moving you from hope to trust as you make the necessary on-the-run choices about what to do.

Horizons 3–5 Whereas the three lower levels have mostly to do with the current state of things—your actions, projects, and areas of responsibility—from Horizon 3 up the factors of the future and your direction and intentions are primary. There is still an inventory to take at these plateaus (especially at the top level, purpose and principles, which represents an ongoing criterion for monitoring and correcting activities and behaviors), but it's more about "What

> When you're not sure where you're going or what's really important to you, you'll never know when enough is enough.

is true right now about where I've decided I'm going and how I'm going to get there?" This can range from one-year goals in your job (Horizon 3) to a three-year vision for your career and personal net worth (Horizon 4) to intuiting your life purpose and how to maximize its expression (Horizon 5).

I'm blending the three uppermost levels together here because situations often can't easily be pigeonholed into one or another of these categories. Also, since *Getting Things Done* is more about the art of implementation and execution than about how to define goals and vision, I won't offer a rigorous examination here. But by its very nature this investigation can broach potentially deep and complex arenas, which could include business strategy, organization development, career planning, and life direction and values.

For our purposes, the focus is on capturing what motivators exist for you in current reality that determine the inventory of what your work actually is, right now (some of which may be stemming from your higher-level commitments and intentions). Whether your directions and goals should be changed or clarified—based on deeper thinking, analysis, and intuition—could be another discussion. Even so, there are probably some things you can identify right now that can help you get current in your own thinking about your work and what's important in it.

> Pick battles big enough to matter, small enough to win.
> —Jonathan Kozol

If you were to intuitively frame a picture of what you think you might be doing twelve to eighteen months from now, or what the nature of your job will look like at that point, what would that trigger? At this level, which is subtler, there may be things personally you need to let go of, and people and systems that may need to be developed to allow the transition. And as the job itself is a moving target, given the shifting sands of the professional world these days, there may need to be projects defined to ensure viability of the outputs in your area.

In the personal arena, this is where you would want to consider things like: "My career is going to stagnate unless I assert my own goals more specifically to my boss [or my boss's boss]." Or "What new things are my children going to be doing in the next couple of years, and what do I need to do differently because of that?" Or

"What preparation do I need to ensure that I can deal with this health problem we've just uncovered?"

Through a longer scope you might assess: How is your career going? How is your personal life moving along? What is your organization doing relative to changes in the environment, and what impact does that have on you? These are the one-to-five-year-horizon questions that, when I ask them, elicit different and important kinds of answers from everyone.

I coached someone in a large international bank who, after a few months of implementing this methodology and getting control of his day-to-day inventory of work, decided the time was right to invest in his own start-up high-tech firm. The thought had been too intimidating for him to address initially, but working from the Ground level up made it much more accessible and a natural consequence of thinking at this horizon. I recently heard of his phenomenal success in the new endeavor.

If you're involved in anything that has a future of longer than a year (marriage, kids, career, a company, an art form, a lifelong passion), you would do well to think about what you might need to be doing to manage things along that vector.

Questions to ask are:

- What are the longer-term goals and objectives in my organization, and what projects do I need to have in place related to them to fulfill my responsibilities?
- What longer-term goals and objectives have I set for myself, and what projects do I need to have in place to make them happen?
- What other significant things are happening that could affect my options about what I'm doing?

Let me emphasize here that setting new goals or raising your standards is not what I'm specifically advocating. I am, rather, directing your focus to what may be inherently true about these situations within your current reality. If they are there in any obvious or subtle way, then addressing them appropriately will be critical to getting into your own clear space.

Here are some examples of the kinds of issues that show up at this level of conversation:

The changing nature of your job, given the shifting priorities of the company. Instead of managing the production of your own training programs in-house, you're going to outsource them to vendors.

The direction in which you feel you need to move in your career. You see yourself doing a different kind of job a year from now, and you need to make a transition out of the one you have while exploring the options for a transfer or promotion.

The organization's direction, given globalization and expansion. You see a lot of major international travel looming on the horizon for you, and given your lifestyle preferences, you need to consider how to readjust your career plans.

Lifestyle preferences and changing needs. As your kids get older, your need to be at home with them is diminishing, and your interest in investment and retirement planning is growing.

At the topmost level of thinking you'll need to ask some of the ultimate questions: Why does your company exist? Why do *you* exist? What is the core DNA of your existence, personally and/or organizationally, that drives your choices? This is the big-picture stuff with which hundreds of books and gurus and models are devoted to helping you grapple.

Why? This is the great question with which we all struggle.

You can have all the other levels of your life and work shipshape, defined, and organized to a T. Still, if you're the slightest bit off course in terms of what at the deepest level you want or are called to be doing, you're going to be uncomfortable.

Getting Priority Thinking off Your Mind

Take at least a few minutes, if you haven't already done so, to jot down some informal notes about things that occurred to you while you were reading this chapter. Whatever popped into your mind at these more elevated levels of your inner radar, write it down and get it out of your head.

Then process those notes. Decide whether what you wrote down is something you really want to move on or not. If not, throw the note away, or put it on a Someday/Maybe list or in a folder called "Dreams and Goals I Might Get Around to at Some Point." Perhaps you want to continue accumulating more of this kind of future thinking and would like to do the exercise with more formality—for example, by drafting a new business plan with your partners, designing and writing out your idea of a dream life with your spouse, creating a more specific career map for the next three years for yourself, or just getting a personal coach who can lead you through those discussions and thought processes. If so, put that outcome on your Projects list, and decide the next action. Then do it, hand it off to get done, or put the action reminder on the appropriate list.

> *Neutral is a state where you are not jumping ahead too quickly or moving too slow. Neutral does not mean being inactive, complacent, or passive. It's about a calm poise that allows for new information and new possibilities to emerge before taking further action. When in neutral you actually increase your sensitivity and intuitive intelligence. Neutral is fertile ground for new possibilities to grow from.*
>
> *—Doc Childre*

With that done, you may want to turn your focus to developmental thinking about specific projects that have been identified but not fleshed out as fully as you'd like. You'll want to ensure that you're set up for that kind of vertical processing.

10

Getting Projects Under Control

CHAPTERS 4 THROUGH 9 have given you all the tricks and methods you need to clear your head and make intuitive choices about what to do when. That's the horizontal level—what needs your attention and action across the horizontal landscape of your life. The last piece of the puzzle is the vertical level—the digging deep and pie-in-the-sky thinking that can leverage your creative brainpower. You may indeed have clarified outcomes and next-action steps for the various projects and situations in which you're involved, but there are times when you will feel called to enhance your relationship with some of them with more creative thinking and detailed how-to development.

That gets us back to refining and energizing our project planning.

The Need for More Informal Planning

After years of working with thousands of professionals down in the trenches, I can safely say that virtually all of us could be doing more planning, more informally and more often, of our projects and our lives. And if we did, it would relieve a lot of pressure on our psyches and produce an enormous amount of creative output with minimal effort.

> *The middle of every successful project looks like a disaster.*
>
> —*Rosabeth Moss Kanter*

I've discovered that the biggest improvement opportunity in planning does not consist of techniques for the highly elaborate and complex kinds of project organizing that professional project managers sometimes use (like Gantt charts). Most of the people who need those already have them, or at least have access to the training and software required to learn about them. The real need is to capture and utilize more of the creative, proactive thinking we do—or *could* do.

The major reason for the lack of this kind of effective value-added thinking is the dearth of easily structured and usable systems for managing the potentially infinite amount of detail that could show up as a result. That is why my approach tends to be bottom-up. If you feel out of control with your current actionable commitments, you'll resist focused planning; an unconscious pushback occurs. As you begin to apply these methods, however, you may find that they free up room for enormous creative and constructive thinking. If you have systems and habits ready to leverage your ideas, your productivity can expand exponentially.

> You need to set up systems and tricks that get you to think about your projects and situations more frequently, more easily, and more in depth.

In chapter 3, I covered in some detail the five phases of project planning that take something from the idea stage into physical reality.

What follows is a compilation of practical tips and techniques to facilitate the natural, informal planning processes I recommend. Although these suggestions are all based on common sense, they're not followed by most people nearly as frequently as they could be. Put them to use whenever and as often as you can, instead of saving up your thinking for big formal meetings.

What Projects Should You Be Planning?

Most of the outcomes you have identified for your Projects list will not need any kind of front-end planning, other than the sort you do in your head, quickly and naturally, to come up with a next action on them. The only planning needed for "Get car inspected," for example, would be to decide to check the Internet for the nearest inspection location and set up a time.

There are two types of projects, however, that deserve at least some sort of planning activity: (1) those that still have your attention even after you've determined their next actions, and (2) those about which potentially useful ideas and supportive detail just show up ad hoc.

The first type—the projects that you know have other things about them that must be decided on and organized—will need a more detailed approach than just identifying a next action. For these you'll need a more specific application of one or more of the other four phases of the natural planning model: purpose and principles, vision/outcome, brainstorming, and/or organizing.

The second type—the projects for which ideas just show up, ad hoc, when you're on a beach or in a car or in a meeting—need to have an appropriate place into which these associated ideas can be captured. Then they can reside there for later use as needed.

Projects That Need Next Actions About Planning

There are probably a few projects you can think of right now, off the top of your head, that you know you want to get more objectified, fleshed out, and under control. Perhaps you have an important meeting coming up and you know you have to prepare an agenda and materials for it. Or you've just inherited the job of coordinating the annual associates' conference, and you've got to get it organized as soon as possible so you can start delegating significant pieces. Or you need to think about and handle plans for an upcoming holiday with your family. If you haven't done it already, get a next action *now* that will start the planning process for each of these, and put it on the appropriate action list. Then proceed with further planning steps.

Typical Planning Steps

The most common types of planning-oriented actions will be your own brainstorming and organizing, setting up meetings, and gathering information.

Brainstorming   Some of the projects that have your attention right now will require you to do your own free-form thinking; this is especially true of those for which you were not clear about what the next action would be when you made that decision. These should all have a next action, such as "Draft ideas re X."

You need to decide where and how you want to do that action, in order to know which action list to put it on. Do you do this kind of thinking best on a computer, or by handwriting your thoughts on paper? I may choose either medium, depending on what my intuition tells me. For me this next action would go either on my "At Computer" list or on "Anywhere" (because I can draw mind maps or take rough notes wherever I am, as long as I have pen and paper).

Organizing You may have some projects for which you have already collected notes and miscellaneous support materials, and you just need to sort through them and get them into a more structured form. In this case, your next action would likely be "Organize Project X notes." If you have to be in your office to do that (because that's where the files are, and you don't want to carry them around), that action should go on your "At Office" action list. If you're carrying the project notes around with you in a folder, or in some digital device, then the "Organize . . ." action would go on an "Anywhere" action list if you're going to do it by hand, or on "At Computer" if you're going to use a word processing or outlining program, or presentation, mind-mapping, or project-planning software.

> One of the greatest blocks to organizational (and family) productivity is the lack of decision by someone about the need for a meeting, and with whom, to move something forward.

Setting Up Meetings Often the next progress to be made on project thinking is to set up a meeting with the people you'd like to have involved in the brainstorming and/or decision making. That usually means sending an e-mail to the whole group or to an assistant to get it calendared, or making a phone call to the primary person to nail down a day and time.

Gathering Information Sometimes the next task on project thinking is to gather more data. Maybe you need to talk to someone to get his or her input ("Call Bill re his thoughts on the managers' meeting"). Or you need to look through the files you just inherited from last year's conference ("Review Associate Conference archive files"). Or you want to surf the Web to get a sense of what's happening "out there" on a new topic you're exploring ("Look into college scholarship funds").

Random Project Thinking

Don't lose any ideas about projects that could potentially be useful. Many times you'll think of something you don't want to forget when you're in a place that has nothing to do with the project. You're driving to the store, for example, and you think of a great way to start off the next staff meeting. Or you're stirring the spaghetti sauce in the kitchen and it occurs to you that you might want to give out nice tote bags to participants in the upcoming conference. Or you're watching the evening news when you suddenly remember another key person you may want to include in the advisory council you're putting together.

If these aren't specifically next actions that can go directly on your action lists, you'll still need to capture and organize them somewhere that makes sense. Of course, the most critical tool for ensuring that nothing gets lost is your collection system—your in-tray, pen and paper, or smartphone. You need to hold all your ideas until you later decide what to do with them.

Tools and Structures That Support Project Thinking

No matter at what level project ideas show up, it's great to have good tools always close at hand for capturing them as they occur. Once they've been captured, it's useful to have access to them whenever you need to refer to them.

Thinking Tools

One of the great secrets to getting ideas and increasing your productivity is utilizing the function-follows-form phenomenon—great tools can trigger good thinking. (I've come up with some of my most productive thoughts when simply exploring a new software application that created an interesting or fun way to generate and capture data.)

> *Luck affects everything. Let your hook always be cast; in the stream where you least expect it there will be fish.*
>
> —*Ovid*

If you aren't writing anything down, or inputting into a digital device, it's extremely difficult to stay focused on anything for more than a few minutes, especially if you're by yourself. But when you utilize physical tools to keep your thinking anchored and saved, you can stay engaged constructively for hours.

Writing Instruments

Keep good writing tools around all the time so you never have any unconscious resistance to thinking due to not having anything to capture it with. If I don't have something to write with or text or type into, I know I'm not as comfortable letting myself think progressively about projects and situations.

> Function often follows form. Give yourself a context for capturing thoughts, and thoughts will occur that you don't yet know you have.

Conversely, I have done some great thinking and planning at times just because I wanted to use my great-feeling, smooth-writing fountain or gel pen! You may not be inspired by cool gear like I am, but if you are, do yourself a favor and invest in quality writing tools.

I also suggest that you keep nice pens at each of the stations where you're likely to want to take notes—at your desk(s), in the kitchen, in your briefcases, satchels, purses, and backpacks.

Paper and Pads

In addition to writing tools, you should always have their functional equivalent—pads of paper—close at hand. Perforated paper is preferable to solid notebooks, because you want to be able to tear off pages with ideas and notes and toss them into your in-tray until you get a chance to process them. Also, you may find it valuable to keep some of your early and informal jotted mind maps and notes (original or scanned) in appropriate files. The handwritten trails often contain rich context memory jogs that prove valuable later on.

> Where is your closest writing pad? Keep it closer.

Easels and Whiteboards

If you have room for them, whiteboards and/or easel pads are very functional thinking tools to use from time to time. They give you plenty of space on which to jot down ideas, and it can be useful to keep them up in front of you for a while, as you incubate on a topic. Whiteboards are great to have on a wall in your office and in meeting rooms, and the bigger the better. Some companies have designed whole internal walls as erasable writing surfaces, fostering brainstorming and ad hoc visual communications. If you have children, I recommend that you install one in their bedrooms (I wish I had grown up with the encouragement to have as many ideas as I could!). Be sure to keep plenty of fresh markers on hand—nothing stifles creative thinking faster than dry and useless writing tools.

> *How do I know what I think, until I hear what I say?*
>
> —*E. M. Forster*

Whenever two or more people are gathered for a meeting, someone should start writing somewhere where the other(s) can see. Even if you erase the thoughts after a few minutes, just the act of writing them down facilitates a constructive thinking process like nothing else. (I've found it immensely helpful at times to draw informal diagrams and notes on paper tablecloths, place mats, or even napkins in restaurants, if I didn't have my own pad of paper at hand.)

Thinking in Your Digital Tools

Many times I like to think on my laptop (and, less frequently, on my tablet), within my word processing, mind-mapping, outlining, presentation, or spreadsheet programs. There are so many things I might want to do later on with my thinking, and it feels terrific to already have it in some digital form for later editing, and cutting and pasting into various other applications. Once I've booted up and the screen is ready in front of me, I find that thinking just automatically starts to happen. This is another good reason to ensure that your typing and keyboard skills are sufficient to make engaging with the computer at least easy, if not downright fun.

Just as larger whiteboards facilitate more creative connections and expanded thought horizons, I have found that larger and additional computer screens provide a similar usefulness. As the world has rapidly become both digital and mobile, people have understandably experienced a tremendous increase in access and efficiency with their ever-smaller devices. I suggest, however, that the value of smartphones and the like is for the execution of the *results* of thinking—not for generating creative thought.* For that I want *more* space, not less.

The Support Structures

In addition to good tools ubiquitously at hand, it is productive to have accessible formats into which project thinking can be captured. Much as a good pen and paper in front of you support brainstorming, having good tools and places for organizing project details facilitates the more linear planning that many projects need.

Create File Folders or Loose-Leaf Pages as Needed

A good general-reference filing system, right at hand and easy to use, is not only critical to manage the general workflow process, but highly functional for project thinking as well. Often a project begins to emerge when it's triggered by relevant data, notes, and miscellaneous materials, and for this reason,

> If you don't have a good system for storing bad ideas, you probably don't have one for filing good ones, either.

you'll want to create a folder for a topic as soon as you have something to put in it. If your filing system is too formal (or nonexistent), you'll probably miss many opportunities to generate a project focus sufficiently early. As soon as you return from that first meeting with your initial notes about a topic that has just emerged on the horizon, create a file and store them in it right away (after you have gleaned any next actions, of course).

---

*A great use of the camera function in smartphones is to snap pictures of whiteboard and easel-pad thinking, so that can be erased for further brainstorming and the results channeled back to the participants for whatever use they might want to make of it.

Many times, while coaching clients, I find that the mere act of creating a file for a topic into which we can organize random notes and potentially relevant materials gives them a significantly improved sense of control. It's a way of physically, visibly, and psychologically getting their "arms around it."

If you like to work with a loose-leaf notebook or planner, it's good to keep an inventory of fresh notepaper or graph paper that you can use to set up a page on a theme or project as it shows up. While some projects may later deserve a whole tabbed section or even an entire notebook of their own, they don't start out that way. And most of your projects may need only a page or two to hold the few ideas you need to track.

Paper Versus Digital

For those who have become increasingly digitally oriented, it is tempting to try to eliminate paper altogether. Theoretically that shouldn't be a problem, with all the digital note-taking, scanning, and character-recognition tools available. In practice, however, paper still provides high value for most of us. Handwritten note taking is not going away, for multiple reasons, not the least of which is the universality of the tools and the range of graphic representations available. We tend to think differently when we express with different equipment, and many people find that writing and drawing by hand unwraps a broader palette of ideas.

Also, paper-based materials allow us to be reminded of information, relationships, and perspectives more readily than what we can see at any one time on a computer screen. I personally know of many digitally savvy people who have returned to using paper planners and notebooks because they found them easier to use to coordinate their own thinking and reminders. Many times I will print documents related to a person, project, or topic, which I then hold in a physical file folder to use in a meeting or for my own writing and research. Though much of that paper will be recycled and the updated information returned to a digital home, the physical materials in the interim serve a function of which the computer by itself is still incapable.

Digital technology will undoubtedly continue to emerge, which will contribute vastly to thinking, planning, and decision support in ways that low-tech materials and tools cannot. But until pens, notepads, Post-its, physical folders, and printed documents can be replaced by something better, they will still need to play some part in your coordinated personal management system.*

Software Tools

I have yet to discover any one perfect project-management tool. The plethora of applications that purport to serve that function are usually either too high-powered or too simplistic for what most of us need to manage. And as I've noted, I have never seen any two projects that needed the same amount of detailing and structure to get them under control. So it would be difficult to create any one application that would suffice for the majority. The rest of us usually find bits and pieces of applications more informal and project-friendly.

That said, there are multiple kinds of digital tools that can be extremely useful. Most professionals are familiar with word processing programs, spreadsheets, and presentation programs, any of which might be the optimal way to structure project plans or portions thereof, especially once the purpose, vision, and brainstorming phases have been handled.

The two types of software that tend to be more useful for informal planning and brainstorming are mind-mapping and outlining applications. I personally use a digital mind-mapping tool for most all of my projects as a way both to do focused brainstorming and to capture random thoughts about the projects as they show up ad hoc. In most cases the final mind map itself is sufficient organization for me to feel comfortable that I have the project under control.

Another option for brainstorming is an outlining program, which allows the creation of headings and subheadings, in limited or expanded detail. Most good word processing programs also provide this functionality. The nice thing about these programs is that they

---

*What if paper was *just* discovered? Wow! Something that allows you a visual map of your digital information, which you can manipulate and communicate physically and visually? And something that can capture, facilitate, and share creative thinking, without batteries or electricity? Wow.

DIGITAL OUTLINING

can handle a wide range of complexity—from the simplest few bullet points about organizing a party to generating the structure for a whole book you're writing. Though outlining and word processing programs tend to support more structured thinking, because of the ease of cutting, pasting, and rearranging text in the digital world, they still allow for plenty of creative thought development.

On the high end of the spectrum is complex project-management software. Professionals and organizations that have very specific needs for which the rigor and details managed by those applications are required usually have and use these tools already, in order to function. And they are most often customized for company-specific projects. This is the software that is used to launch Mars probes, coordinate building construction, and deliver airplanes and pharmaceuticals.

On the lowest end of the digital project-management scale is jotting ideas in the Notes section of a Task item that lists one of your projects, or using generic note-generating and organizing software, creating a note for a project with its associated thoughts.

If you are computer savvy, you will no doubt use several of these modalities for developing and capturing project plans and collateral material. Make sure you create comfort with the applications, so you can focus more on your project thinking than on the software. It will also behoove you to do regular reviews and updating of this content, wherever it is, and keep it current with consistent purging and reorganizing. Remember that the computer is a bit of a black hole, and as memory and storage capacity continue to expand and new cool applications for pieces of this functionality continue to proliferate, it becomes easier to keep *everything* and then lose a coordinated orientation of your active stuff.

How Do I Apply All This in My World?

Clear the deck, create a context, and do some creative project thinking. You'll then be way ahead of most people.

Just as your Next Actions lists need to be up-to-date, so, too, does your Projects list. That done, give yourself a block of time, ideally between one and three hours, to handle as much of the vertical thinking about each project as you can.

At the very least, right now or as soon as possible, take those few of your projects that you have the most attention on or interest in right now and do some thinking, collecting, and organizing on them, using whatever tools seem most appropriate.

Focus on each, one at a time, top to bottom. As you do, ask yourself, "What about this do I want to know, capture, or remember?"

Let our advance worrying become our advance thinking and planning.

—Winston Churchill

You may just want to mind-map some thoughts on a piece of paper, make a file, and toss the paper into it. You may come up with some simple bullet-point headings to attach as a note in your digital/mobile organizer. Or you could create a word processing document and start an outline on it.

The key is to get comfortable with having and using your ideas. And to acquire the habit of focusing your energy constructively, on intended outcomes and open loops, before you *have* to.

part

The Power of the
Key Principles

11

The Power of the Capturing Habit

THERE'S MUCH MORE to these simple techniques and models than may appear at first glance. Indeed, they offer a systematic method to keep your mind distraction-free, ensuring a high level of efficiency and effectiveness in your work. That in itself would be sufficient reason to implement these practices.

> Demonstrating integrity in managing internal and external agreements optimizes all of your relationships.

But there are even greater implications for the fundamental principles at work here. What follows in the next three chapters is an accounting of my experience, over the past thirty years, of the subtler and often more profound effects that can transpire from the implementation of these basic principles. The longer-term results can have a significant impact on you as an individual, and they can positively affect larger organizational cultures as well.

When people with whom you interact notice that without fail you receive, process, and organize in an airtight manner the exchanges and agreements they have with you, they begin to trust you in a unique way. More significantly, you incorporate a level of self-confidence in your engagement with your world that money cannot buy. Such is the power of capturing placeholders for anything that is incomplete or unprocessed in your life. It noticeably enhances your mental well-being and improves the quality of your communications and relationships, both personally and professionally.

And when organizations expect and reinforce this best practice of allowing nothing to fall through a communication crack, with everyone accountable for resulting actions, and commitments clarified and tracked by the appropriate persons, it can significantly increase a culture's productivity and reduce its stress.

The Personal Benefit

How did it feel to go through the collecting and downloading activity? Most people say it feels so bad, and yet so good. How can that be?

If you're like most people who go through the full capturing process, you probably felt some form of anxiety. Descriptive terms like *overwhelmed*, *panic*, *frustration*, *fatigue*, and *disgust* tend to come up when I ask seminar participants to describe their emotions in going through a minor version of this procedure. And is there anything you think you've procrastinated on in that stack? If so, you have guilt automatically associated with it—"I could have, should have, ought to have done this before now."

At the same time, did you experience any sense of release, or relief, or control as you did the drill? Most people say yes, indeed. How does that happen? Totally opposite emotional states showing up as you're doing a single exercise, almost at the same time—anxiety and relief; overwhelmed and in control. What's going on here?

When you understand the source of your negative feelings about all your stuff, you'll discover, as I did, the way to get rid of them. And if you experienced any positive feelings from collecting your stuff, you actually began the process of eliminating the negativity yourself.

The Source of the Negative Feelings

Where do the not-so-good feelings come from? Too much to do? No, there's always too much to do. If you felt bad simply because there was more to do than you could do, you'd never get rid of that feeling. Having too much to do is not the source of the negative feeling. It comes from a different place.

How have you felt when someone broke an agreement with you, told you they would meet you Thursday at four p.m. and never showed or called? How did that feel? Frustrating, I imagine. The price people pay when they break an agreement in the world is the disintegration of trust in the relationship—an automatic negative consequence.

> The sense of anxiety and guilt doesn't come from having too much to do; it's the automatic result of breaking agreements with yourself.

But what are all those things in your in-tray? Agreements you've made or at least implicitly accepted with yourself—things you somehow have told yourself you should deal with in some way. Your negative feelings are simply the result of breaking those agreements—they're the symptoms of disintegrated self-trust. If you tell yourself to draft a strategic plan, when you don't do it, you feel bad. Tell yourself to get organized, and if you fail to, welcome to guilt and frustration. Resolve to spend more time with your kids and then don't—voila! anxious and overwhelmed.

How Do You Prevent Broken Agreements with Yourself?

If the negative feelings come from broken agreements, you have three options for dealing with them and eliminating the negative consequences:

• Don't make the agreement.
• Complete the agreement.
• Renegotiate the agreement.

All of these can work to get rid of the unpleasant feelings.

Don't Make the Agreement

It probably felt pretty good to take a bunch of your old stuff, decide that you weren't going to do anything with it, and just shred, recycle, or toss it into the trash. One way to handle an incompletion in your world is to just say *no!*

You'd lighten up a lot if you would just lower your standards. If you didn't care so much about things being up to a certain level—your parenting, your school system, your team's morale, the software code—you'd have fewer things to do or have attention on.*

I doubt you're going to lower your standards. But once you

---

*It has been a popular concept in the self-help world that focusing on your values will simplify your life. I contend the opposite: the overwhelming amount of things that people have to do *comes from* their values. Values are critical elements for meaning and direction and decision making. But don't kid yourself—the more you focus on them, the more things you're likely to feel responsible for taking action on. Your values make it easier for you to make choices, but don't think they will make things any simpler.

Maintaining an objective and complete inventory of your work, regularly reviewed, makes it much easier to say no with integrity.

really understand the consequences, you'll probably make fewer agreements. I know I did. I used to make a lot of them, just to win people's approval. When I realized the price I was paying on the back end for not keeping those agreements, I became a lot more conscious about the ones I made. One insurance executive I worked with described the major benefit he derived from implementation of this system: "Previously I would just tell everyone, 'Sure, I'll do it,' because I didn't know how much I really had to do. Now that I've got the inventory clear and complete, just to maintain my integrity, I have had to say, 'No, I can't do that, I'm sorry.' The amazing thing is that instead of being upset with my refusal, everyone was impressed with my discipline!"

Another client, an entrepreneur in the personal coaching business, recently told me that making an inventory of his work had eliminated a huge amount of worry and stress from his life. The discipline of putting everything he had his attention on into his in-tray caused him to reconsider what he really wanted to do *anything* about. If he wasn't willing to toss a note about it into "in," he just let it go!

I consider that very mature thinking. One of the best things about this whole method is that when you really take on the responsibility to capture and track what's on your mind, you'll think twice about making commitments internally that you don't really need or want to make. In my many years of working with people to get their list of Projects clear and current, every single person has decided that something was not worth doing that they thought they were committed to. Not being aware of all you have to do is much like having a credit card for which you don't know the balance or the limit—it's a lot easier to be careless with your commitments.

Complete the Agreement

Of course, another way to get rid of the negative feelings about your stuff is to just finish it and be able to mark it off as done. You actually love to *do* things, as long as you get the feeling that you've completed something. If you've begun to take less-than-two-minute actions as they surface in your life, I'm sure you can attest to the psychological benefit. Most people I work with feel fantastic after just a couple of hours of processing their piles, simply because of how many things they accomplish using the two-minute rule.

One of your better weekends may be spent just finishing up a lot of little errands and tasks that have accumulated around your house and in your personal

> Out of the strain of the doing, into the peace of the done.
> —*Julia Louise Woodruff*

life. Invariably when you capture all the open loops, little and big, and see them on a list in front of you, some part of you will be inspired (or creatively disgusted or intimidated enough) to go knock them off the list.

We all seem to be starved for a win. It's great to satisfy that by giving yourself doable tasks you can start and finish easily. Have you ever completed something that wasn't initially on a list, so you wrote it down and checked it off? Then you know what I mean.

There's another issue here, however. How would you feel if your list and your stack were totally—and successfully—completed? You'd probably be bouncing off the ceiling, full of creative energy. Of course, within three days (if not three minutes!), guess what you'd have? Right—another list, and probably an even bigger one, with more potentially daunting things to do on it! You'd feel so good about finishing all your stuff you'd likely take on bigger, more ambitious things to do.

Not only that, but if you have a boss (or a board), what do you think he or she or they are going to do after noticing the high levels of competency and productivity you're demonstrating? Right again—give you more things to do! It's the irony of professional development—the better you get, the better you'd *better* get.

So, since you're not going to significantly lower your standards or stop creating more things to do, you'd better get comfortable with the third option, if you want to keep from being stressed out.

Renegotiate the Agreement

Suppose I'd told you I would meet you Thursday at four p.m., but after I made the appointment, my world changed. Now, given my new priorities, I decide I'm *not* going to meet you Thursday at four. But instead of simply not showing up, what had I better do, to maintain the integrity of the relationship? Correct—call and change the agreement. A renegotiated agreement is not a broken one.

It is the act of forgiveness that opens up the only possible way to think creatively about the future at all.

—*Father Desmond Wilson*

Do you understand yet why getting all your stuff out of your head and in front of you makes you feel better? Because you automatically renegotiate your agreements with yourself when you look at them, think about them, and either act on them that very moment or say, "No, not now." Here's the problem: it's impossible to renegotiate agreements with yourself that you can't remember you made!

The fact that you can't remember an agreement you made with yourself doesn't mean that you're not holding yourself liable for it. Ask any psychologist how much of a sense of past and future that part of your psyche has, the part that was storing the list you dumped: zero. It's all present tense in there. That means that as soon as you tell yourself that you should do something, if you file it only in your short-term memory, that part of you thinks you should be doing it *all the time*. And *that* means that as soon as you've given yourself two things to do, and filed them only in your head, you've created instant and automatic stress and failure, because you can't do them both at once, and that (apparently significant) part of your psyche will continue to hold you accountable.

If you're like most people, you've probably got some storage area at home—maybe a basement that you told yourself a while back (maybe even ten years ago!) you ought to clean and organize. If so, there's a part of you that likely thinks you should've been cleaning your basement twenty-four hours a day for the past ten years! No wonder people are so tired! And have you heard that little voice inside your own mental committee every time you walk by that area? "Why are we walking by the basement? Aren't we supposed to be cleaning it?" Because you can't stand that whining, nagging part of yourself, you never even go into that area anymore if you can help it. If you want to shut that voice up, you have three options for dealing with your agreement with yourself:

1 | Lower your standards about your garage (you may have done that already). "So I have a crappy garage . . . who cares?"
2 | Keep the agreement—clean the garage.
3 | At least put "Clean garage" on a "Someday/Maybe" list. Then, when you review that list weekly and you see that item, you

can tell yourself, "Not this week." The next time you walk by your garage, you won't hear a thing internally, other than "Ha! Not this week."

I'm quite sincere about this. It seems that there's a part of our consciousness that doesn't know the difference between an agreement about cleaning the basement and an agreement about buying a company or improving our personal finances. In there, they're all just agreements—kept or broken. If you're holding something only internally, it will be a broken agreement if you're not moving on it in the moment.

The Radical Departure from Traditional Time Management

This method is significantly different from traditional time-management training. Most of those models leave you with the impression that if something you tell yourself to do isn't that important, it's not worth it to track, manage, or deal with. But in my experience that's inaccurate, at least in terms of how a less-than-conscious part of us operates. It *is* how our conscious mind operates, however, so every agreement must be made conscious. That means it must be captured, clarified, and reviewed objectively and regularly in full conscious awareness so that you can put it where it belongs in your self-management arena. If that doesn't happen, it will actually take up a lot more of your internal energy than it deserves.

In my experience, anything that is held only in your head will take up either more or less attention than it deserves. The reason to collect everything is not that everything is equally important; it's that it's *not*. Incompletions, uncaptured, take on a dull sameness in the sense of the pressure they create and the attention they tie up.

How Much Capturing Is Required?

You'll feel better collecting *anything* that you haven't captured yet. When you say to yourself, "Oh, that's right, I need to get butter the next time I'm at the store," and you write it on your grocery list, you'll feel better. When you remember, "I've got to call my financial adviser about the trust fund," and you write that down someplace

When the only thing on your mind is the only thing on your mind, you'll be "present," in your "zone," with no distinction between work and play.

where you know you'll see it when you have a phone and time, you'll feel better. But there's still a light-year's difference when you know you have it *all*.

When will you know how much you have left in your head to capture? Only when there's nothing left. If some part of you is even vaguely aware that you don't have it all, you can't really know what percentage you have collected. How will you know when there's nothing left? When nothing else shows up as a reminder in your mind.

This doesn't mean that your mind will be empty. If you're conscious, your mind will always be focusing on something. But if it's focusing on only one thing at a time, without distraction, you'll be in your "zone."

I suggest that you use your mind to think *about* things, rather than think *of* them. You want to be adding value as you think about projects and situations, not creating stress by simply reminding yourself they exist and you need to do something about them. To fully realize that more productive place, you will need to capture it all. It takes focus and a change of habit to train yourself to recognize and download even the smallest agreements with yourself as they're created in your mind. Doing the capturing process as fully as you can, and then incorporating the behavior of gathering all the new things as they emerge, will be more empowering and productive than you can imagine.

When Relationships and Organizations Have the Capture Habit

What happens when everyone involved on a team—in a marriage, in a department, on a staff, in a family, in a company—can be trusted not to let anything slip through the cracks? Frankly, once you've achieved that, you'll hardly think about whether people are dropping the ball anymore—there will be much bigger and better things to occupy your attention.

But if communication gaps are still an issue, there's likely some layer of frustration and a general nervousness in the relationship or the culture. Most people feel that without constant babysitting and hand-holding, things could disappear in the system and then blow up at any time. They don't realize that they're feeling this because they've been in this situation so consistently that they relate to it as if it were a permanent law, like gravity. It doesn't have to be that way.

> Having to bail water in a leaky boat undermines your ability to direct it and move it forward.

I have noticed this for years. Good people who haven't incorporated these behaviors come into my environment, and they stick out like a sore thumb. I've lived with the standards of a clear head and hard, clean edges on in-trays for more than three decades now. When a note sits idle in someone's in-tray unprocessed, or when he or she nods, "Yes, I will," in a conversation but doesn't otherwise capture that in some way, my "uh-oh" bell rings. This is unacceptable behavior in my world. There are much bigger fish to fry than worrying about leaks in the system.

I need to trust that any request or relevant information I put in an e-mail, on a voice mail, in a conversation, or in a written note will get into the other person's system and that it will be processed and organized soon, and available for his or her review as an option for action. If the recipient is managing voice mails but not e-mail and paper, I have now been hamstrung to use only his or her trusted medium. That should be unacceptable behavior in any organization that cares about whether things happen with the least amount of effort.

When change is required, there must be trust that the initiatives for that change will be dealt with appropriately. Any intact system will ultimately be only as good as its weakest link, and often that Achilles' heel is a key person's dulled responsiveness to communications in the system.

I especially notice this when I walk around organizations where in-trays are either nonexistent or overflowing and obviously long unprocessed. These cultures usually suffer from serious "interrupt-itis" because they can't trust putting communications into the system. I come across executives whose calendars are insanely overbooked but who, when they begin to give timely responses to their e-mails, experience a dramatic relief from that pressure. When their staff and others are getting what they need in terms of appropriate feedback and decisions through that virtual medium, they no longer need the kind of face-to-face time they previously tried to get with meetings.

Where cultures do have solid systems, down through the low-tech level of paper communications, the clarity is palpable. It's hardly even a conscious concern, and everyone's attention is more focused. The same is true in families that have installed in-trays—the parents, the children, the nanny, the housekeeper, or anyone else with whom family members frequently interact. People often grimace when I tell them that my wife and I put things in each other's in-trays, even when we're sitting within a few feet of each other; to them it seems cold and mechanical. Aside from being an act of politeness intended to avoid interrupting the other's work in progress, the practice actually fosters more warmth and freedom between us, because mechanical things are being handled in the system instead of tying up our attention on the relationship.

Unfortunately, you can't legislate personal systems. Everyone must have his or her own way to deal with what he or she has to deal with.

> Organizations must create a culture in which it is acceptable that everyone has more to do than he or she can do, and in which it is sage to renegotiate agreements about what everyone is *not* doing.

You can, however, hold people accountable for outcomes, and for tracking and managing everything that comes their way. And you can give them the information in this book. Then, at least, they'll have no excuse for letting something fall through the cracks.

This doesn't mean that everyone has to do everything. I hope I have described a way to relate to our knowledge-based world that provides room for everyone to have a lot more to do than he or she *can* do. The critical issue will be to facilitate a constant renegotiation process with all involved, so they feel OK about what they're *not* doing. That's real knowledge work, at a more sophisticated level. But there's little hope of getting there without having bulletproof capture systems in play. Remember, you can't renegotiate an agreement with yourself that you can't remember you made. And you certainly can't renegotiate agreements with others that you and they have lost track of.

When groups of people collectively adopt the 100 percent capture standard, they have a tight ship to sail. It doesn't mean they're sailing in the right direction, or even that they're on the right ship; it just means that the one they're on, in the direction it's going, is sailing with the most efficient energy it can.

12

The Power of the
Next-Action Decision

I HAVE A personal mission to make "What's the next action?" part of our global thought process. I envision a world in which no meeting or discussion will end, and no interaction cease, without a clear indication of whether or not some action is needed—and if it is, what it will be, or at least who has accountability for it. I envision organizations adopting a standard that anything that lands in anyone's field of awareness will be evaluated for action required, and the resulting decisions managed appropriately. Imagine the freedom that would provide for people and organizations to focus their attention on bigger issues and opportunities.

> When a culture adopts "What's the next action?" as a standard operating query, there's an automatic increase in energy, productivity, clarity, and focus.

Over the years I have noticed an extraordinary shift in energy and productivity whenever individuals and groups installed "What's the next action?" as a fundamental and consistently asked question. As simple as the query seems, it is still somewhat rare to find it fully operational where it needs to be.

One of the greatest challenges you may encounter is that once you have gotten used to "What's the next action?" for yourself and those around you, interacting with people who aren't asking it can be highly frustrating. It clarifies things so quickly that dealing with people and environments that don't use it can seem nightmarish.

We are all accountable for defining what, if anything, we are committed to make happen as we engage with others and ourselves. And at some point, for any outcome that we have an internal commitment to complete, we must make the decision about the next physical action required. There's a great difference, however, between making that decision when things *show* up and doing it when they *blow* up.

The Source of the Technique

I learned this simple but extraordinary next-action technique more than thirty years ago from a longtime friend and management-consultant mentor of mine, Dean Acheson (no relation to the former U.S. Secretary of State). Dean had spent many prior years consulting with executives and researching what was required to free up the logjams many of them had regarding projects and situations they were involved in, in order to release and galvanize energy for significant change required in their organizations. One day he just started picking up each individual piece of paper on an executive's desk and forcing him to decide what the very next thing was that he had to do to move it forward. The results were so immediate and so profound for the executive that Dean continued for years to perfect a methodology using that same question to process the in-tray. Since then, given what I've developed using Dean's insights, hundreds of thousands of people have been trained and coached with this key concept, and it remains a foolproof technique.

Doing a straightforward, clear-cut task that has a beginning and an end balances out the complexity-without-end that often vexes the rest of my life. Sacred simplicity.

—Robert Fulghum

This thought process is not something we are born doing, nor does it seem to come to us naturally. When you were born, it probably didn't occur to you to ask your mother, "So, what are we doing here, and what's the next action, and who has it?" It is a learned technique of thinking, decision making, and consciously directed focus. It will happen automatically for you when the situation obviously demands it, as in a crisis, or when the pressure in a situation (from the boss, a client, your child, or the unexpected circumstance) forces a next-action decision to avert painful consequences. But incorporating this as a proactive behavior, before the circumstances are so obvious and actions so immediately necessary, is an acquired practice.* Making it a part of your personal and organizational life never fails to improve both your productivity and peace of mind.

Creating the Option of Doing

How could something so simple be so powerful—"What's the next action?"

To help answer that question, I invite you to revisit for a moment your mind-sweep list (see page 115)—or at least to think about all the projects that are probably sitting around in your head. Do you have a sense that any of them haven't been moving along as consistently and productively as they could be? You'll probably admit that yes, indeed, a few have been a little bit stuck.

If you haven't known for sure whether you needed to make a call, send an e-mail, talk to someone, surf the Web about something, or buy an item at the store as the very next thing to move on, it hasn't been getting done. What's ironic is that it would likely require only about ten seconds of thinking to figure out what the next action would be for almost everything on your list. But it's ten seconds of thinking and decision making that most people haven't done about most things on their lists.

For example, someone will have something like "tires" on a list. I then ask, "What's that about?"

He responds, "Well, I need new tires on my car."

"So what's the next action?"

At that point he usually wrinkles up his forehead, ponders for a few moments, and expresses his conclusion: "Well, I need to check the Web for stores and prices for the tires."

That's about how much time and cognitive investment is required to decide what the "doing" would look like on almost everything. It's

---

*I am tempted, but hesitant, to use the word *skill* in this case. We all already have the *ability* to make a next-action decision. We do it all the time, thousands of times a day, but mostly unconsciously. Yet making that decision before we *have* to about things we're committed to move on is a powerful and elegant cognitive behavior pattern that can be learned, practiced, and integrated. It is a core element of "knowledge-work athletics." And most people don't do it in that manner, about even the most important things in their lives.

just the few seconds of focused thinking that most people have not yet done about most of their still unfinished stuff.

The secret of getting ahead is getting started. The secret of getting started is breaking your complex overwhelming tasks into small, manageable tasks, and then starting on the first one.

—*Mark Twain*

It will probably be true, too, that the person who needs tires on his car has had that on his radar for quite a while. It's also likely that he's been on his computer hundreds of times, often with just enough time and energy to take that action. Why didn't he do it? Because in that state of mind, the last thing in the world he felt like doing was considering all his projects, including getting tires, and what their next actions were. In those moments he didn't feel like thinking at all.

What he needed was to have already figured those things out. If he gets that next-action thinking done, then when he happens to have fifteen minutes before a meeting, at his computer, and his energy is about 4.2 out of 10, he can look at the list of things to do and be delighted to see "Research new tires" on it. "That's something I can do and complete successfully!" he'll think, and then he'll actually be motivated to surf the Web about it, just to experience the "win" of completing something useful in the time and energy window he's in. In this context he'd be incapable of starting a large proposal draft for a client, but he has sufficient resources for searching the Internet and getting simple information quickly. It's highly probable that at some point he'll look at a new set of tires on his car and feel on top of the world.

Defining what real doing looks like on the most basic level and organizing placeholder reminders that we can trust are master keys to productivity enhancement and creating a relaxed inner environment.

Often even the simplest things are stuck because we haven't made a final decision yet about the next action. People in my seminars often have things on their lists like "Get a tune-up for the car." Is "Get a tune-up" a next action? Not unless you're walking out to

Without a next action, there remains a potentially infinite gap between current reality and what you need to do.

your car with wrench in hand, dressed to get greasy.

"So, what's the next action?"

"Uh, I need to take the car to the garage. Oh, yeah, I need to find out if the garage can take it. I guess I need to call the garage and make the appointment."

"Do you have the number?"

"Darn, no . . . I don't have the name and number for the garage. Fred recommended that garage to me, and I don't have that information. I knew something was missing in the equation."

And that's often what happens with so many things for so many people. We glance at the project, and some part of us thinks, "I don't quite have all the pieces between here and there." We know something is missing, but we're not sure what it is, so we quit.

"So, what's the next action?"

"I need to get the name and phone number. I guess I could get it from Fred."

"How could you do that?"

"I can e-mail Fred!"

So the next action really is "E-mail Fred for info re: the garage."

Did you notice how many steps had to be tracked back before we got to the real next action on this project? That's typical. Most people have many things just like that on their lists and on their minds.

Why Bright People Procrastinate the Most

It's really the smartest and most sensitive people who have the highest number of undecided things in their lives and on their lists. Why is that? Think of how our bodies respond to the images we hold in our minds. It appears that the nervous system can't tell the difference between a well-imagined thought and reality.

To prove this to yourself, picture walking into a food market and approaching the brightly lit fruit-and-vegetable section. Are you there? OK, now go to the citrus bins—oranges, grapefruits, lemons. Now see the big pile of yellow lemons. There's a cutting board and a knife next to them. Take one of those big yellow lemons and cut it in half lengthwise. Smell that citrus smell! It's

> Bright people have the capability of freaking out faster and more dramatically than anyone else.

really juicy, and there's lemon juice trickling onto the board. Now take a half lemon and cut *that* in half, so you have a quarter lemon wedge in your hands. OK, now—remember how you did this as a kid?—put that quarter of a lemon in your mouth and bite into it! Scrunch!

If you played along with me, you probably noticed that the saliva content in your mouth increased at least a bit. Your body was actually trying to process citric acid! And it was just in your mind. If your body responds to the pictures you give it, how are you likely to feel physically when you think about, say, doing your taxes? Are you sending yourself easy, let's go, completion, success, and "I'm a winner!" pictures? Probably not. For just that reason, what kinds of people would logically be the most resistant to being reminded about a project like that—that is, who would procrastinate the most? Of course, it would be the most creative, sensitive, and intelligent people—because their sensitivity and creativity give them the capability to produce in their minds lurid nightmare scenarios about what might be involved in doing the project, and all the negative consequences that might occur if it isn't done perfectly! They just freak out in an instant and quit!

> *I am an old man, and I have known a great many troubles, but most of them never happened.*
>
> —*Mark Twain*

Who doesn't procrastinate? Often it's the insensitive oafs who just take something and start plodding forward, unaware of all the things that could go wrong. Everyone else tends to get hung up about all kinds of things.

Do my taxes? Oh, no! It's not going to be that easy. It's going to be different this year, I'm sure. I saw the forms—they look different. There are probably new rules I'm going to have to figure out. I might have to read all that damn material. Long form, short form, medium form. File together with my partner? File separate? We'll probably want to claim some new deductions, but if we do we'll have to back them up, and that means we'll need all the receipts. Oh, my God—I don't know if we really have all the receipts we'll need, and what if we didn't have all the receipts but we claimed the deductions anyway and we got audited? Audited? Oh, no—tax fraud! Jail!

And so a lot of people psychologically put themselves in jail, just glancing at their tax forms—because they're so smart, sensitive, and creative. In my many years of coaching individuals, this pattern has been borne out more times than I can count—usually it's the brightest and most sophisticated folks who have the most stuck piles in their offices, homes, e-mail, and heads. Most of the executives I work with have at least several big, complex, and amorphous projects stacked either on top of a file cabinet or on a mental shelf. There always seem to be hobgoblin thoughts lurking inside them—"If we don't look at or think about the projects, maybe they'll stay quiet!"

So what's the solution? There's always having a drink. Numb it. Dumb it down. Notice what happens to many people when they get a little alcohol in their brain. It should drop their energy immediately, because it's a depressant; often, though, the energy lifts, at least initially. Why? The alcohol is depressing something—it's shutting down the negative self-talk and

> Ceasing negative imaging will always cause your energy to increase.

uncomfortable visions that are going on in these folks' minds. Of course my energy will increase if I stop depressing myself with overwhelming pictures of not handling something successfully. But the numbing solutions are temporary at best. The stuff doesn't go away. And unfortunately, when we numb ourselves, we can't do it selectively—the source of inspiration and enthusiasm and personal energy also seems to get numbed.

Intelligent Dumbing Down

There is another solution: intelligently dumbing down your brain by figuring out the next action. You'll invariably feel a relieving of pressure about anything you have a commitment to change or do, when you decide on the very next physical action required to move it forward. Nothing, essentially, will change in the world. But shifting your focus to something that your mind perceives as a doable task will create a real increase in positive energy, direction, and motivation.

> *No matter how big and tough a problem may be, get rid of confusion by taking one little step toward solution. Do something.*
>
> *—George F. Nordenholt*

If you have truly captured all the things that have your attention during the mind sweep, go through the list again now and decide on the single very next action to take on every one of them. Notice what happens to your energy.

You are either attracted or repelled by the things on your lists; there isn't any neutral territory. You are either positively drawn toward completing the action or reluctant to think about what it is and resistant to getting involved in it. Often it's simply the next-action decision that makes the difference between the two extremes. Thinking and deciding require energy. And when you notice something unfinished in your world but haven't determined what the next action is yet, you'll tend to be reminded of your fatigue and sense of being overwhelmed! Hence most people's reaction to their own lists and organizers is negative—not because of the contents per se, but rather because sufficient appropriate thinking has yet to be applied to them.

Everything on your lists and in your stacks is either attractive or repulsive to you—there's no neutral ground when it comes to your stuff.

In following up with people who have begun to implement this methodology, I've discovered that one of the subtler ways many of them fall off the wagon is in letting their action lists grow back into lists of tasks or subprojects instead of discrete next actions. They're still ahead of most people because they're actually writing things down, but they often find themselves stuck, and procrastinating, because they've allowed their action lists to harbor items like:

"Meeting with the banquet committee"

"Johnny's birthday"

"Receptionist"

"Slide presentation"

You can only cure retail but you can prevent wholesale.

—Brock Chisholm

In other words, things have morphed back into "stuff" instead of starting at the action level. There are no clear next actions here, and anyone keeping a list filled with items like this would send her brain into overload every time she looked at it.

Is this extra work? Is figuring out the next action on your commitments additional effort that you don't need to expend? No, of course not. If you need to get your car tuned, for instance, you're going to have to figure out that next action at some point anyway. The problem is that most people wait to do it until the next action is "Call the Auto Club for tow truck!"

So when do you think most people really make a lot of their next-action decisions about their stuff—when it shows up, or when it blows up? And do you think there might be a difference in the quality of their lives if they handled this knowledge work on the front end instead of the back? Which do you think is the

Avoiding action decisions until the pressure of the last minute creates huge inefficiencies and unnecessary stress.

more efficient way to move through life—deciding next actions on your projects as soon as they appear on your radar screen and then efficiently grouping them into categories of actions that you get done in certain uniform contexts, or avoiding thinking about what, exactly, needs to be done until it *has* to be done, then sputtering through your actions as you try to catch up and put out the fires?

That may sound exaggerated, but when I ask groups of people to estimate when most of the action decisions are made in their companies, with few exceptions they say, "When things blow up." One of our global corporate clients surveyed its population about sources of stress in its culture, and the number one complaint was the last-minute crisis work consistently promoted by team leaders who failed to make appropriate decisions on the front end.

The Value of a Next-Action Decision-Making Standard

I have had several sophisticated senior executives tell me that installing "What's the next action?" as an operational standard in their organization was transformative in terms of measurable performance output. It changed their culture permanently and significantly for the better.

Why? Because the question forces clarity, accountability, productivity, and empowerment.

Clarity

Too many discussions end with only a vague sense that people know what they have decided and are going to do. But without a clear conclusion that there *is* a next action, much less what it is and who's got it, more often than not a lot of stuff gets left up in the air.

I am frequently asked to facilitate meetings. I've learned the

Talk does not cook rice.

—*Chinese proverb*

hard way that no matter where we are in the conversation, twenty minutes before the agreed end time of the discussion I must force the question: "So what's the next action here?" In my experience, there is usually twenty minutes' worth of clarifying (and sometimes tough decisions) still required to come up with an answer.

This is radical common sense—radical because it often compels discussion at deeper levels than people are comfortable with. "Are we serious about this?" "Do we really know what we're doing here?" "Are we really ready to allocate precious time and resources to this?" It's very easy to avoid these more relevant levels of thinking. What prevents those issues from slipping away into amorphous stuff is forcing the decision about the next action. Some further conversation, exploration, deliberation, and negotiation are often needed to put the topic to rest. The world is too unpredictable these days to permit assumptions about outcomes: we need to take responsibility for moving things to clarity.

You have to have some experience of this to really know what I mean here. If you do, you're probably saying to yourself, "Yes!" If you're not sure what I'm talking about, I suggest that in your next meeting with anyone, you end the conversation with the question, "So what's the next action here?" Then notice what happens.

Accountability

The dark side of collaborative cultures is the allergy they foster to holding anyone responsible for having the ball. "Mine or yours?" is unfortunately not in the common vocabulary of many such organizations. There is a sense that that would be impolite. "We're all in this together" is a worthy sentiment, but seldom a reality in the hard-nosed day-to-day world of work. Too many meetings end with a vague feeling among the players that something ought to happen, and the hope that it's not their personal job to make it so.

The way I see it, what's truly impolite is allowing people to walk away from discussions unclear. Real togetherness of a group is reflected by the responsibility that all take for defining the real things to do and the specific people assigned to do them, so everyone is freed of the angst of still-undecided actions.

Again, if you've been there, you'll know what I'm talking about. If you haven't, test it out—take a small risk and ask, "So what's the next action on this?" at the end of each discussion point in your next staff meeting, or in your next family conversation around the dinner table.

Productivity

Organizations naturally become more productive when they model and train front-end next-action decision making. For all the reasons mentioned, determining the required physical allocation of resources necessary to make something happen as soon as the outcome has been clarified will produce more results sooner, and with less effort.

> *There are risks and costs to a program of action, but they are far less than the long-range risks and costs of comfortable inaction.*
> —*John F. Kennedy*

Learning to break through the barriers of the sophisticated creative thinking that can freeze activity—that is, the entangled mental webs we spin—is a superior skill. "Productivity" has been touted for decades as a desirable thing to improve in organizations. Anything that can help maximize output will do that. But in the world of knowledge work, all the computers and telecom improvements and leadership seminars on the planet will make no difference in this regard unless the individuals involved increase their operational responsiveness. And that requires thinking about something that lands in your world *before* you have to.*

> Productivity will improve only when individuals increase their operational responsiveness. And in knowledge work, that means clarifying actions on the front end instead of the back.

---

*One of the biggest productivity leaks I have seen in some organizations is the lack of next actions determined for long-term projects. Long-term does not mean "someday/ maybe." Those projects with distant goal lines are still to be done as soon as possible; long-term simply means "more action steps until it's done," not "no need to decide next actions because the day of reckoning is so far away." When every project and open loop in an organization is being monitored, it's a whole new ball game.

Empowerment

Perhaps the greatest benefit of adopting the next-action approach is that it dramatically increases your ability to make things happen, with a concomitant rise in your self-esteem and constructive outlook.

Start by doing what's necessary, then what's possible, and suddenly you are doing the impossible.

—*Saint Francis of Assisi*

People are constantly doing things, but usually only when they have to, under fire from themselves or others. They get no sense of winning, or of being in control, or of cooperating among themselves and with their world. People are starving for those experiences.

The daily behaviors that define the things that are incomplete and the moves that are needed to complete them must change. Getting things going of your own accord, before you're forced to by external pressure and internal stress, builds a firm foundation of self-worth that will spread to every aspect of your life. You are the captain of your own ship; the more you act from that perspective, the better things will go for you.

Asking yourself, "What's the next action?" undermines the victim mentality. It presupposes that there is a possibility of change, and that there is something you can do to make it happen. That is the assumed affirmation in the behavior. And these kinds of assumed affirmations often work more fundamentally to build a positive self-image than can repeating, "I am a powerful, effective person, making things happen in my life!" a thousand times.

Is there too much complaining in your culture? The next time someone moans about something, try asking, "So what's the next action?" People will complain only about something that they assume could be better than it currently is. The action question forces the issue. If it can be changed, there's some action that will change it. If it can't, it must be considered part of the landscape to be incorporated in strategy and tactics. Complaining is a sign that someone isn't willing to risk moving on a changeable situation, or won't consider the immutable circum-

People are always blaming their circumstances for what they are. I don't believe in circumstances. The people who get on in this world are the people who get up and look for the circumstances they want, and, if they can't find them, make them.

—*George Bernard Shaw*

stance in his or her plans. This is a temporary and hollow form of self-validation.

Although my colleagues and I rarely promote our work in this way, I notice people really empowering themselves every day as we coach them in applying the next-action technique. It increases the light in their eyes and the lightness in their step, and a sparkle shows up in their thinking and demeanor. We are all already powerful, but deciding on and effectively managing the physical actions required to move things forward seems to exercise that power in ways that call forward the more positive aspects of our nature.

When you start to make things happen, you begin to believe that you can make things happen. And *that* makes things happen.

13

The Power of Outcome Focusing

THE POWER OF directing our mental and imaginative processes to create change has been studied and promoted in thousands of contexts—from early "positive thinking" books to recent discoveries in advanced neurophysiology.

My own interest has been in applying the principle in terms of practical reality: Does it help get things done? And if so, how do we best utilize it in managing the work of our lives? Can we really use this information in ways that allow us to produce what we want to have happen with less effort? The answer has been a resounding yes.

Focus and the Fast Track

Over the years I have seen the application of the method presented in this book create profound results for people in their day-to-day worlds. As you begin to use it habitually as your primary means of addressing all situations—from processing e-mails to buying a house or a company to structuring meetings or having conversations with your kids—your personal productivity can go through the roof.

Many of the professionals I have worked with who integrated this method now find themselves experiencing enhanced or even new jobs, careers, and lifestyles. These processes really work in the arena of the ordinary things we must deal with daily—the stuff of our work. When you demonstrate to yourself and to others an increasing ability to get things done "in the trenches," you probably won't stay in the same trench for very long. Of course, those attracted to implementing *Getting Things Done* are usually already on a self-development path and don't assume that they'll be doing the same things a year from now that they're doing now, anyway. But they love the fact that this method gets them there faster and more easily. It's interesting to note that the people who need this methodology the least are usually the ones who engage with it the quickest and the most. That puzzled me for a while until I realized that one of the most important results of its implementation is the relief of drag (as in "retarding force"). Who is the most interested in that? Those who are the most invested in moving themselves forward, quickly and easily.

It's been inspiring for me to learn and coach others how to deal with the immediate realities down where the rubber meets the road—and how to tie in the power of positive imagery to practical experiences in all our daily lives.

The "fast track" alluded to here is a bit of a misnomer. For some, slowing down, getting out of the squirrel cage, and taking care of themselves may be the major change precipitated by this methodology.* The bottom line is it makes you more conscious, more focused, and more capable of implementing the changes and results you want, whatever they are.

"Create a way to spend more time with my daughter" is as specific a project as any, and equally demanding of a next action to be determined. Having the vague, gnawing sense that you "should" do something about your relationship with your daughter, and not actually doing anything, can be a killer. I often work with people who are willing to acknowledge the real things of their lives at this level as "incompletes"—to write them down, define real projects about them, and ensure that next actions are decided on—until the finish line is crossed. That is real productivity, perhaps in its most awesome manifestation.

The Significance of Applied Outcome Thinking

What I want to emphasize now is how learning to process the details of our work and lives with this clear and consistent system can affect us and others in significant ways we may not expect.

Defining specific projects and next actions that address real quality-of-life issues is productivity at its best.

---

*An interesting phenomenon I have noticed more than once is that for some highly energetic people, incorporating the *Getting Things Done* mind-set turbocharges their busy and creative lifestyle to a new level of discomfort ("Now I can really get a lot *more* done, and faster!"), and they then take the opportunity for healthy self-examination about how important that really is versus more quality-of-life kinds of outcomes they may crave.

As I've said, employing next-action decision making results in clarity, productivity, accountability, and empowerment. Exactly the same results happen when you hold yourself to the discipline of identifying the real results you want and, more specifically, the projects you need to define in order to produce them.

It's all connected. You can't really define the right action until you know the outcome you're after, and your outcome is disconnected from reality if you're not clear about what you need to do physically to make it happen. You can get at it from either direction, and you must, to get things done.

As Steven Snyder, an expert in whole-brain learning and a friend of mine, put it, "There are only two problems in life: (1) you know what you want, and you don't know how to get it; and/or (2) you don't know what you want." If that's true (and I think it is) then there are only two solutions:

• Make it up.
• Make it happen.

This can be construed from the models of yin/yang, right brain/left brain, creator/destroyer, visionary/implementer—or whatever equivalent framework works best for you. The truth is, our energy as human beings seems to have a dualistic and teleological reality—we create and identify with things that aren't yet real on all the levels we experience; and when we do, we recognize how to restructure our current world to morph it into the new one, and experience an impetus to make it so.

We are constantly creating and fulfilling.

Things that have your attention need your *in*tention engaged. "What does this mean to me?" "Why is it here?" "What do I want to have be true about this?" ("What's the desired outcome?") Everything you experience as incomplete must have a reference point for "complete."

Once you've decided that there is something to be changed and a mold to fill, you ask yourself, "How do I now make this happen?" and/or "What resources do I need to allocate to make it happen?" ("What's the next action?")

By this point you've probably noticed that *Getting Things Done* is not some new technology or invention—it simply makes *explicit* the principles at work within what we all do *implicitly*. But with that awareness, you can then leverage those principles consciously to create more elegant results.

Your life and work are made up of outcomes and actions that you engage in more or less consciously. Whether they are merely less-than-conscious responses to your environment or more conscious results of your directed focus is the choice you will always have. If you have any intention to expand your experiences and expressions beyond simply being at the mercy of the world as it comes at you, the opportunity is there to recognize, develop, and master the art of getting things done. The challenge will continually be to apply the two essential elements of this art: defining what *done* means and what *doing* looks like. This is not always that easy, especially when dealing with some of the more subtle and sublime areas of your life experience; but without challenges, you would never learn or grow.

> *Life affords no higher pleasure than that of surmounting difficulties, passing from one step of success to another, forming new wishes, and seeing them gratified.*
>
> —Dr. Samuel Johnson

The good news is that when your operational behavior is grooved to engage with everything that comes your way, at all levels, based upon those dynamics, a deep alignment occurs, and wondrous things emerge. You become highly productive. You make things up, and you make them happen.

> *Wisdom consists not so much in knowing what to do in the ultimate as in knowing what to do next.*
>
> —Herbert Hoover

The Magic of Mastering the Mundane

People often wonder how I can sit with them at their desks, often for hours on end, as they empty their drawers, unpack all their unprocessed e-mails, and painstakingly go through the minutiae of stuff that they have let accumulate in their minds and their physical and virtual spaces. Aside from the common embarrassment they feel about the volume of their irresponsibly dealt-with details, they assume I should be bored to tears. Quite the contrary. Much to my own surprise, I find it to be some of the most engaging work I do with people. I know the release and relief and freedom that sit on the other side of dealing with these things effectively. I know that we all need practice and support and a strong, clear focus to get through them, until we have the built-in standards and behaviors we need to engage with them as they demand. Every time I notice a client identifying something in his environment or mind that is pulling on him and in a few moments he processes it to silence, I know he's deepening a critically important pattern of behavior. And I know how significant a change these people may then experience in their relationships with their bosses, their partners, their spouses, their kids, and themselves over the next few hours and (we hope) days and years.

It's not boring. It's some of the best work I do.

Multilevel Outcome Management

I'm in the focus business. As a consultant, coach, and educator I ask simple questions that often elicit very creative and intelligent responses from others (and even myself!), which in turn add value to the situation and work at hand. People aren't any smarter after these sessions than they were before—they just direct and utilize their intelligence more productively.

> The challenge is to marry high-level idealistic focus to the mundane activity of life. In the end they require the same thinking.

What's unique about the practical focus of GTD is the combination of effectiveness and efficiency that these methods can bring to every level of your reality. There are lots of inspirational sources for the high-level "purpose, values, vision" kind of thinking, and many more mundane tools for getting hold of smaller details such as phone numbers and appointments and grocery lists. The world has been rather barren, however, of practices that relate equally to both levels and tie them together.

> *An idealist believes that the short run doesn't count. A cynic believes the long run doesn't matter. A realist believes that what is done or left undone in the short run determines the long run.*
>
> *—Sydney J. Harris*

"What does this mean to me?" "What do I want to be true about it?" "What's the next step required to make that happen?" These are the cornerstone questions we must answer, at some point, about everything. This thinking, and the tools that support it, will serve you in ways you may not yet imagine.

The Power of Natural Planning

The value of natural project planning is that it provides an integrated, flexible, aligned way to think through any situation. Whereas the basic five-step process of capturing, clarifying, organizing, reflecting, and engaging is a coherent way to achieve stability across the whole spectrum of your life, natural planning produces relaxed, focused control in more specific areas.

Challenging the purpose of anything you may be doing is healthy and mature. Being comfortable making up visions of success, before the methods are clear, is a phenomenal trait to strengthen. Being willing to have ideas, good or bad, and to express and capture all of them without judgment is critical for fully accessing creative intelligence. Honing multiple ideas and types of information into components, sequences, and priorities aimed toward a specific outcome is a necessary mental discipline. And deciding on and taking real next actions—actually moving on something in the physical world—is the essence of productivity.

> I respect the man who knows distinctly what he wishes. The greater part of all mischief in the world arises from the fact that men do not sufficiently understand their own aims. They have undertaken to build a tower, and spend no more labor on the foundation than would be necessary to erect a hut.
>
> —Johann Wolfgang von Goethe

Being able to bring all these ingredients together, with appropriate timing and balance, is perhaps the major component of competence for this new millennium. But it's not yet the norm of much professional and personal behavior; far from it. It's still a daunting task to apply this awareness to all the aspects of one's life. The natural planning model is natural, but in many cases it is not automatic.

But even when only portions of the model are inserted, tremendous benefit ensues. The feedback I've gotten over the years with this model has continued to validate that even the slightest increase in the use of natural planning can bring significant improvement.

To see brainstorming about almost every aspect of their lives becoming a standard for so many people is terrific. To hear from executives who have used the model as a way to frame key meetings and discussions and have gotten great value from doing so is gratifying. It all just affirms that the way our minds naturally work is what we should focus on to make anything happen in the physical world.

The model is simply the basic principle of determining outcomes and actions for everything we consider to be our work. When those two key focus points become the norm in our day-to-day lives, the baseline for productivity moves to another level. The addition of brainstorming—the most creative means of expressing and capturing ideas, perspectives, and details about projects—makes for an elegant set of behaviors for staying relaxed and getting things done.

Shifting to a Positive Organizational Culture

It doesn't take a big change to increase the productivity standards of a group. I continually get feedback indicating that with a little implementation by a few key people, immediately things start to happen more quickly and more easily.

The constructive evaluation of activities, asset allocations, communications, policies, and procedures against purposes and intended outcomes has become increasingly critical for every organization I know of. The challenges to our companies continue to mount, with pressures coming these days from globalization, competition, technology, shifting markets, erratic economic swings, and raised standards of performance and production, making outcome/action thinking a required twenty-first-century behavior.

"What do you want to have happen in this meeting?" "What is the purpose of this form?" "What would the ideal person for this job be able to do?" "What do we want to accomplish with this software?" These and a multitude of other, similar questions are still sorely lacking in many quarters. There's plenty of talk in the big meetings that sounds good, but learning to ask, "Why are we doing this?" and "What will it look like when it's done successfully?" and to apply the answers at the day-to-day, operational level—*that* will create profound results.

Commonly the productivity issues expressed at senior levels in companies we work with are centered around e-mail and meetings—too many of both, and too much time having to be spent dealing with seemingly nonstrategic stuff within them. It is very easy for these communication media to morph into an unproductive maelstrom, draining energy. Unfocused meetings lead to unnecessary e-mails, which then produce the need for clarifying meetings, which produce more e-mail, and so on. Both e-mail and meetings are critical to organizational life, but too often they fall into the category of necessary evils, primarily because there is a lack of rigor relative to their purposes and desired outcomes.

Empowerment naturally ensues for individuals as they move from complaining and victim modalities into outcomes and actions defined for direction. When that becomes the standard in a group, it creates significant improvement in the atmosphere as well as in the output. There are enough other problems and opportunities to be concerned with; negativity and passive resistance need to continually give way to a focus on the desired results at the appropriate horizons.

> *A vision without a task is but a dream; a task without a vision is but drudgery; a vision and a task is the hope of the world.*
> *—From a church in Sussex, England, ca. 1730*

The microcosm of how people deal with their in-trays, e-mail, and the conversation with others will be reflected in the macro-reality of their culture and organization. If balls are dropped, if decisions about what to do are resisted on the front end, if not all the open loops are managed responsibly, that will be magnified in the group, and the culture will sustain a stressful fire-and-crisis siege mentality. If, in contrast, individuals are implementing the principles of *Getting Things Done*, the culture will expect and experience a new standard of high performance. Problems and conflicts will not go away—they remain inherent as you attempt to change (or maintain) anything in this world. The operational behaviors of this book, however, will provide the focus and framework for addressing them in the most productive way.

I am often asked, "How can this methodology improve an organization?" In fact, all the principles I've put forward are as applicable to an enterprise as they are to an individual. Capturing what has a group's attention, getting clarity about the inherent outcomes desired and actions required, regularly reviewing status and incorporating new realities, and consistently recalibrating and reallocating resources—all are core best practices for any team or company. But just like you can't teach an organization to read, you can't expect to "improve an organization," per se, with *Getting Things Done*. To function at all in a knowledge economy, most organizations need people who read; the culture can provide training and support to ensure that occurs. They will also need people who have mastered the art of effectively getting things done, to operate at the new levels being demanded in this century. When that is manifest in a company through its expectations, training, and modeling, from the top down, the results in organizational output can be profound.

GTD and Cognitive Science

SINCE THE FIRST edition of *Getting Things Done* was published, significant research in the field of social and cognitive psychology has documented and validated the efficacy of the principles that underlie the methodology. Until recently these practices could be confirmed only experientially and anecdotally. Anyone who had ever applied the GTD techniques of capturing, clarifying, organizing, and reflecting on the resulting inventory acknowledged the same results: greater clarity, control, and focus, along with all the resulting personal and organizational benefits associated with that experience. If you have to any degree begun to implement the practices I have put forward so far, you will no doubt have noticed some positive increase in your own demeanor.

Rigorous studies compiled by experts in the field of cognitive science, ranging from personal to organizational aspects, have begun to provide data that gives foundational support to this methodology and why and how its improvements are produced. In some sense this may seem like someone's proving that gravity exists after we've all been experiencing it and dealing with it since we were conscious. But from another perspective it gives perhaps needed credence to the advice for mastering workflow I've put forward here, and to why such seemingly simple processes and behaviors described in *Getting Things Done* have such a compelling result.

The supporting research has emerged within several frameworks and categories:

• Positive psychology
• Distributed cognition: the value of an external mind
• Relieving the cognitive load of incompletions
• Flow theory
• Self-leadership theory

• Goal-striving via implementation intentions
• Psychological capital (PsyCap)

GTD and Positive Psychology

In 2000 Martin Seligman took on the presidency of the American Psychological Association. For his presidential address he challenged the profession to shift its focus away from simply describing, studying, and diagnosing the negative aspects of the human condition and to begin devoting more attention to the positive aspects of what it means to be human. Of course, his message was simply a more mainstream embodiment of Abraham Maslow's ideas from the mid-twentieth century of personal fulfillment as the richest arena of psychology. But since Seligman's call to action, positive psychology has blossomed into a full-fledged component of the field.

The research generated by this change in perspective has been conducted at both the basic and applied levels. It has added to our understanding of a myriad of psychological constructs and has been used to improve the lives of many. Positive psychology is a vast discipline, but a sampling of its relevant aspects includes happiness, psychological well-being, flow/optimal experience, meaning, passion, purpose, authentic leadership, strengths, values, character, and virtue. Graduate education programs in these areas have emerged across the world and continue to expand.

How is this relevant to *Getting Things Done*? GTD is more than just a way to manage tasks and projects. In many respects it is more concerned with fundamental issues of meaningful work, mindful living, and psychological well-being than simply offering methods for being more efficient or productive for their own sake. The emphasis (and requirement) of outcome thinking concerning the stuff we encounter, as well as achieving a functional way to capture, clarify, organize, and assess the results so we can think more clearly, describes the core practices that truly make the actual experience of life better.

That said (and experienced, if you have!), it is still quite interesting to examine some of the various theories and studies that have focused on the more specific aspects of the relationship of our psyche, our well-being, and our performance—all with close correlation to the principles and practices of *Getting Things Done*.

Distributed Cognition: The Value of an External Mind

In 2008 a fascinating paper, "Getting Things Done: The Science Behind Stress-Free Productivity," was published in a professional journal by two researchers in Belgium who analyzed my methodology specifically from the perspective of verifiable data and working theories from cognitive science.* Their brilliant and detailed assessments and conclusions extend far beyond what I can do justice to here (the paper is worthy of multiple reads), but suffice it to say that its thesis is profound: your mind is designed to have ideas, based upon pattern detection, but it isn't designed to remember much of anything!

> Your mind is for *having* ideas, not for *holding* them.

Because of the way the mind developed, it is brilliant at recognition, but terrible at recall. You can glance at today's calendar and in the course of a few seconds get a coherent sense of the day and its contents and contexts. But you'd have a terrible time trying to recall the contents of the next fourteen days on your calendar merely from memory.

A wonderful exposition of the new discoveries in the science of cognition, related to our limited capacity to manage and maintain awareness of relevant data in the information age, and the necessity of building and utilizing an "external brain," was put forward by Daniel Levitin in his book *The Organized Mind.*†

The bottom line is that when you use your memory as your organizing system (as most everyone on the planet still does, for most of what they're doing to manage their lives), your mind will effectively become overwhelmed and incompetent, because you are demanding of it intense work for which it is not well equipped.

---

*Francis Heylighen and Clément Vidal, "Getting Things Done: The Science Behind Stress-Free Productivity," *Long Range Planning* 41, no. 6 (2008): 585–605.
†*The Organized Mind: Thinking Straight in the Age of Information Overload,* Daniel J. Levitin (New York: Dutton, 2014).

If, however, you are able to bring its attention to bear appropriately and efficiently to create the optimal triggers for later thinking and action (such as reading an e-mail, then setting a meeting on your calendar to deal with its issue or opportunity), then it gets to relax and rely on the automatic and elegant thinking it can do when presented specific things on which to focus, in the proper context. You trust you'll see that meeting on your calendar sufficiently in advance to be prepared for it.

GTD provides the methodology for identifying those things that need focused attention, applying it efficiently on the front end and organizing the triggers for appropriate thinking at the right time. The Belgian researchers crafted an elegant exposition of the science behind efficiently maximizing what our minds are good for and what they're not, creating a framework for how we can more effectively produce profound results with minimal thinking!*

Relieving the Cognitive Load of Incompletions

Much fruitful work has been done in the early part of this century by Dr. Roy Baumeister et al. in determining the effects on consciousness of unfinished items—goals, projects, outcomes, etc.— that have been committed to but not yet completed. His conclusions simply verify what I've experienced for decades: uncompleted tasks take up room in the mind, which then limits clarity and focus.†

But interestingly, in alignment with the GTD practices, Baumeister has also proven that completion of such items is not required to relieve that burden on the psyche. What is needed is a trusted plan that ensures forward engagement will happen.‡

---

*Heylighen's background and expertise is in analyzing insect behavior—how relatively brainless creatures produce phenomenally effective results. He makes a fascinating case for us humans to do likewise, with *Getting Things Done* as a key platform.
†Roy F. Baumeister and E. J. Masicampo, "Unfulfilled Goals Interfere with Tasks That Require Executive Functions," *Journal of Experimental Social Psychology* 47, no. 2 (2011): 300–11.
‡Roy F. Baumeister and E. J. Masicampo, "Consider It Done! Plan Making Can Eliminate the Cognitive Effects of Unfulfilled Goals," *Journal of Personality and Social Psychology* 101, no. 4 (2011): 667–83.

In Baumeister's model merely determining the next action to fulfill a commitment is a sufficient end result of "planning"—as long as the trigger or reminder is parked in a place that we trust we'll look within a reasonable amount of time. My thinking and model were heavily cited in his wonderful book *Willpower*, which positions them within a rich context of managing the mental "muscle" we must continually employ, especially in knowledge work.*

Flow Theory

One of the more popular concepts in this field, which has often been associated with GTD, has been the idea of "flow"—the state of optimal performance and engagement. Flow is what the athletes refer to as being "in the zone," and it can be closely correlated with the idea of "mind like water," which I introduced in the first chapter.

The flow experience is marked by various distinct components, several of which are already implemented by the GTD approach. To experience flow, it is necessary that your skills in a given task match the challenge at hand. If the challenge exceeds your requisite skill level, you will experience anxiety, and if your skills exceed the challenge, you will most likely feel bored during the activity.[†] Flow is usually accompanied by complete concentration on the given task, and you typically feel in control and have clear goals in sight. Individuals in flow generally have an idea of what is coming next and receive immediate feedback throughout the task. They also experience a merging of action and awareness, during which they lose both their self-consciousness and their sense of time. They are usually intrinsically motivated, performing an activity for its own sake and not for an external reward. Those in flow often are performing at an optimal level and are completely absorbed in what they are doing. Once individuals have experienced flow, they are often compelled to repeat the activities that enabled them to experience it.

---

*Roy F. Baumeister and John Tierney, *Willpower*: Discovering the Greatest Human Strength (New York: Penguin Press, 2011).
[†]Mihaly Csikszentmihalyi, *Flow: The Psychology of Optimal Experience* (New York: Harper Perennial, 1990).

While flow was originally conceptualized by investigating leisure activities (e.g., rock climbing, painting), Csikszentmihalyi and Le-Fevre* found that individuals are engaged in high-skill, high-challenge activities more often at work (54 percent) than at leisure (18 percent). Csikszentmihalyi explained that many jobs inherently contain the type of goals and feedback structures that would allow one to experience flow at work, a phenomenon that is associated with higher levels of subjective well-being.†

> You can only put your conscious attention on one thing at a time. If that's all that *has* your attention, you're in flow.

The GTD approach includes several conditions of the flow experience—namely, having clear goals and receiving feedback. GTD's emphasis on focusing attention on one task at a time is closely associated with the crux of the flow experience: being completely absorbed in a singular activity, in which one's stimulus field is limited. Adopting GTD enables individuals to find flow more easily in their work and personal lives. By getting tasks out of the mind and into an external system, they can more easily see and track progress, which is a form of feedback. Having a complete picture of one's commitments in work and life can help individuals make better decisions about what to pay attention to in any given moment, which, in turn, will allow them to engage more fully in the task at hand, making flow a more likely outcome.

Self-Leadership Theory

Self-leadership can be traced back to the mid-1980s as an expansion of the concept of self-management. According to Neck and Manz,‡ self-leadership is a process through which individuals control their own behavior, influencing themselves through the use of

---

*M. Csikszentmihalyi and J. LeFevre, "Optimal Experience in Work and Leisure," *Journal of Personality and Social Psychology* 56, no. 5 (1989): 815–22.
†Clive Fullagar and E. Kevin Kelloway, "Work-Related Flow," in *A Day in the Life of a Happy Worker*, ed. Arnold B. Bakker and Kevin Daniels (New York: Psychology Press, 2013), 41–57.
‡Christopher P. Neck and Charles C. Manz, *Mastering Self-Leadership: Empowering Yourself for Personal Excellence*, 6th ed. (Upper Saddle River, NJ: Pearson Prentice-Hall, 2012), 192.

specific behavioral and cognitive strategies. The popularity of self-leadership has soared via a large number of practitioner-oriented books, theoretical and empirical journal publications, inclusion in management and leadership textbooks, and the growth of self-leadership training programs.

The strategies that comprise self-leadership are commonly separated into three categories: behavior-focused, natural reward, and constructive thought pattern.

Behavior-focused strategies are usually centered on raising individual self-awareness with the goal of facilitating behavioral management. In the context of work, these strategies commonly place an emphasis on doing necessary but unpleasant tasks. This family of strategies includes self-observation, self–goal setting, self-reward, self-punishment, and self-cuing.

Natural reward strategies are intended to create situations in which an individual is motivated or rewarded by the activity itself. These strategies revolve around reshaping unpleasant tasks or activities to make them more enjoyable and deliberately focusing attention on the inherently rewarding aspects of the activities.

Constructive thought pattern strategies relate specifically to creating ways of thinking that can positively impact performance. Examples of these strategies include self-talk, mental imagery, and replacing dysfunctional beliefs and assumptions.

> Providing yourself the right cues, which you will notice at the right time, about the right things, is a core practice of stress-free productivity.

There are aspects of GTD that connect to each of the three overall types of self-leadership. One of the most evident is the concept of self-cuing. A well-constructed GTD system provides for a physical artifact that spurs future action. The GTD methodology also embodies the component of natural reward strategies. There is a sense of pleasure in identifying small yet annoying tasks and taking care of them—something a thorough mental RAM dump and some free time certainly make possible. Finally, a key element of GTD is the mental component of thinking of your work not simply as a series of large projects but more directly as concrete next actions. This shift from a defeatist/overwhelmed attitude to the motivational state that enables you to move forward on such tasks is a great example of shifting your mind-set in a positive way.

Using self-leadership strategies has been shown to improve people's sense of self-efficacy, and self-efficacy is one of the most well-researched constructs when it comes to organizational psychology. It has been connected to job satisfaction, job performance, and other positive organizational behaviors for both traditional employees and entrepreneurs.

Goal-Striving/Attainment Via Implementation Intentions

Goals (desired outcomes) are a vital part of life, and GTD can serve to facilitate both personal and professional goals. Gollwitzer and Oettingen have conducted a major line of research on goal achievement, incorporating the idea of "implementation intentions."* In a nutshell they argue that the best way to ensure goal striving (taking actions toward a stated goal) is to create a cause-and-effect link in your mind about when certain goal-relevant actions will be taken. When you make plans (implementation intentions) ahead of time and decide what actions will be carried out in which contexts, the proper behavior is nearly automatically enacted instead of being drawn from your limited reserve of willpower. In other words, if you can trust that something you will more or less do automatically will provide sufficient direction and juice to move you toward your outcome, you'll have that juice when needed. It won't be depleted by your constant worrying or thinking about what you should do and when.

GTD and implementation intentions are linked through using the system as the trigger or prompt for taking outcome-directed action. For example, you could set the implementation intention, "When I'm in my office with more than an hour of free time and a high level of energy, I'll look at my task list and select something challenging and important to work on." Or, "When it is Sunday afternoon I will conduct a Weekly Review." Or, "When I'm feeling flustered and overwhelmed I'll do a mental RAM dump." The number of such possible implementation intentions is truly endless.

---

*Peter M. Gollwitzer and Gabrielle Oettingen, "Planning Promotes Goal Striving," in Kathleen D. Vohs and Roy F. Baumeister, eds., *Handbook of Self-Regulation: Research, Theory, and Applications*, 2nd ed. (New York: Guilford, 2011), 162–85.

Psychological Capital (PsyCap)

Psychological capital (PsyCap) is a relatively new framework within which organizational psychologists are beginning to evaluate the overall resourceful state of workers and its effect. It consists of four definable aspects: self-efficacy, optimism, resilience, and hope.

- *Self-efficacy* is the confidence to take on and devote the necessary effort to succeed at challenging tasks.
- *Optimism* involves making positive attributions about succeeding now and in the future.
- *Hope* means persevering toward goals and, when necessary, redirecting paths to those goals.
- *Resilience* involves bouncing back to an original—or even better—state of being after facing adversity and problems.

Individually each of these variables can predict various outcomes to a certain degree. For example, someone's degree of optimism can correlate statistically with particular results or behaviors. However, when these four components are considered together in what psychologists now call PsyCap, you can predict much more than merely the sum of the effects of its component elements. In its relatively short history as a construct, PsyCap has been connected to many positive individual and organizational outcomes, such as job performance[*][†] and psychological well-being.[‡]

PsyCap is more of a description of a state than a trait itself—that is, it is something that can change or be changed, developed, or undermined, almost minute to minute, as in the example of one's mood. In familiar terms it would reflect the difference between

[*]F. Luthans, B. J. Avolio, J. B. Avey, and S. M. Norman, "Positive Psychological Capital: Measurement and Relationship with Performance and Satisfaction," Personnel Psychology 60, no. 3 (2007): 541–72.

[†]T. Sun, X. W. Zhao, L. B. Yang, and L. H. Fan, "The Impact of Psychological Capital on Job Embeddedness and Job Performance Among Nurses: A Structural Equation Approach," *Journal of Advanced Nursing 68*, no. 1 (2012): 69–79, doi:10.1111/j.1365 -2648.2011.05715.x.

[‡]J. B. Avey, F. Luthans, R. M. Smith, and N. F. Palmer, "Impact of Positive Psychological Capital on Employee Well-being Over Time," *Journal of Occupational Health Psychology 15*, no. 1 (2010): 17–28, doi:10.1037/a0016998.

your experiencing a good day or a bad day. Are you feeling on top of your game, or buried by it? The good news is that such states are malleable—you can do things that can change and improve them without having to change some inherent aspect of yourself.

Getting Things Done relates directly to all four ingredients of a high PsyCap and its intended results. By enabling people to create and maintain a complete picture of their commitments to themselves and others in order to make good decisions about what to do (or not do) at any given moment, it automatically builds a sense of confidence and control (*self-efficacy*). Simply identifying all open loops and moving them from memory to an external mind while systematically identifying concrete and doable next actions is a pure exercise in self-control and directedness. An individual utilizing GTD knows exactly what needs to be done and exactly what action he can take to achieve it, given the restrictions of available time, energy, and contextual restraints.

Adopting GTD sets people up for greater *optimism* because it enables them to draw connections between the successful completion of projects and their own purposeful and goal-directed efforts. Individuals identify meaningful projects, articulate the next steps needed to complete them, and then ideally follow through the process until the project is completed. As each "win" is achieved, it produces greater capacity for making more positive commitments.

In addition, the focus on front-end decision making in GTD—doing "the work to define the work"—can be viewed as an exercise in both aspects of *hope* (setting goals and identifying pathways to those goals). Individuals set goals ("What does 'done' look like?") and identify the tasks needed to achieve those goals ("What's the next action?") during this front-end decision-making process.

While no empirical data yet exists for the idea that those individuals who utilize GTD are more successful in recovering from failure (*resilience*), it's certainly been validated anecdotally for me from scores of the best and brightest individuals on the planet. Dealing with serious family emergencies or tumultuous changes in their jobs and careers, people have provided abundant testimonials to attest to their retained sanity, stability, and productivity by utilizing GTD practices. The methodology gives an individual a sense of calm and control over a difficult situation that allows them to use their mental faculties to address the task at hand and recalibrate multiple vectors in real time, as needed. In a time of stress or other adversity, those individuals who are able to think most clearly and process the results more efficiently will be more likely to emerge from the stress in better shape than those who do not.

The PsyCap model also provides a framework within which to understand why groups who have integrated GTD as a cultural standard experience a significant degree of "moving up the food chain," relative to how their organization responds, interacts, and produces results. Whether or not PsyCap develops further as a definable, verifiable, and developmental arena in organizational psychology, it's a great way to describe the mental, emotional, reflective, and even physical benefits of what you get from using GTD.

Undoubtedly during the coming years we will see a continual stream of new scientific data that will validate what I've known was true from day one of my experience with this model, and what has been shared by countless others: when all of our potentially meaningful things are captured, clarified, organized, and reflected upon, the more mature, elegant, and intelligent part of who we really are can show up at the table. That produces experiences and results that can't be beat.

The Path of GTD Mastery

GTD IS ACTUALLY a lifelong practice with multiple levels of mastery. It is very similar to playing an instrument like the violin, a sport like tennis, or a game like chess. It's like mathematics, pottery, art history, or even parenting. All of these endeavors involve learning and applying a particular set of moves and techniques, and there's no end to how good you can become at them, or how many subtleties there are to explore.

GTD is the art of dealing with the stream of life's work and engagements, which itself is constantly evolving for all of us, at any age or station. It's about identifying and navigating your commitments and interests from a state of confidence and flow. Your work and focus will change, often dramatically, over time. But engaging with all of it masterfully is a defined practice that can be learned and refined over a lifetime.

Mastery does not refer to some final end state of a Zen-like peacefulness and enlightenment on a mountaintop (though that could be an optional nice expression of it). Rather, it's the demonstrated ability to consistently engage in productive behaviors as a means to achieve clarity, stability, and focus when it's desired or required—no matter what the challenge.

How well you have developed that ability will be tested when you're confronted with things that are unclear, unstable, and distracting, which are natural and normal symptoms of any change in your world. The idea of "mind like water" doesn't assume that water is always undisturbed. On the contrary, water engages appropriately with disturbance, instead of fighting against it. Over the course of life such disturbances can range from dealing with your homework in the sixth grade to the demands of your new job to the vague sense of uneasiness about what to do when you retire.

GTD mastery involves learning and incorporating its various

best practices, and then integrating them in a holistic manner, which results in a much more dynamic experience than simply the sum of its parts. When you learn to play tennis, you focus on specific components of its moves, like the backhand, the forehand, the lob, and the serve. When you actually play a game of tennis, you then put them all together. As you increase your mastery, your focus matures to encompass an overall strategy. Similarly, mastering GTD involves an initial mastery of its segments, techniques, and tools and then incorporating them as you play your whole life and work game. Your expertise will be reflected in your using an optimally integrated system and approach, without thinking about it.

The Three Tiers of Mastery

Over the many years of engaging with people who have adopted the GTD methodology, I have noticed generally three stages of maturity they have demonstrated in using the model:

1 | Employing the fundamentals of managing workflow;
2 | Implementing a more elevated and integrated total life management system; and
3 | Leveraging skills to create clear space and get things done for an ever-expansive expression and manifestation.

A good analogy here is the experience of learning to drive a car. The first stage is getting the basics under control, so that you can handle the machine without hurting yourself or anyone else. The moves feel awkward and often counterintuitive. But once you're good enough to get your license, your world changes dramatically for the better, because now you can go places and do things that you couldn't previously. Then there comes a time when you are able to drive down a road without actually thinking about the act of driving—it's become an almost automatic part of your life. And finally, you decide to graduate to a really high-performance vehicle, in which the prime challenge and opportunity is how well you can focus ahead, making yourself essentially one with your vehicle, experiencing elevated levels of satisfaction and fulfillment with driving.

Each of those stages is represented by the horizons of your focus and the application of specific techniques. At first you're making what look like small, jerky movements but what are actually very smooth movements focused on very short horizons. Then, as you gain comfort and familiarity with the process, you extend your focus to the next street corner or freeway exit. Then you can graduate to a more conscious and directed focus at multiple horizons, driving across town with total situational awareness. Similarly, as the techniques of *Getting Things Done* become increasingly second nature, you shift your attention from the mechanics of your system to the results it produces.

Mastering the Basics

As simple as they may seem at first, building proficiency with the fundamental components of *Getting Things Done*—the basics—can take a while. Though it's easy to understand and agree with its concepts and principles, putting them fully into practice is not necessarily a smooth or automatic process. It's the same as with any sophisticated practice—driving a car, throwing a karate punch, or playing the flute—the beginning moves are not familiar or comfortable. Once you've done them a thousand times, however, you can manifest elegance, power, and fluidity that would be inaccessible any other way. The same may be true for you about learning GTD.

For example, capturing *everything* potentially meaningful into trusted external buckets, so that nothing remains rattling around in your head, is a behavior that can be as daunting to employ as learning to manually shift easily in a car. As with most aspects of the GTD model, writing things down is itself not a new skill, but rather a practice that can easily seem unworthy of the effort, if not downright counterintuitive. ("If it's not immediately important, why should I bother?") Becoming sensitized to the need to externalize those kinds of thoughts as well as building the habit to actually carry out the necessary actions with a ubiquitous tool at hand, without exception, is the real challenge.

Other basic practices, which, even if implemented initially, easily regress into incomplete, out-of-date, and therefore dysfunctional usage, include:

- Avoiding next-action decision making on "stuff to do"
- Fully utilizing the "Waiting For" category, such that *every* expected deliverable from others is inventoried and reviewed for follow-up in adequate timing
- Using Agenda lists to capture and manage communications with others
- Keeping a simple, easily accessible filing and reference system
- Keeping the calendar as pure "hard landscape" without undermining its trustworthiness with extraneous inputs
- Doing Weekly Reviews to keep one's system functional and current

It's Easy to Get Off Track . . .

If you are sincere about implementing *Getting Things Done*, it's actually not that difficult to get started, as I've tried to assure you with the instructions given in the earlier sections of the book. At some point, though, the rest of your reality will inevitably come flooding at you full force, and if the new practices haven't yet had time to root themselves in your behavior patterns, it's relatively easy to get blown off course.

Most people are so used to keeping things in their heads that it's very easy to slip back into that familiar pattern. Deciding next actions requires a thrust of cognitive effort that seductively can be avoided if a particular situation is not in some critical mode. Making time for the Weekly Review, if it's not been instituted as a habit, can be a daunting challenge. All of that begins to result in a personal system that is incomplete and out of date—you'll no longer be able to trust your lists to give you the whole picture, and because the system is not really relieving pressure, you'll conclude it's not worth keeping up with anymore, and you might as well take it back into your head. In those circumstances it's not uncommon for someone to wander off the track exponentially quickly.

. . . and Easy to Get Back On

The good news is that it's as easy to get back *into* your productive groove as it may have been to get knocked out of it. It simply requires revisiting the basics: get a pen and paper and empty your head again; clean up your lists of actions and projects; identify and add new projects and next actions to bring your lists current; clean up what's leaked outside your system.

This cycle of getting off track and getting back on again happens to almost everyone—particularly during this first level of mastering the basics of the game. In my experience it can easily take as long as two years to finally get this stage of practice fully integrated into one's life and work style, and consistently maintained.

Another piece of good news is that even if a person has gleaned only a few concepts from this material, or has not implemented the system regularly, it can bring marked improvement. If you "get" nothing more than the two-minute rule, it will be worth its weight in gold. If you just write down a few more things on your mind than you would have previously, you'll sleep better. If you clean up e-mail to zero at least every once in a while, you will have great cause for celebration. And if you simply ask, "What's the next action?" of yourself or anyone else when you might not have otherwise, it will add to your stress-free productivity.

Of course, the more those techniques begin to work together as a whole, systematically and consistently, the more dramatic will be the increase in the experience of relaxed, focused control. Mastering the basics is transformative for most everyone who achieves it. If you reach that stage, you will be getting many more things done, more quickly and more easily, and operating with greatly increased confidence in how you're dealing with the operational details of life. At this first tier of GTD mastery you will be generally keeping yourself under control and focused on an hour-by-hour, day-by-day basis.

Graduate Level—Integrated Life Management

At this point, you are ready to graduate to the next level—having your hand on the helm of your life on a week-to-week, month-to-month (and even longer) basis. This requires a more subtle level of awareness and practice. As I mentioned earlier, as you get better at driving a car, you are able to extend your horizon, which creates smoother moves, and you can focus more on where you're going than on the mechanism that's getting you there. Similarly, when you reach a certain level of maturity with the GTD process, you won't be as focused on the system itself or how you're working it, but will utilize it in more flexible, customized ways, as your trusted tool to facilitate control and focus over longer and larger spans.

Whereas the first level of mastery involves in-trays, meetings, e-mail, phone calls, agendas, waiting-fors, reference systems, list management, getting the right tools, etc., this next tier is concerned with getting rigorous with the bigger issues that are driving the contents of the basic level. These specific actions and information exist because of their relevance to things larger than themselves— the projects we have to complete, the problems we need to solve, the areas of focus and interest we have in our complex lives. Why are you getting that e-mail? What's the purpose of that meeting, and why do you have to attend? What's coming up next quarter that you need to start dealing with now? What "projects" need to become "someday/maybes," and vice versa, because of some of the larger changes going on?

Mastery of the fundamentals, which provides the basics of effective and efficient execution, also provides the ability and room to address a higher level of control and focus—projects, and how they are identified, managed, and understood in relation to one another and to the larger frameworks within which we operate. Developing comfort with an external mind frees up and leverages one's cognitive abilities, paving the way for many more creative and productive uses of an integrated self-management system.

The hallmarks of this next level of maturity with *Getting Things Done* are:

- a complete, current, and clear inventory of projects;
- a working map of one's roles, accountabilities, and interests— personally and professionally;
- an integrated total life management system, custom tailored to one's current needs and direction and utilized to dynamically steer out beyond the day-to-day; and
- challenges and surprises trigger your utilization of this methodology instead of throwing you out of it.

When Projects Become the Heartbeat of
Your Operational System

Further down the path of mastering this methodology you will reach a stage at which your Projects list becomes more the driver, rather than a reflection, of your Next Action lists, and your projects themselves will become a truer reflection of your roles, areas of focus, and interests. At this point the center of gravity of your self-management system will have moved from the Ground-level horizon to somewhere between Horizon 1 and Horizon 2 (refer to page 55 in chapter 2).

Though it is central to an ongoing experience of stress-free productivity, very few people—even among those who have been engaged with *Getting Things Done* for years—actually walk around with a complete inventory of their projects, objectively and regularly reviewed. Those who do reach this level, however, and come to realize its power, make *that* the principle list from which they navigate.

Given my broad definition of *project* (any outcome requiring more than one step that you're committed to achieve within a year), it might be challenging enough for you to delineate all of those, even if they are clear ("Get new tires," "Fix the printer," "Find a new babysitter," etc.). But the real expression of maturity here is the inclusion of the more subtle desired outcomes definable as doable events ("Clarify Frank's new role on the team," "Research options for improving Bettina's math grades," "Resolve property boundary issue with neighbor," etc.). A signpost of GTD mastery at this stage—and, indeed, *life* mastery!—is when one recognizes *anything* that has his or her attention (concerns, worries, problems, issues, tensions) and translates them into achievable outcomes (projects), to be executed with concrete next actions. Most people resist acknowledging issues and opportunities until they know they can be handled successfully, not realizing that exploring, looking into, or in some way accepting or putting something to bed because there is no solution is an appropriate outcome (project) itself. The ability to create appropriate engagement with your neighbor's boundary issue, your daughter's math grades, or the role of a new team member—no matter how ambiguous or unclear the actual path for achieving each may be—by identifying the inherent project and taking steps to resolve it is quite an extraordinary and mature self-management practice.

Assessing and Populating Your Projects List from Your Areas of Focus

Everything we do is serving some aspect of the roles and account-abilities we have taken on or an area of interest and engagement in our lives. I call my brother just to check in and say hello because "family relationships" has meaning for me. I buy groceries because I consider "health and vitality" important. I produce an agenda for a board meeting because I need to maintain "corporate oversight" in my role in my company.

Whenever people actually produce a checklist for this horizon—the areas of professional and personal focus they can identify—they invariably realize that there are more projects they need to add. They will also usually realize that they have not been paying ap-propriate attention to some aspect of either their work or their per-sonal life, or both, and they are motivated to bring more balance and wholeness to their Projects list.

An Integrated Total Life-Management System

The third aspect of this stage of mastery is that your system will have become not just a conglomeration of various lists, information, applications, and tools but rather a cohesive "control room" with all its components working together to engage effectively with what-ever circumstance arises. You will have attained the ability to cus-tomize your lists and categories, and how you use them, in response to changes in your world and your own increasing sophistication with the possibilities.

This is a reflection of a *functional awareness* of GTD. You un-derstand the essence and recognize the value of the various parts of the model and therefore have the freedom to tailor how they are implemented to best serve your needs. You could build your own application of the GTD system from scratch, if need be, with your own tools at hand. You are guided by the principle of creating and engaging with the necessary orientation "maps" to ensure you are appropriately focused as required for a given situation.

You're not at a loss about what to do with anything—a business card you collected at a lunch meeting, a harebrained idea you woke up with this morning about a project you might want to launch, an unexpected private invitation to a major gala event, or your blood panel report from your last medical checkup. You can create the right placeholder for any type of potentially meaningful data. You can also easily get a sense of your priorities for an upcoming trip; you have everything you need at hand for the next webinar you're conducting; it would take minimal effort to pull together a company overview for your bank; and you can quickly create a rich context for a family conversation about plans for the next two years. You have a dynamic, working dashboard that serves your orientation for virtually any context, whether at home, at the office, or in transit, seamlessly.

Pressure Produces Greater Rather Than Reduced Utilization of These Practices

One of the most common observations I hear from people who have at some point bought into the GTD process but have not progressed particularly far with it is that they fell away from it because they had an intense series of back-to-back business trips, or an extended bout of the flu, or an unexpected crisis occur with a major client, or were asked to run a major project in addition to their regular job, or . . . and so on.

And one of the most common things I hear from people who *have* matured with their application of and experience with the methodology is that applying *Getting Things Done* is the very thing that enabled them to negotiate these kinds of tense situations with much more effectiveness and much less stress.

So, a significant hallmark of progress in the path of mastery at this stage is that very transition point when issues and opportunities galvanize GTD practices instead of causing its users to abandon them. When a new problem explodes at work, you can get back in control quickly with a new mind sweep instead of taking everything back up into your head. You identify desired outcomes, projects, and next actions about this circumstance as soon as you can, as opposed to simply worrying about what's happened. You actually do a Weekly Review in the middle of the week because you need that kind of elevated focus to recalibrate your work, instead of reverting back to latest-and-loudest as your priority criterion.

Operating at this level of GTD mastery is achievable and truly elegant. The experience, for those who do achieve it, is one of *establishing the conditions to flourish*. What *flourish* means and looks like for a twenty-four-year-old rock musician will likely be very different than for a fifty-four-year-old attorney with three kids, but the expanded experience and the process of how they got there with GTD are identical.

Postgraduate: Focus, Direction, and Creativity

Once you have incorporated the basic elements of *Getting Things Done* and integrated the more elevated aspects of your commitments of life and work into a trusted and customized systemic approach, the next frontier opens: using clear internal space to optimize your experience, ad infinitum.

This mastery level involves two key aspects:

• Utilizing your freed-up focus for exploring the more elevated aspects of your commitments and values
• Leveraging your external mind to produce novel value

Freedom to Engage in the Most Meaningful Things

Once you really know and trust you can and will execute effectively anything that lands in your in-tray, you will have the freedom to toss *anything* into your own in-tray, whether it's your next crazy idea, a possible new technology to research, a book you might want to write, or an NGO Web site that almost brought you to tears that you'd like to support. The power to produce produces powerful possibilities.*

And, as I hope I've made clear throughout this book, the ability to put your attention on the more subtle and elevated levels of your life and work to a large degree depends on your being able to "put to bed" the inevitably necessary more operational and mundane aspects that, without your appropriate engagement, can easily distract and exhaust your creative focus.

I applaud the people who can sufficiently compartmentalize their consciousness to be able to draft a movie script, craft a vision statement for their NGO, or write the perfect poem for their wedding vows, with all the stuff of unanswered e-mails, crashed computer, taxes to be filed, mother-in-law's complaints about the wedding program, and needed bank credit line extension still impinging on their psyches. I do know that if all of those issues were quieted with appropriate engagement from a GTD perspective, the space and inspiration for the more creative activities would be tremendously enhanced. The negative effect on focus and performance of the cognitive load of these kinds of open loops has now been documented. Many people attest to their ability to leave work at work and drop everything to focus on the creative pursuits that interest them, but in my experience that's only because they don't have a reference point of what their lives would be like without that pressure to begin with.

The lack of pervasive angst about the details of your daily life also makes it much easier to shift your attention to the direction and qualities of experience that really matter. As I indicated in chapter 2, the upper Horizons of Focus—goals, vision, purpose, and principles—are the defining criteria for your priorities. But most people find the ability to concentrate on and execute them effectively elusive at best and avoided (and guilt producing!) at worst. A distraction-free mind won't by itself get you to think about wild success scenarios five years in the future—you still have to consciously

---

*One of my favorite sayings is, "The better you get, the better you'd better get!" The more confidence you have that you can actually manifest things before you have all the knowledge and resources you might need, the more you can potentially overwhelm yourself with your own possibilities. So the clarity and confidence that your GTD practices allow simultaneously demand their ongoing utilization.

direct your attention to those matters—but it does make it infinitely easier to engage in such an exercise productively.

Leveraging Your External Mind

Once you are regularly functioning at this level of mastery, the creative thrust of your "GTD-ing" shifts from implementing the most effective way of dealing with the inputs and inherent demands of your day-to-day world to optimally taking advantage of self-created contexts and triggers to produce creative ideas, perspectives, and actions that wouldn't normally occur.

For instance, if you have ever needed to purge and bring up-to-date a contact manager, as you've reviewed old and potentially out-of-date entries of people and businesses, you've invariably come across items that caused you to tell yourself, "You know, I really ought to get in touch with her again, given what I'm now doing in my business." If that kind of catalyzed thought has ever turned into something in any way valuable, then you've tasted at least a tiny bit of what could be infinitely more utilized. How many more ideas could any of us have had today that would have potentially added value to some aspect of our relationships, work, and creative expressions, had we only brought the right things into our conscious focus with the ability to capture what might show up?

> Wouldn't it be great not to have to think too hard about what you need to think about?

This highly creative and productive reflection activity automatically occurs in something like the Weekly Review, when you are glancing at past and future calendar items ("Oh, that reminds me . . . !") and updating your Projects and Next Actions lists ("Ah . . . now I need to . . . !"). Regularly reassessing your Someday/Maybe contents offers an even more expansive berth ("You know, I think I really *am* going to take a painting class!"). But how many other aspects of your experience and relationships could be enhanced with the same kind of triggers for reflection? What other contents, reviewed with some consistency, might reveal valuable ideas? It's challenging enough to build in regular catch-up behaviors, but the possibilities of going beyond them are endless.

This is the stage of maturity along the GTD path of mastery in which the simple idea of checklists takes on sublime significance. As cognitive scientists have validated, your mind is terrible at recalling things out of the blue, but it is fantastic at doing creative thinking about what it has directly in front of it to evaluate. When freed from the remembering function, the mind is a fabulous mechanism to put in play by putting things "in front of the door" so you don't have to think too hard about what to think about.

How often would you like to be reminded to think about your significant family members? What, specifically, would be good to remind yourself to think about when you think about your partner, your son, your sister? Whom would you consider to be on your A-list in your professional network (the people whose influence and interactions with you are most valuable)? How often should you review that list? What affirmations and inspirational writings would serve you to reconnect with, and at what intervals?

There are obviously an infinite number of opportunities any of us could take advantage of to add value to our world, with the right kind of structure established to relieve our psyche of the jobs it does not do well and to leverage what it does wonderfully. But that will not happen by itself. It is a hallmark of this advanced level of GTD mastery that you recognize that dynamic and use your intelligence to leverage itself. It's having the freedom to generate and develop ideas, without constraint, and then utilizing the practice of processing and organizing those notes and thoughts appropriately. It's the smartest individuals who realize they are only randomly in their "smarts" and inspired. They're the ones who intelligently build in systems and processes to take advantage of the brilliance that often simply lies sleeping behind the dullness required to deal with the brutish world we inhabit.

This path of GTD mastery—incorporating the fundamentals, utilizing an elevated and integrated system, and leveraging creative directional focus—is not actually as limited sequentially as I have laid it out. Most everyone manifests aspects and portions of all of these levels in his or her own practices, and I have often met novices in some field who had some extraordinarily advanced moves. But in my experience, when the whole gestalt of stress-free productivity is taken into consideration, it requires a solid progression that does not have shortcuts. You can't really maintain a sense of week-to-week control if your e-mail is in chaos. You won't really be free to engage with your long-range planning or vision if you don't have a grip on the current reality of the actual inventory of your seventy-five projects.

You are continually involved in all of these levels, consciously or unconsciously, explicitly or implicitly. You have appointments, projects, actions, goals, and values, and as a professional you will find that your work has its own set of commitments within which you must operate. Your mastery of *Getting Things Done* will simply reflect the elegant equanimity with which you are engaged with *all* of them. The unexpected e-mail with the major problem that just appeared, your aunt Martha's birthday this week, the potential change in strategy for your company, and the new piece of cookware you realize you want—each is dealt with quickly, smoothly, and in an appropriate context, leaving nothing on your mind other than what's present in the moment.

Conclusion

I hope this book has been useful—that you have started to reap the rewards of getting more done with less effort and stress. And I *really* hope you have tasted the freedom of a "mind like water" and the release of your creative energies that can be the result of the application of these techniques. Those who begin to implement GTD methods always discover there's more here than meets the eye, and you may have already begun to experience your own version of that.

I'm willing to bet that *Getting Things Done* has validated much of what you already know and have been doing to some degree in your personal and professional life all along. Perhaps, though, this book will make it much easier for you to apply that common sense more systematically in a world that seems to increasingly confound us with its intensity and complexity.

My intent is not to add more to the plethora of modern theories and models about how to be successful. I have tried, on the contrary, to define the core methods that don't change with particular fashions, and that, when applied, always work. As with gravity, when you understand the basic principle, you can operate a lot more effectively, no matter what you're doing. Perhaps this is the leading edge of back to basics!

Getting Things Done is a road map to achieve the positive, relaxed focus that characterizes your most productive state. I invite you to use it, like a road map, as a reference tool to get back there whenever you need to.

Here are some final tips for moving forward:

• Get your personal physical organization hardware set up.
• Get your workstation organized.
• Get in-trays.

- Create a workable and easily accessed personal reference system—for work and home.
- Get a good list-management organizer that you are inspired to play with.
- Give yourself permission to make any changes that you have been contemplating for enhancing your work environments. Hang pictures, buy pens, toss stuff, and rearrange your workspace. Support your fresh start.
- Set aside time when you can tackle one whole area of your office, and then each part of your house. Gather everything into your system, and work through the *Getting Things Done* process.
- Share anything of value you've gleaned from this with someone else. (It's the fastest way to learn.)
- Review *Getting Things Done* again in three to six months. You'll notice things you might have missed the first time through, and I guarantee it will seem like a whole new book.
- Stay in touch with people who are broadcasting and reflecting these behaviors and standards.*

Have a great rest of your life!

---

*We're available. Visit www.gettingthingsdone.com anytime for tons of free support material, conversations and stories about these best practices from people like you, current information about supportive products and services, and access to our global network of people sharing in this methodology.

Appendix

Glossary of *Getting Things Done* Terms

The following are terms used throughout the exposition of the *Getting Things Done* methodology.

actionable—Describes something on which one intends to take action

action support—A category of physical or digital materials that relate to next actions. To be used as reference when taking those actions rather than as reminders for action.

appropriate engagement—The state of being sufficiently OK with something's status to eliminate its pull on one's attention

backlog—The inventory of still-unprocessed stuff that has accumulated in one's mind and physical environment

capture—To gather (and at times generate) items and ideas identified as potentially meaningful, about which one has any attention or interest in possibly deciding or doing something. See also **collect**.

categories—Groupings of similar content items, usually on a list, in a folder or file, or in a discrete physical location

checklist—Any list used to remind one of or to evaluate optional steps, procedures to follow, and/or ingredients of an activity (e.g., Travel Checklist; Computer Backup Process; Ready-for-School Tasks for kids)

clarify—To determine exactly the meaning of something that has emerged or landed in one's environment from the capture phase (e.g., "Is there something I now need to do about this, and if so, what? Or is it reference? Or is it trash? Or is it on hold for later review?"). See also **process**.

collect—To group together items and ideas about which some assessment, decision, or action is required. See also **capture**.

context—The physical or psychological environment within which reminders and information are most effectively sorted for access (e.g., when one is at home, in a staff meeting, out for errands, at the computer, feeling creative, near a phone, having a conversation with a partner, etc.)

control—One of the two key elements of self- and organizational management (along with perspective). Used to refer to having something stable and "under control," rather than attempted manipulation (e.g., having a car, a meeting, or the kitchen under control).

Getting Things Done—Usually referring to the methodology described in this book, as in, "Maria was just a beginner at implementing *Getting Things Done*"

GTD—The acronym for *Getting Things Done*; the shorthand for referring to this methodology

Horizons of Focus—The discrete levels of commitments we make and thoughts we have, personally and/or organizationally

   Ground: Next actions—The things we deal with at the physical, visible level of activity, such as e-mails, phone calls, conversations, errands, and meetings

   Horizon 1: Projects—Anything we're committed to finish within the next year that requires more than one discrete action step. Includes short-term outcomes such as "Repair brake light" and larger-scope projects such as "Reorganize Western Region." The critical inventory of the Weekly Review. See also **project**.

Horizon 2: Areas of focus and accountability—The segments of our life and work that we need to maintain, to ensure stability and health of ourselves and our enterprises (e.g., health, finances, customer service, strategic planning, family, career)

Horizon 3: Goals and objectives—The mid- to longer-term outcomes to accomplish (usually within three to twenty-four months); e.g., "Finalize acquisition of Acme Consulting," "Establish profitable online version of our leadership training course," "Get Maria's college plans finalized"

Horizon 4: Vision—Long-term desired outcomes; ideal scenarios of wild success (e.g., "Publish my memoir," "Take the company public," "Have a vacation home in Provence")

Horizon 5: Purpose, principles—Ultimate intention, raison d'être, and core values of a person or enterprise (e.g., "To serve the growth of our community in ways that sustainably provide the greatest good for the greatest number of our citizens")

horizontal thinking—Assessing and managing content across a particular equal level (e.g., overviewing all the projects one has, personally and professionally)

incubate—To allow something to remain within a system without a commitment to take action yet, but to be reassessed at a later time. Reminders are usually held within Someday/Maybe lists, tickler files, or triggered-for-later calendar items.

integrated life-management system—The combination of tools, structures, content, and practices used to maintain appropriate engagement with one's world. A workflow, organization, and review process that incorporates every aspect of one's work and life, ensuring a seamless and current inventory of commitments, reminders, and information for optimal control and focus anywhere, at any time.

in-tray—A holding bin, either physical or digital, for incoming items still to be processed

map—Any tool for orienting appropriate focus and direction (e.g., a calendar, lists of actions and projects, agendas for meetings, strategic plans, job descriptions, travel checklist, Weekly Review checklist). See also **review**.

natural planning model—The instinctual five-stage thought process our minds follow when executing any desired outcome

next action—The next physical, visible activity that progresses something toward completion. It is specific enough so that you know where it happens, and with what tools (if any). What "doing" looks like.

open loop—Anything considered unfinished, which, if inappropriately managed, consistently engages one's mind inefficiently

organize—To physically, visually, or digitally sort items of similar meaning into discrete categories and locations (e.g., a list of phone calls to make, a shelf for books to read, a list of projects to complete)

organized—Where something is matches what it means to you

orientation maps—Custom lists or reference documents that support appropriate engagement with one's circumstances (e.g., meeting agendas, calendars, checklists, action and project lists)

outcome—A final result, at any level. Usually refers to "desired outcome"—i.e. the specifics of a successful conclusion.

path of GTD mastery—The lifelong learning, refining, and adaptation of managing one's life and work. The development and utilization of a completely integrated life-management system, dynamically steered, providing optimal orientation for any circumstance for the rest of one's life.

perspective—One of the two key elements of self- and organizational management (along with control). Refers to point of view, focus, altitude of horizon.

predefined work—One's predetermined actions and projects, reflected in a set of lists and reminders, accessible for review and evaluation against unplanned and unexpected options

process—To decide what, exactly, a captured or collected item means, the nature of any of its derivatives, and what you intend to do with the results. See also **clarify**.

productive experience—The condition of being in control, relaxed, focused, meaningfully engaged, and fully present. Optimal state for performance and experience.

productivity ecosystem—All potentially meaningful information, relationships, and inputs that may trigger one's attention and direction of focus

project—Any multistep outcome that can be completed within one year. Any commitment within that time frame needs to be reviewed at least weekly. See also **Horizons of Focus: Horizon 1**.

project support—Any collateral materials and information connected to a specific project. Can include project plans and any potentially relevant reference content. Best organized by project, theme, or topic.

reflect—To assess contents of any horizon or category of items from a broader perspective. See also **review**.

review—To analyze appropriate maps on a consistent basis or as needed for clarity and focus. See also **reflect; map**.

someday/maybe—A common category used to organize projects and actions one is committed to review only for potential action at a later date

stuff—Anything that has appeared in one's physical or psychological environment about which some decision or action is required but which is yet undetermined or unorganized

threefold nature of work—The categories of what we do as we go through our day: (1) work we've previously defined (actions predetermined); (2) unplanned activity; and (3) defining our work (processing inputs)

tickler file—A physical or digital organizational tool that provides a date-related reminder to be assessed only at or beyond a specific future date (also referred to as a "perpetual file," "bring-forward file," "follow-up file," or "suspense file")

total life ecosystem—The contents within the boundary of one's sensing self. The world as one perceives it, one's situational awareness and correlative behavior that may be more or less effective on the scale from physical survival to full spiritual presence.

vertical thinking—Examining and creating multiple levels of content within a particular sphere (e.g., planning a project from intended purpose through next actions)

waiting for—Category of expected items pending receipt from other sources

Weekly Review—The best practice recommended of regrouping at an operational level once a week, "bringing up the rear guard," by getting clean, clear, current, and creative to sustain week-to-week control and focus

weird time—The random and usually small open-time windows that show up spontaneously throughout the day, during which one can often still be productive by utilizing reminders and material appropriate within that framework

work—Anything one is committed to accomplish that is unfinished

workflow—The sequence of activities that takes inputs and commitments from initiation to completion

Index

An invitation . . .

The David Allen Company provides training, coaching, assessment, and consulting programs that continue to serve many of the global Fortune 100 organizations, small- and medium-size businesses, and a vast array of creative individuals worldwide. Our Academy is the source of the best practices of the Getting Things Done methodology and offers certification programs and a forum for a worldwide community of professionals who are dedicated to ensuring consistent top-quality education through all of our certified global trainers, coaches, and partners.

- Could you use more in-depth coaching and training to install, implement, maintain, and leverage these practices for yourself personally and/or professionally?

- Are you interested in connecting and engaging with a global community of people who have embodied and endorsed this methodology both personally and professionally?

- Are you part of an organization that could benefit from these practices?

- Would you simply like to get immediate tips and inspiration for gaining greater control and perspective with the least amount of effort?

If you answered "yes" to any of the above, explore the wide range of products and services on our Web site and feel free to communicate with us directly.

At whatever level you choose to participate, we at the David Allen Company welcome you into our dynamic global community of GTD practitioners. It doesn't take much involvement with this material to make a lot of difference—for yourself and the world around you.

Stay engaged, and stay in touch.

gettingthingsdone.com
info@gettingthingsdone.com

Making It All Work
*Winning at the Game of Work
and the Business of Life*

Since its publication in 2001, *Getting Things Done* became "the defining self-help business book" of the decade. In the sequel, *Making It All Work,* Allen unlocks the full power of his methods across the entire span of life and work. *Making It All Work* is an invaluable road map, providing both bearings to help you determine where you are in life and directions on how to get to where you want to go.

Ready for Anything
*52 Productivity Principles
for Getting Things Done*

Based on Allen's highly popular e-newsletter, *Ready for Anything* shows readers how to increase their ability to work better, not harder—every day. With wit, inspiration, and know-how, Allen shows readers how to make things happen—with less effort and stress, and lots more energy, creativity, and effectiveness. *Ready for Anything* is the perfect book for anyone wanting to work and live at his or her very best.

**PENGUIN
BOOKS**